A Hole Gets Bigger Whenever You Work on It

Cho Moo-jung
(C. Bonaventure)

Book Lab Press
SEOUL, KOREA

A Hole Gets Bigger Whenever You Work on It(구멍은 깎을수록 커진다)

발행일	2021년 4월 30일		
지은이	Moo-Jung Cho		
펴낸이	손형국		
펴낸곳	(주)북랩		
편집인	선일영	편집	정정두철, 윤성아, 배진용, 김현아, 박준
디자인	이현수, 한수희, 김민하, 김윤주, 허지혜	제작	박기성, 황동현, 구성우, 권태련
마케팅	김회란, 박진관		
출판등록	2004. 12. 1(제2012-000051호)		
주소	서울특별시 금천구 가산디지털 1로 168, 우림라이온스밸리 B동 B113~114호, C동 B101호		
홈페이지	www.book.co.kr		
전화번호	(02)2026-5777	팩스	(02)2026-5747
ISBN	979-11-6539-727-2 04740 (종이책)		979-11-6539-729-6 05740 (전자책)
	979-11-6539-728-9 04740 (세트)		

잘못된 책은 구입한 곳에서 교환해드립니다.
이 책은 저작권법에 따라 보호받는 저작물이므로 무단 전재와 복제를 금합니다.

(주)북랩 성공출판의 파트너

북랩 홈페이지와 패밀리 사이트에서 다양한 출판 솔루션을 만나 보세요!

홈페이지 book.co.kr   •   **블로그** blog.naver.com/essaybook   •   **출판문의** book@book.co.kr

To

June (주영)

And

Korean ancestors, who have continuously
refined their proverbs over centuries

CONTENTS

서언

조무정 박사와는 1961년 고등학교 졸업 후 만나지 못했다. 조 박사는 서울대 약대를 나온 후 곧바로 미국으로 건너가 학문의 길을 매진했고 나는 서울에서 미국의 AP와 같은 news agency 기자 생활로 일관했으니 가다 오다 우연히 만날 일도 없었다. 그러다 접선이 이루어진 게 2020년 4월 고등학교 단체 카톡방에 조 박사가 돌연 등장하면서부터였다. 60년 동안 다른 세상에 살던 두 사람이 時空을 초월해 옆에 있는 듯 자유자재로 소통이 이루어지다니! 참으로 좋아진 세상 덕을 톡톡히 본 셈이다. 우리 둘은 한국전쟁의 상처로 도로와 교통과 숙박 시설이 극도로 열악했던 고등학교 2학년 여름방학 때 미국의 hitchhiker처럼 트럭과 화물열차를 얻어 타며 제2의 금강산이라는 설악산에서 동해안을 거쳐 경상도까지 이른바 무전여행을 함께 했던 사이이다. 대학교수를 역임한 미국 박사가 쓴 책에 왈가왈부할 처지도 아니지만 친구로서 '뭐라도 써보라'는 압박에 응할 수밖에 없었다.

스스로 그동안의 삶이 '나그네 길'이었다고 토로한 조 박사는 은퇴 후 라스베이거스에 정착했다. 오로지 한국에서만 사는 나로서는 일생에 한 번 가볼까 말까 한 세계의 환락가에서 느긋하게 노년을 엔조이하는 조 박사가 한없이 부럽기만 하다. "약학박사 된 후 40년간 죽어라 일만 했고 이제 죽기 전에 다른 일 하고 싶어 글을 쓰기 시작했다"는 조 박사는 "공부하느라 장가를 늦게 가 자식들이 없다"면서 손녀가 대학생이라는 나를 보고 "부럽다"라고 한다. 정말 진심으로 그렇다는 건지 한국 속담 '無자식 上팔자'를 강조하면서 놀리는 건지 잘 와닿지는 않는다. 본인 말처럼 그동안 일만 했으면 마침 라스베이거스에 둥지를 틀었으니 이제 gamble도 하면서 좀 쉬어도 될 텐데, 그 부지런함과 왕성한 지적 탐구 자세가 놀랍다.

조 박사는 영어로 한국 속담집을 내면서 "뜻있는 국제평화는 각 나라의 문화와 전통을 제대로 이해하는 데서 비롯된다고 생각한다. 조상의 지혜가 담겨있는 우리 속담을 소개하는 것도 효과적인 방법 중의 하나이겠지. 그래서 이 책이 조금이라도 영어권 내에 사는 외국인들과 한국 2세들에게 한국 문화와 전통을 이해하는 데 도움이 되기를 바란다. 과거가 미래를 알리듯 한국 속담들이 우리의 미래도 이끌어줄 것"이라고 강조한다. 지극히 당연하면서도 겸손한 말이다.

    제1권 '사람의 혀는 뼈가 없어도 사람의 뼈를 부순다'와 제2권 '드는 정은 몰라도 나는 정은 안다'에 이어 제3권을 완성했다. 300번째는 'Ugly trees keep a mountain pretty'(굽은 나무가 선산을 지킨다)이다. "병신자식이 효도한다"는 속담과 일맥상통한다. 자식들 간에 부모 재산 상속 싸움이 빈번하고 막상 부모가 늙거나 병들었을 땐 서로 미루고 거들떠보지 않는 풍조 속에서 평소 부모덕을 보지도 못했던 병신자식이 묵묵히 옆을 지키며 보살피는 경우를 일컫는, 요즘 한국에서 재조명 받는 사회현상을 지적하는 안성맞춤의 선택이다. 동부에 사는 부모가 병들어 죽음이 임박했을 때 평소 찾아오지도 않던 서부 거주 친척이 마지못해 왔으면서 이러쿵저러쿵 잔소리만 해대는 경우를 일컬어 'daughters from California syndrome'이라고 하는 것과도 비슷하다.

    특히 미국 독자들에게 한국 속담의 오묘한 의미를 전달하는 것은 또 다른 한류를 개척했다는 평가가 가능하다. 한국인이 읽어도 새삼스럽고 영어 공부도 된다. 한국에 거주하는 외국인에게는 한국말을 배우고 한국 문화와 한국인 정서를 이해하는, 아주 좋은 지침서가 될 것으로 믿는다. 지금 한국에서도 속담 같은 거 알려고 하는 젊은이들이 드물다. 휴대폰 들고 바쁘게 살아가는 세상, 오히려 국적 불명의 카톡용 줄임말이 유행하는 안타까운 처지에서 조 박사의 시도는 그를 '한국 문화 전도사'라고 불러도 과언이 아니다. 고마울 뿐이다.

    속담은 그 지방의 역사, 문화, 환경, 풍토가 녹아든 바로 그곳 사람들의 생각을 나타낸다. 그래서 지구의 공기를 함께 호흡하고 사는 같은 인간으로서 금방 공감하는 것도 많은 반면 역사나 문화를 모르면 이해하기 어려운 것들도 적지 않다. 직설적이고 끝까지 파헤쳐서 철저하게 끝장을 보는 게 서양식 사고방식이라면, 적당한 선에서 그칠 줄도 아는 게 어쩌면 동양식이다. 적당하게, 정도껏, 애매하게 놔두기도 한다. 어딘가 좀 부족한 느낌이지만 깊은 해학과 지혜가 번뜩이기도 한다. 결국 동서양을 막론하고 지극히 인간적이면서도 교훈적 메시지를 담고 있는 속담을 통한 상호 이해 증진은 당연히 귀중하고, 그런 데 착안한 약학박사 친구 조무정의 혜안에 경의를 표한다. (끝)

이 문 호
전 연합뉴스 기자

FOREWORD

I had not seen nor heard of this man - I will call him MJ for Moo-jung (무정) - since 1961 when we graduated high school together. MJ completed a pharmacy program and I did journalism. He had gone to North America for further studies while I became a reporter for Yonhap News Agency. Then, out of nowhere, MJ started to participate in a chatroom of Kakao-talk among our high school classmates. It was in April of this year. Two of us, who had lived in two different worlds, thousands of miles apart, and more than 60 years later, were connected again, all thanks to the modern age we live in now! It would be an understatement to say that we used to be bosom buddies back then: close enough, during our sophomore year, we had hitchhiked together all the way to Seorak Mountain and down to Gyeoungsango-do, most of the way as hobos on open trains "without any pennies" (무전여행). Now, he is asking me for a few words about this book. It suffices to say, "His wish is my command." Do I have any other choice? He doesn't think so.

A self-proclaimed wanderer, MJ finally retired to, of all places, Las Vegas. It looks like he plans to enjoy the rest of his life frequenting the bustling Vegas Strip. I can only envy this man. But, then, he confesses that he rather envies me because I have a granddaughter who is already attending college. He claimed that he had been too busy to have a family during his 40-year professional life. The truth may well be that MJ is a luckier man without any children. As they say, "Blessing is having no kid." All said and done, MJ amazes me with his diligent and thriving quest for intellectual challenges.

MJ states: "Meaningful global peace will come about only through mutual understanding of culture and history. One way of promoting Korean culture to the Western World, as well as the next generations of Koreans therein, must be through introducing our ancestral wisdom embedded in Korean proverbs. As history tells us about the future, the old Korean sayings must provide us with pointers. " I couldn't agree with him more and salute his humble, but an ambitious project.

His first two books, *The Tongue Can Break Bones* and *Easier to See Jeong (Love) Leaving than Arriving*, are now followed by this book that ends

14

with #300, "Ugly Trees Keep a Mountain Pretty." If I may, this particular one likens to: "A Handicapped Child Takes Better Care of Parents." Nowadays we often hear about a wealthy family where siblings fight for an inheritance, without much care for the ailing parents. And yet it is the handicapped son who has stepped up to look after those ailing parents. To add insult to injury, here comes "a daughter from California," arriving belatedly and asserting herself as a caregiver of the dying parents. This proverb sheds new light on such a contemporary social issue.

Disseminating our ancestor's unique wisdom to English speakers, through Korean proverbs, may well be a novel way to promote Korean culture. His books should not only refresh our own thoughts on proverbs but also help us learn English. As a reference book, it would help those foreigners residing in Korea to understand her culture, as well as our collective mentality. In this day and age, young Koreans do not read, not to mention write: They are simply too busy with their cell phones and inventing baseless abbreviated words for social media. In such a climate, MJ keeps his quixotic efforts alive and well. We should call him an emissary of Korean culture. I am just thankful for what he has been doing.

A proverb is an amalgam of history, culture, environment, and nature. As such, it reflects the collective thought of people at a given place and at a given time. Although we, as world citizens, breathe the same air and thus share an opinion, there are many events and phenomena that we cannot rationalize or explain without a true understanding of the underlying given culture and history. If Western culture reflects thoroughness and assertion, Oriental culture is all about compromise and harmony. We tend to leave things ambiguous and perhaps intentionally incomplete, and yet this very act of imperfection encompasses humor, as well as wisdom. Regardless of time and place, the didactic message of humanity one can extract from an old saying should enhance the mutual understanding of all people involved. And thus, in conclusion, I will have to highly commend MJ's purpose, well-focused with his penetrating eyes.

Lee Moon-ho
Former reporter for Yonhap News Agency

ACKNOWLEDGMENT

A Hole Gets Bigger Whenever You Work on It is a sequel to the earlier two books, *The Tongue Can Break Bones* (under a pen name, C. Bonaventure) and *Easier to See* Jeong (*Love*) *Leaving than Arriving*. They were published in the spring of 2018 and 2020, respectively, both in Korea and the United States. As before, this book also introduces 100 proverbs, starting with #201 and ends with #300. Unlike other storybooks, each entry is independent of the others, and has no formal beginning and end. Every two-page essay starts on the left side of the book so that one can open the book at any place for quick reading in a rush.

As I believe that the incidental interpretation of a proverb to be the best way to offer its underlying nuance, I have heavily quoted the Korean (hi)story as well as happenings in the United States. Although I had planned to use more time-tested old events, there has been much distraction from contemporary news, particularly those involving President Donald Trump: my apology for this lazy and easy way out on my part. Likewise, I have cited many novels and films that many readers may have read or seen them. Even with my long life, there is a limit to my own stories and experience.

In English, we do not have a gender-neutral third-person pronoun. Linguistics scholars suggest us to use "they-their-them" instead of "he/she - his/her - him/her." Thanks to the LGBTQ movement, the use of "they-their-them" is gaining significant acceptance. Throughout this book, I will adopt their recommendation in italic whenever gender is irrelevant. This convention begins in Entry #207 (see its footnote) and was reminded whenever it appears.

I would also like to acknowledge the fine job of my Editor, Paul Kim of San Diego. But for his help, the essays herein would still have shown rough edges: those are all mines, never his neglects. Since each essay is only two-page long, INDEX is in the entry number. As before, I dug out the primary references from Wikipedia as well as NAVER whenever research of a given topic was warranted.

INTRODUCTION

The beauty of proverbs lies in their simplicity. Spoken and written in plain language, any child can memorize them as soon as he or she learns to speak. However, the deep-rooted meaning of these idioms evolves as we age. Most likely, children hear a given proverb for the first time from an older and thus wiser person who relates it to one occasion, and then, they hear the same proverb spoken later by others in slightly different situations. Soon, these proverbs become children's own.

At least, that was how I acquired the essence of Korean proverbs. There was no class at school, neither at the elementary school nor at the university, where we learned what Korean proverbs are all about. Now sitting here, several thousand miles away from Korea, without any reputable references or teachers to consult with, I am trying to present what I believe to be the true element of the Korean proverb. Even if there were books and articles written about the topic, I would probably not have read them lest they should affect my own understanding, thoughts, and feelings.

If there is one unique feature in Korean old sayings, it would be gentleness, often with humor derived from the everyday lives of average citizens. They are as if the sharp edges have been worn down through continuous use over many years. They are rolling hills under the blue sky peppered with lazy white clouds, never the Alps or the Himalayas under a windy snowstorm. They are small, gentle streams and the peaceful sound of a lullaby, never the deafening thunder of Niagara Falls. Many Korean proverbs end with a question mark. Instead of stating outright, "The first spoonful of food will never give you satiety," one asks "Would the first spoonful of food bring about satiety?" You will come up with the same conclusion in the end, but it asks you with some level of subtlety. The gentleness and subtleness that I identify Korean proverbs with must be from the people's life as well as the geographic and terrestrial surroundings of Korea. Describing these two factors alone will take up a tome, and I will instead let these proverbs speak themselves.

And the wisdom therein! The oral history of Korea goes back for 5,000 years. The traceable history for the two millennia preceding the 15th century has been recorded in Chinese characters and our own alphabets since then. Although many idioms were thus written in Chinese, especially those four-letter phrases in Chinese characters, I suspect that they could not have been very popular among our ancestors, since most of them were simply illiterate in Chinese. The class division itself, between learned men, or 양반 (yang-ban), and the ordinary citizens, or 서민 (seo-min), has been a popular subject among the latter, sprinkled with their ridicule and wit. These ordinary people, who shared barely-won happiness as well as various adversities in their lives, invented and used the proverbs. They are the collective consciousness of Korean people, which defines who we are now.

Some 40 years ago, my sister who lived in Phoenix, Arizona, sent me *One-Thousand Korean Proverbs* in several loose pages. I do not know where they were originally from, but I knew that one day I would try to interpret them for English-speakers. I have kept them in a drawer for all these years. As I tried to translate a few of them in English just to gauge the scope of the job, I immediately encountered the difficulty of keeping alive those rhymes that are perfect in the Korean language, which has survived for decades, if not centuries. They are poetries. I do not know how to translate them into English. All I can say is that I did my best. In some fortunate cases, however, some English versions are almost mirror images of Korean proverbs. I hurriedly copied them in this book. If there is an English version that is similar in its implication to a Korean proverb, I introduce it in the text.

As to the implied content of a proverb, I take my prerogative: others may interpret it in different ways. The proverb may talk about an earthworm or spider, but I am more interested in learning about what their behaviors teach us about human interaction and interactions among institutions, communities, or even nations. I will be the first to admit that my thought in the interpretation process tends to drift widely and wildly. Japanese kamikaze pilots appear in a story involving tiger cubs. The story about smoke from a chimney introduces those cheaters in contemporary baseball. Quite often, I find great pleasure in submitting my own opinion on various topics as I have not yet had opportunities to do so. Be it cynical or sounding ridiculous, the writing is, to the truest sense, my voice: good as well as bad that have been accumulated during my life of over 70 years.

Language is a culture, which leads to the next problem of how to take care of the stark differences between the two cultures. I naively thought that I should be in a good position to address this issue since I have, after all, lived approximately one-third and two-thirds of my life in Korea and the United States, respectively. It was once again my guesswork to determine to what extent I ought to cover cultural background in these essays. I apologize in advance if I have too many superfluous words or too little on the Korean culture.

Then, there are many words with different nuances and meanings: krill and shrimp are completely different from each other, but we Koreans call them both 새우, or *saewoo*. Tangerine and orange are both 귤, or *gule*. Since the topic of proverbs varies widely and since there is no framework for sorting them in some rational manner, I list them completely at random. As far as I can tell, the *One-Thousand Korean Proverbs* that I received many years ago do not appear to have any discernable order either. I simply present them in chronological order with the date of write-up at the end of each entry. I have tried to avoid discussing ongoing events: instead, I cited time-tested, well-established historical accounts. However, I could not let the episodes involving the 45th President of the U.S. just pass by unnoticed. He has provided an immeasurable amount of priceless examples of how one should not lead the nation and its citizens. I am thus thankful for his contribution.

The most impressionable and formative period of my life in Korea was just after the Korean War (1950-1953). There was a large contingent of American soldiers in the country. Whether we liked it or not, their presence offered us a great deal of exposure to the American culture. We read Hemingway and Steinbeck, followed the fights of Cassius Clay (Mohammad Ali since then), admired Mickey Mantle's career at Yankees, hummed along with Beatles, watched American films like *From Here to Eternity*, and even monitored closely what was happening in the political arena of the United States. At night, my ears were glued to the AFKN (American Forces Korea Network) radio station, which carried songs requested by the loved ones back at home for the American soldiers in Korea, largely what I later realized was country music. My poor English did not allow me to fully understand what the lady announcer was saying, but I figured it was all about boosting troop morale. I still vividly remember the alluring voice she spoke in. As I look back now, I understood America far better than they did about Korea.

Imbalance in cultural understanding between nations has undoubtedly added fuel to ongoing animosity, often igniting a full-blown war. Even at that tender age, I found myself wondering how many Americans

19

knew anything about Korea, the exception being the Korean War and our cold winter. Years later, I discovered that the Peace Corps campaign by the Kennedy administration was to help Americans understand the culture of developing countries. I just hope that this book could also similarly contribute to the understanding of Korean culture among English-speakers. It is one tiny grain of sand on the vast oceanic beach but is better than nothing.

Having been a scientist, it has become a habit to always reveal the source of a given piece of information in my writing. Here, I am greatly indebted to Wikipedia and NAVER. Even with these online encyclopedias, whenever warranted, I went back to the primary literature to confirm that what I was writing is indeed correct. My Korean is no longer what it used to be when I was a college kid in Korea. Inevitably, I had to consult Korean-English as well as English-Korean dictionaries, both by Dong-A Publishing and Printing Company. To my delight, they often introduce an English version of a Korean proverb. These occasions were like finding a few coins between the cushions on a sofa.

I used a pseudonym, C. Bonaventure, as the author of the first volume, *The Tongue Can Break Bones.* It was published in the U.S. in June 2018. As writing essays has never been my profession, my real name would not mean anything. Bonaventure was the Christian name given to me when I was baptized as a Catholic. There is neither more nor less significance associated with the pseudonym. Just accept it as is. Now that both the first book and *Easier to See* Jeong (*Love*) *Leaving than Arriving* coming out in Korea, there is no reason not to use the name given to me when I was born. Some of my old Korean friends may still recognize the name.

I immensely enjoyed writing these essays. I hope that readers find this collection somehow meritorious and enjoy reading as much as I did with my writing. (adopted from *The Tongue Can Break Bones:* 11/15/2020)

A Hole Gets Bigger Whenever You Work on It

Cho Moo-jung
(C. Bonaventure)

Book Lab Press
SEOUL, KOREA

201. No means yes in bribery.
싫어 싫어 하면서 손 내민다.

The party who receives a bribe usually pretends not to know what is being transferred at the very moment, often diverting his attention to irrelevant topics or uttering words of nonsense like, "No, you don't need to do this," or "What a beautiful day." Likewise, the party who is offering the bribe tends to hide what he is giving: If the "gift" is cash it is inside an envelope, lest the receiver gets embarrassed by the directness. This is even though each side knows that the other party understands exactly what is happening. They still have some level of decency and humility, but it is hypocrisy at its best. The above proverb thus describes a scene where the receiving party keeps saying "no," but extends a hand at the same time, to reach for what is being offered.

Practicing unwarranted modesty among Koreans is not limited only to bribery. More often, it is about the food being offered. Even if you are still hungry and have room for further nourishment, just like most Koreans, you would say that you have had enough and politely refuse a further offering. Knowing this "tradition," the host of a dinner party ignores what you are saying and continuously places more food on your plate. Out of politeness, you will have to consume everything presented, even if you are truly full. If, by slim chance, the host accepts what you are saying at face value, you could go home still hungry, accusing the host of being insensitive. This is a nightmare of over-analyzed, reverse psychology, which most Koreans have experienced. It is a case of marginal hypocrisy.

Before Bill Clinton was elected as the 42nd President in 1993, he had been the Governor of Arkansas for almost a decade. One evening in May 1991, a certain Paula Jones, then a state employee, was escorted to Clinton's room at a Little Rock hotel by State Troopers, where, according to Jones, Clinton exposed himself to her. Three years later, Jones filed a sexual harassment suit against Clinton, now a duly elected, sitting President of this country. Between November 1995 and March 1997, Clinton had nine sexual encounters with a White House intern, Monica Lewinsky, in no other place than the Oval Office. According to her, these interactions between a 50-year old married man and a 23-year old young woman, consisted of fellatio and other sexual acts but not intercourse.

This story broke out to the public because Lewinsky told her "friend" about the affair, who secretly recorded their conversation. The lawyers representing Jones somehow obtained a written testimony from Lewinsky and used it to generalize Clinton's behavior towards female employees. The audiotape was also given to Independent Counsel, Kenneth Starr, who was investigating unrelated matters involving Clinton and some obscure land use in Arkansas. Now, Starr expanded his investigation into the Lewinsky affairs, just to make sure there was no perjury in all three cases.

Clinton was impeached on December 19, 1998 by the House of Representatives, on grounds of perjury to a grand jury and obstruction of justice. The former charge included lying about his relationship with Lewinsky, false statements he made in the Jones case, and witness tampering. The second charge was primarily concerned with encouraging Lewinsky, his lawyers, and his secretary to lie. As incredible as it may sound now, these events were quite entertaining on one hand and also disgusting at the same time. The Lewinsky scandal was particularly amazing; with many juicy details, like the announcement of "semen on a blue dress" and the definition of "is" questioned by Clinton.

However, the real story relevant to the current proverb involves the hypocrisy displayed by House Republicans, who came out in droves to "murder" Democrat President, Bill Clinton. The House Speaker, Newt Gingrich, spearheaded the impeachment of President Clinton based on moral grounds. Then, his extramarital affair with a congressional employee became known to the public and he promptly resigned. Gingrich's successor, Bob Livingston, also withdrew his candidacy at the last minute because of his own marital infidelity. Many prominent Republican members of Congress, who voted for impeachment, turned out to have had their own marital infidelities. Larry Flynt, the publisher of the notoriously lewd adult magazine *Hustler*, offered a reward for such information. As I look back now, it was an interesting segment of modern American history. (01/01/20)

202. No smell, no musk.
싸고 싼 사향도 냄새난다.

People use perfume to present an alluring scent to others close by. Its use is said to be as old as human civilization. The fundamental purpose may well be to lure a mate, although it also gives the user a sense of well-being. The aftershave lotion I used in the morning, for instance, ushers me to a fresh start of a brand new day with a renewed vigor and hope. Modern perfumes are prepared through blending chemically synthesized aroma compounds on a trial-and-error basis until a consensus arises from a test panel. It has to be a judgmental call, not only because of underdeveloped olfactory science but also because of individual variation in preference. Since perfume is consumed in a small quantity and considered part of luxurious cosmetics, there seems to be a perception of "the higher the price, the better." Just check the price of the iconic French perfume Chanel No. 5.

When the above proverb was in use among our Korean ancestors, ingredients for perfume must have been from natural sources, one of which was *sa-hyang* (사향) from musk deer. Musk is a class of smelly compounds secreted from a glandular organ, which is attached to the scrotum of male musk deer. The egg-shaped gland is usually sliced and dried for long-term storage. When its extract is diluted, it produces fragrance and thus is used in perfumery. In old China and Korea, it is also used as herbal medicine as a cardiac stimulant as well as an anticonvulsant. Just like ammonia spirit, it was commonly used for reviving a fainted person with its pungent smell.

The upshot of all this is that musk was very expensive, resulting in many bogus products in the market. However expensive musk might have been, the above proverb says that even cheap musk, from a questionable origin, still gives off an odor, albeit possibly not the same as the authentic scent. Now, what does this proverb imply? First and foremost, if one tries to sell fake musk, it must smell: No odor, no musk. As such, it defines the minimum but an absolute requirement. In any transaction involving musk, being smelly is a necessary condition.

In a similar vein, we could raise a question as to such basic elements required in a human being. Physically, one can list a pair of eyes, ears, legs, arms, etc. One of the non-tangible features of human beings must be that we all have a wide range of emotions and feelings. Together with the ability of thinking, they form the hallmark of humanity. Without emotion, one is not a human being, just like anything without smell can't be musk. We are to condemn such emotions as hatred and jealousy, while others, such as empathy and compassion, are highly prescribed: especially in a divided society and a nation with diverse views of various topics such as religion and politics. And yet, the goodness in each of us, as a manifestation of humanity, is always looking for a heart-warming story.

A couple of months ago, a homeless, petite, blond woman named Emily Zamourka, was singing the aria "*O mio babbino caro*" from Puccini's one-act opera, *Gianni Schicchi*, at a subway platform in Los Angeles that offered "outstanding" acoustics. Beside her, plastic bags on a shopping cart carried all her possessions. The videotape that a Los Angeles police officer posted online immediately went viral, along with a brief biography of the 52-year old Zamourka. She immigrated to the States from the Soviet Republic Moldova in 1992, and had survived primarily as a music teacher before a string of bad luck hit upon her. Without any steady income, she was not able to catch up with her ever-increasing rent and became homeless about three years ago. Soon after the story was posted, outpouring support followed, via a GoFundMe campaign.

Samantha Savitz was born deaf in the small town of Newton Massachusetts. At the age of three, she began walking around the neighborhood with her parents. "We really wanted to communicate and play with her," said a neighbor who lives across the street from the Savitzes. "And since she couldn't learn our language, we thought we wanted to learn hers." At first, only three other neighbors signed up for a class in American Sign Language, but by December 2019, the whole town had decided to learn the sign language so that Samantha could feel at home. Here, the compassion of the town folks to humanity is what the fragrance is to musk. (01/04/20)

203. A master with a full stomach doesn't see the hunger of servants.
상전 배 부르면 종 배고픈 줄 모른다.

Any mid-level managers in an organization would have subordinates as well as a boss. Ideally, they should be in firm control of underlings with consistent fairness, and yet should be "slow to anger but quick to kindness." Here, empathy must be the foundation of their guiding principle. If I were one of those managers, I would ask myself, "Could they finish the assignment I am about to give without breaking their back? If I push them too hard, would the quality of the outcome be compromised? Do I know about their domestic situation sufficient enough to ask them for occasional over-time work? Or shall I completely ignore the personal aspect and drive them as hard as I can? How would I handle the assignment, if I were one of them?"

Towards the immediate supervisor, the manager must be responsive to a given directive as well as responsible for what his or her department has been contributing to the goal of the organization. The manager should try to be as transparent as one can be about the pressure from the upper management, without sacrificing any confidentiality involved. This sincere effort may bring about a great deal of empathy and possibly sympathy from subordinates. They may share the difficulties of a given project as if their well-being is indeed on the line. These are all part of an ideal scenario.

One's own emotional experience must play a role in developing the ability to understand another person's emotions and feelings. Parents who have lost a child must understand much better the other families with a similar tragedy. Having quit smoking in the past, I can sympathize with those who struggle to do the same. Alcoholics and drug addicts empathize with others in similar situations. Surprisingly, however, sharing another person's emotions based on one's similar past is not as universal as one may assume. Does the poverty I experienced, as a child of the Korean War, make me more compassionate towards the poor? Sad to say, the short answer is, not really. When old friends, who grew up together, meet nowadays, we seldom talk about the shared misfortune of the long past. I do not know why, but it may be the same reason why war veterans often avoid sharing their memories and experiences with others.

Medical training demands a long period of arduous effort from students. In this country, after a four-year college, those who are successfully admitted to a medical school, go through another four-year program, the last two in clinical practices. After eight years of schooling, they take up internship and residency for three to seven years, along with board exams for formal certificates. Sleep deprivation, and lack of personal time are the hallmarks of this training. Most of the young physicians swear to themselves that they would change this seemingly ridiculous tradition once they become established in the profession. However, tradition is still striving and well. Is this a case of absence of empathy and compassion among practicing physicians? Or does the mantra, "I did suffer and thus so do you also," vaguely insist that the hardship was indeed an essential part of the training that makes the medical profession a "profession of pride?" Or perhaps they might have simply forgotten what they have gone through as in Entry #58, "Frogs don't remember they were once tadpoles."

Now that you are full in the stomach, you have forgotten that other people might still be hungry. This is essentially what the above proverb is complaining about. The proverb refers to this selfish man with little empathy as *sang jeon* (상전), or simply as "master" or "lord." He was most likely born into a wealthy family, with a silver spoon in his mouth, and was probably never exposed to any adverse conditions, certainly not hunger. How could he then learn about the hunger of his servants?

During the French Revolution, the underprivileged commoner eventually retaliated, with a non-stoppable vengeance, by guillotining both King Louis XVI and Queen Marie Antoinette, along with persecuting the Catholic clergy! Immediately after the communist North Korean military captured Seoul in 1950, many citizens that had been "suppressed" thus far carried out an uprising of revenge against the bourgeois families with democratic inclination. In summary, the proverb emphasizes the ease with which a lord or any influential person becomes deficient in empathy. (01/14/20)

204. You can't tell the size of a snake in a narrow tunnel.
구멍에 든 뱀 길이를 모른다.

A snake is entering a narrow underground tunnel for some reason: perhaps it caught a scent of prey through his flickering tongue, or just wanted to get some rest in a warm place. Maybe the snake was looking for company or was simply curious about the hole. No matter what the motive might be, if we witnessed the slithering snake from the moment of its head entering the hole till the end when its tail disappeared, we have seen the whole body of the snake. Then, and only then, we may be able to say a few facts about the snake: its length, thickness, the color of its scales, or even its type, or species. If you happen to be an expert in reptiles, you may even be able to tell us its sex from its tail. But, if we saw only the tail end quickly disappearing into the entrance, we may not know anything about the snake. The above proverb says the same thing.

One inference we can derive from the proverb is that we simply cannot learn about a person we have just met very briefly for the first time. The first impression we form is greatly influenced by the person who makes the introduction, usual words of praise like, "This man is the head of the so-and-so corporation or institute," or "He's a recipient of the presidential award in the this-or-that field." Perhaps you will hear, "He wrote the highly acclaimed book such-and-such that I am sure you have read already," or "He's a national treasure in Korean something," etc. If you are an unmarried lady, the guy who introduces the man may even say, "Watch out, this guy is a notorious womanizer," with a conspiratorial wink in the eyes.

The man we have just met is so impressive a man in this small nation, even school kids can recognize his name. With such a delightful encounter, we tend to advertise the occasion to everybody within earshot as well as the whole world, if you are a big-time namedropper. Besides a long-drawn description of the encounter, you begin to add your own supplemental material about him. In no time, you become one of his bosom buddies. I came across a few questionable Korean characters who knew everything about this country, after a few visits to Koreatown in Los Angeles. These are all good examples of a man who saw the tail end of the snake, describing the creature in minute detail. As far as I can tell, they are the blind man describing an elephant.

Bluntly, we should not judge a man from appearance. It would be like judging a book by its cover. Admittedly, a man driving a Porsche 911 and wearing a tailored Armani suit is likely a rich man, but a guy in plain clothes and with a modest attitude can also be a rich and famous man. He might be simply a humble person. If a man, who is struggling financially, lives a pretentious life beyond his means, he could well be a con man who is trying very hard to impress a wealthy widow.

The 1997 American film *Good Will Hunting* presents a case to the point raised above. Twenty-year-old Will Hunting (played by Matt Damon) works as a janitor at MIT. One night, he leaves the answer to a tough mathematical problem posted on a blackboard by a professor. The perfect solution left by this anonymous person surprises the professor as well as his graduate students. To further challenge this unknown genius, the professor leaves a more difficult problem. Late at night, when the professor catches him writing the solution on the blackboard, Will flees. As it turns out, Will has been unconsciously but deliberately, sabotaging himself in the anticipation of future failure in a relationship with strangers. This is just to avoid any potential emotional pain.

There are many instances where a person tries to hide his or her true identity. A con man introduced above is with a bad intention. Pretending he is nobody, an *amhaeng-uhsa*, a royal secret ombudsman, during the Joseon Dynasty, tried to uncover the wrongdoings of corrupt government officials: see Entry #77, "Hot tea doesn't show steam." In the film industry, a body double is a professional who plays an impersonator of a major character in certain shots: often used for shots involving a nude scene or a steamy scene, if an actress flatly refuses to be seen naked for one reason or another. Stunt doubles are used when a special skill is required, which the actor is lacking. Usually, their face is obscured so that the audience can be fooled. They only show their "tails." (01/19/20)

205. Getting flogged is preferred to bad food.
싫은 매는 맞아도 싫은 음식은 못 먹는다.

The corporal punishment we used to receive for having misbehaved, when we were school children, is something all of us had to endure. There was no way to avoid it. We just bit the bullet and tried to get it over with as quickly as we could. The mental fortitude of "better to face the whipping early," or "매도 먼저 맞아라," is another famous piece of Korean wisdom. Punishments were usually in the form of getting whipped on the calf, or open hands, with a wooden ruler or some such thing. Most of the time we knew we deserved the punishment for such "crimes" as incomplete homework, a fistfight with fellow students, whispering to a nearby classmate during a lecture, being late to class, etc. If I recall, some teachers were on the borderline of being a sadist. When you received punishment from such fearful teachers, you were to convince yourself it was just your bad luck. The severe pain you remembered forces you to avoid him at all costs from then on. But time eventually heals all.

The gastrointestinal (GI) tract can be considered a tube starting from the mouth and ending at the anus. In adult humans, it can be as long as 9 m (30 feet) and consists of the stomach, small intestine, large intestine, and colon. The food we eat is digested and resulting nutrients are absorbed mainly in the duodenum of the small intestine and delivered to the liver. The surface area of the small intestine alone can be as large as 30 m^2, perfect for its function. The surface of the track is, in a sense, still exposed to ambient surroundings, just like our skin: thus epithelium in jargon. People often suffer from GI ailments, especially associated with tainted or spoiled food. Diarrhea, fever, abdominal pain, and dysentery are the consequence of food we ingest that is contaminated with bacteria, such as *E. coli*, *Salmonella*, and *Shigella*. There is no simple way to determine if hamburger meat or lettuce we buy at a grocery store is tainted with any of these pathogens. In contrast, we can usually avoid spoiled food, as we can smell, taste, or see the problem. The above proverb is asking which I prefer, getting flogged or forced to eat spoiled food. I would choose neither if I can, but I am now cornered.

The choices presented in the proverb are similar to the case of a broken leg versus cancer, acute but severe pain versus sustained but tolerable pain; death by a firing squad versus a life sentence without any possible parole; or a sudden downpour versus the lingering rain of a monsoon season. I suppose it all depends on personal philosophy and given circumstance, but for the record, I usually take care of the side dish I like least first, saving my favorite till the end. I would also prefer surgical intervention to chemotherapy. That is, I prefer, "facing the whipping early."

Dan Brown's 2003 bestseller, *The Da Vinci Code*, introduces a religious fanatic who tries to rob a valuable item from good guys. This albino monk, who belongs to the powerful organization *Opus Dei,* within the Catholic Church, always wears a Discipline Belt known as *cilice*. It constantly gives him pain, often with bleeding. No one would enjoy the pain unless the person is such a believer of suffering as the monk in the novel, or a bona fide masochist found in the fictional work of Marquis de Sade. And yet, the above proverb says that such pain pales in comparison to spoiled food.

As they say, you can bring a horse to a stream, but cannot force him to drink. There is only so much one can impose upon another person or a group of people, with forced demands such as having them eat spoiled food. "Liberty or death!" was the motto that prevailed in the early stage of the American Revolution. On March 1, 1919, 33 like-minded, prominent civil activists gathered together at noon, in *Tap-Gol* Park (탑골공원), on Jong-ro Street, to declare the independence of Korea from the Imperial Japanese occupation. This peaceful demonstration of our ancestors precedes Gandhi's anti-colonial movement in India by at least a decade, and the civil rights movement of this country by at least three decades. The fundamental right of any human being, to live a peaceful and happy life with dignity, is something no government or dictator can deny.

History is rich with painful struggles for liberty, often accompanied by horrendous atrocity and human sacrifice. Our Korean ancestors must have known that any pain would be easier to endure than a corrupt life, much like spoiled food. (01/22/20)

206. The winter complains about the spring chill.
겨울 바람이 봄바람보고 춥다고한다.

This proverb personifies both winter and spring, and the winter says that the spring is chilly. We have come across a similar one in Entry #115, "The pot calls the kettle black. 똥묻은개가겨묻은개나무란다." There, I introduced numerous hypocritical U.S. Congressmen, who were having illegitimate romantic affairs and yet were pointing fingers at other politicians in a similar situation. The above proverb seems to carry a slightly different nuance though. After a long and cold winter, we are looking forward to warm spring weather. According to the calendar, we are now in the middle of spring, and yet feel chilly on a cloudy day, maybe murmuring "Indian winter?" If what we feel or see now is different from what we have been expecting, we would say something, usually a surprise, complaint, or resentment.

A case in point would be the 2016 Presidential election in this country. Unlike other elections that I had gone through before, I went to bed quite early, believing that this election was Hilary's to lose. The following morning, it was, therefore, quite a shock to learn that our new president was D. J. Trump. The disappointment, together with my perception of this man, has been lingering for a long time, and remained a sour point. Some political pundits are saying that the impeachment Trump received recently from the House is nothing but the consequence of this frustration, appearing as a mere political retaliation by Democrats. At this very moment, a Senate trial is taking place. As Jack Nicklaus was replacing the all-time favorite, Arnold Palmer, as a golf champion, fans including me did not like this young man with blond hair from Ohio, called the Golden Bear. The difference from the case of Trump was that I eventually liked the new champion and rooted for him all the time.

The winter complaining about the spring chill is a matter of frame of reference, in terms of time. As pointed out in Entry #155, "The butcher looks down on ordinary people," entertainers used to belong in the lowest class of Korean society, as late as my parent's generation. They were part of the so-called *cheon-min* class. Now, look at the wild, almost fanatic, fans of K-pop like BTS. Crazy is an understatement for their fandom. Last night, they appeared at the 2020 Grammy Award ceremony. *Cheon-min*? What *cheon-min*? They are idols of the current generation.

Korea was freed from the Imperial Japanese occupation in 1945, with the victory of the Allies of the Second World War. Likewise, South Korea was at the brink of total collapse when the U.N. troops, primarily led by the U.S. army, intervened and saved our nation from the War. Koreans, especially my generation, who witnessed these historic events, are eternally grateful to the United States for their unselfish aid. Now that the current U.S. administration insists on sharing the defense cost, many Koreans have become resentful. Needless to say, the United States has a right to ask the Korean government for participating in the defense budget, but still, we feel that we are being betrayed by an old ally. At this writing, the new U.S Ambassador to Korea, Harry Harris, is unduly receiving a cold shoulder from the host country. The fact that his mother is Japanese and his mustache reminds Koreans of Imperial Japanese generals certainly does not help his case right now. As pointed out several times in the past, Koreans are not the most rational people on this planet.

What we expect, or consider normal, changes not only with time but also more significantly, with the place and thus culture. A murder in a small town, say in Iowa, can be a big deal, but probably not so in Chicago or Washington, D.C. In the modern world, killing a wild animal for food sounds rather unnatural: we may unconsciously think that turkey meat is from a local grocery store. We may not even associate it with a turkey farm, not to mention wild turkeys. Although wild animals were a natural source of meat among human ancestors, the meat markets in Wuhan, China, which sold wild animals for sustenance, are suspected to be ground zero of the recent coronavirus outbreak.

We welcome a warm and sunny day, right in the middle of winter, as much as we dislike a chilly and cloudy spring day. This is regardless of what they call each other. It is just human nature and could well be the origin of the phrase, "fair-weather fan," for those fans who support only a winning team in sports. (01/27/20)

207. The dragon runs with a cloud, the tiger with the wind.
용 가는데 구름 가고 범 가는데 바람 간다.

The tiger to Eastern culture is what the lion is to the Western world. As far as Korean children are concerned, the tiger is at the top of the predatory world. Many of the old stories and fables we heard as children dealt with tigers, seldom lions. We were introduced to the lion as another formidable beast, much later in childhood. The occasion immediately brought us to imagine a fight between a tiger and a lion: Who is going to win the fight? This question still intrigues me, at an age close to 80. But, then, there is another beast, a dragon. As in Western culture, it exists only in our imagination. It is truly the most ferocious and powerful animal in the imaginary world. The above proverb says a dragon, wherever he goes and whenever he appears, is accompanied by a dark cloud, whereas a tiger is with a strong wind. I don't think which follows which is significant here, but that each of the beasts has their footprint is the crux of the proverb. By extension, we may say that each individual has *their** own signature in character and personality, just like their own fingerprint.

In the Chinese zodiac, each of the 12 years in a repeating cycle, is assigned to an animal. We can start with a rat, which is followed by the ox, tiger, rabbit, dragon, snake, horse, sheep, monkey, rooster, dog, and pig. Note that both the dragon and the tiger are in but not the lion. The year 2020 happens to be a year of the rat/mouse. Although rats are almost 100 times bigger than mice, the Korean language does not distinguish between them: both are *juee* (쥐). Unlike a dragon or tiger, the movement of this small animal is not associated with any earth-shattering wind or dark cloud that is promising a tornado. The daily whereabouts of ordinary citizens are not the business of others, but that of important people is constantly under scrutiny. They could be politicians like presidents and congressmen, entertainers like BTS members, film actors, sports figures like Kobe Bryant who was killed yesterday in a helicopter accident, or celebrities in various social media. Most of us are "nobody," whose life amounts to very little to others and society as a whole. Yet, collectively the world belongs to this mass of average Joes and Janes.

Wherever Jesus went, a crowd followed. Often the followers witnessed a miracle. They sought wisdom and learned from Him how to serve God best. He taught the followers in parables and offered healing without any demand for payment in return. He was arrested by fellow Jews, delivered to the Romans, and eventually crucified by Pontius Pilate, the Roman governor. In classic Christian paintings, an ascending Jesus is entering heaven in the sky, while blessing a crowd, as well as the entire church on the ground. The four Gospels; Matthew, Mark, Luke, and John, are devoted to His life and messages. Together, these are what accompanied Jesus.

Fast forward two millennia to the current time, the President of the United States, Donald Trump, is still arguably the most powerful man on this planet. Wherever he goes on Air Force One, or "Cadillac One," controversies follow, usually in the form of lying. It ranges from a claim that he does not know some dubious associates of his errand man, Rudy Giuliani, simply because they speak ill of him. This is despite numerous photos of Trump with these men and the audio recording of their conversations. More serious lies have just led him to impeachment in the House. As of December 10, 2019, the *Washington Post* reported that Trump has stated a total of 15,413 untruths during his presidency of fewer than three years. This is the legacy that accompanies the President.

All said and done, we ought to ask ourselves what or who is following each of us. Or, would this be a more relevant question: Whom have I been following in my life? (01/27/20)

---

* For centuries, people have recognized that English is missing a gender-neutral third-person pronoun that could be used in place of "he" or "she" when gender is unknown or irrelevant. Linguistics scholars now suggest we use "they-their-them" instead of "he/she-his/her-him/her." Thanks to the LGBTQ movement, the use of "they" is gaining significant acceptance. Throughout this book, I will also use "they" in italic as a third-person singular when gender is irrelevant in the context. (from *What's Your Pronoun?* by D. Baron)

208. A cow needs a post for back-scratching.
소도 언덕이 있어야 비빈다.

A cow, in a typical Korean farm, must be one of the most docile animals one can imagine. Day in and day out, without much complaint, she would till the field with a farmer, who may well be the only company she has ever known in the past and will know for the rest of her life. She demands so little, people may not realize that she could have a "wish list." The farmer may be an exception: He knows that one of the items on the list is a back scratcher and thus erects a post in the field for his cow. A nuanced translation of the above proverb would be, "Even a cow with seemingly few demands would at least need a wall so that she could rub her back against it." The word for "wall" was originally "hill," but it really meant a back scratcher. I am lost as to why the original expression used the word "hill" or "*un-deok* (언덕)," as it can hardly offer back-scratching. These illogical Korean ancestors are often inscrutable.

If a cow needs something to get rid of an itch on its back, then what about us? There is always a spot on the back that we cannot reach, even with long nails on a long arm. And that's usually where serious itching is taking place. Twenty-some years ago, my wife and I took a two-week tour in China. While my wife was busy purchasing silly stuff like *jinju* cream, stoneware, hand-held foldable fans with fancy drawings on them, and other useless knickknacks, I couldn't find anything appealing to me. In one dusty corner of an equally dusty shop, a back scratcher made of bamboo was sitting along with other interesting items made of bamboo. It was about a foot and a half long, and an inch and a half wide. One end was bent, I am sure through the use of an open fire, with five "fingers" distinctly separated by four open nicks. This was the part that does the scratching. The other end, or handle, offered three openings, each with a small roller, hung by a crossing rod. I assumed that these rollers were for massaging or just for decoration. The whole bamboo strip was curved here and there, rendering a very appealing look. Another small item I brought home was an inner ear scratcher, again made of thin bamboo, about one-eighth-inch thick and five-inch long. One end offered a small carved spoon, while the top end was capped off with a decorative ball with a smiling face drawn on. This, I use for scooping ear wax.

Both items have been quite dear to me. They are always very close to my desk so that I can get them almost with my eyes closed, whenever I need them. Do I need these items in "surviving" every minute of every day? However nice it is to have them around, I can live without them. Even for such a seemingly trivial inconvenience, we look for a way to circumvent it. Then what do we have to do for real survival? This rhetorical question is asking a practical question: how do we make money? As money brings in more money, the question boils down to, how do we earn the first dollar?

Andrew Carnegie (1835 – 1919) was born in a small town in Scotland to a poor family. His father was a weaver and the family barely made ends meet. When Carnegie was 13, with borrowed money, they moved to Allegheny, Pennsylvania for a better life. Both the father and the son worked for a Scottish-owned cotton mill. Carnegie's first job was as a bobbin boy in a Pittsburgh cotton factory, changing spools of thread in a cotton mill, 12 hours a day and six days a week. His starting wage was $1.20 per week, equivalent to about $35 at present. From this humble beginning, he moved on to found the U.S. Steel Corporation. At his financial peak, he was certainly the richest man, not just one of the richest men, in the country.

How do other people earn their first buck then? After all, most of us are not born with a job secured. As I look back at my own life, it was education that rendered feasible what I am now. At the age of two, my parents had to flee from the communist regime of North Korea. We crossed the 38th parallel that divided the Korean Peninsula, me on the back of a drunken "guide," in the darkness of the darkest night, a vivid, 75-year old memory. See more in Entry # 298, "In a day you come across a horse and a cow." Our family somehow survived the Korean War. Education was what we needed as a cow needed a back-scratcher. Even without the education that I have received, I am sure that I would have survived; however, it would have been a completely different life. (02/04/20)

209. A full water bottle makes no noise, even when shaken.
병에 가득찬 물은 저어도 소리가 안난다.

A direct, word-by-word translation of the above proverb would be: "Brimful water in a bottle does not make any noise when stirred." The original offers a slightly different nuance from what I wrote above in the heading and the writing below. It says that water when "stirred," not the bottle when "shaken," does not make noise. It goes without saying that water needs some headspace to make swashing sounds when the bottle is shaken. If we consider the noise undesirable, such as nonsense just out of a chatty person's mouth, then the crux of the proverb is the same as what we encountered before: see Entry #10, "An empty wheelbarrow makes more noise," or "Eloquent speech is silver, silence is gold." If, on the other hand, a full bottle means that there is no room for further accommodation of anything new or fresh, in a person or a nation, then fullness is not so good.

The proverb may be relevant in the relationship between the amount of food we consume and our health or longevity. Here, the fullness is in a negative connotation. We have heard quite often that we ought to stop eating when we want another spoonful of food that will bring about full satiety. That way, we live longer, is what they used to say. In a recent research report published in a respectful journal, the authors compared a group of mice that were fed every other day in a controlled fashion throughout their lives, with another group that was fed ad libitum. In terms of the progress in molecular, cellular, physiological, and histopathological aging, the researchers presented little evidence for retardation of the aging rate in every-other-day fed mice. Supporting other old studies, this cohort indeed lived longer. Interestingly, the researchers attribute this finding to less occurrence of life-limiting neoplastic disorders that were found in the group fed ad libitum, not to just a slowing of the aging process (*Nature Communications*, Volume 8, Article No. 155, 2017). If we extrapolate the results of the above study to humans, it is indeed commendable not to indulge every meal to its fullness. Besides, a full stomach yields lightheadedness, and a lethargic body, for a while after the heavy meal.

Being an old man, I never like the idiom, "You can't teach an old dog new tricks." I will be the first to admit that everything has slowed down in me lately, the exception being time. But there is no reason to insult an old man, saying that I cannot learn something novel. Unwillingness to learn something new, however unconscious it may be, perhaps reflects just laziness. Lack of adaptability or elasticity in my present life might be because I often question the necessity of it, rather than lack of ability. Either way, this sort of stubbornness may indicate that my mind has been, by now, fully pre-occupied with old conventions that I am unwilling to replace with new ones. Just like a bottle of brimful water, perhaps I must empty some to replace with fresh water. After all, the emptying of the mind is the first step in meditation, including religious ones. It is often said that the mind that has been emptied of distracting thoughts offers an agreeable detachment from chaotic thoughts so that it can see everything more clearly.

In 212 B.C., Archimedes discovered that "any object is buoyed up by a force equal to the weight of the fluid displaced by the object," tersely defining buoyancy as the weight of the displaced fluid. The Law taught me how an ironclad boat does not sink and that not all empty space is a waste. In fact, a bottle completely filled with water would sink, so long as the density of glass is greater than that of water.

The lungs of a drowned man are usually filled with water. Otherwise, the person could have been floating. Ancient Chinese must have also realized the significance of emptiness: "What appears to be empty can be full inside," or 허즉실 (虛則實). On a battlefield, you are supposed to be particularly alarmed when your enemy looks disarrayed and weak, as the appearance can be rather deceiving. Your enemy might have taken such posture just to keep your guard down. See also, Entry #124, "Burning a house down to get rid of bedbugs."

If the emptying of mind is the first step in the detachment of oneself from the practical world, it will be indeed a good practice to exercise for an old man, not only because it will lessen the silly stubbornness but it also renders him ready for his pending departure from this world. (02/07/20)

210. Be quiet when ten mutes speak.
열 벙어리가 말을 해도 가만 있거라.

Imagine a fire broke out in a dormitory of deaf-mute students, you have just arrived on a fire truck, and don't know anything about sign language. You want to ask them where and how the fire started, but all you hear from the students in utter panic is plain guttural noise you cannot comprehend. More or less out of frustration you yell, not necessarily at them, and rush to where the fire is blazing while dragging the water hose along. The above proverb suggests you just be quiet and patient: What good is it to try to communicate with them, shouting your lungs out? The keyword here would be patience.

When I was a professor of pharmaceutical chemistry, I had my share of international graduate students in the lab, including Koreans and Chinese. Through our weekly lab meetings, I would be fully aware of each student's research progress. More importantly, I would know who is slacking and who got stuck at a difficult stage of their research project. We all tried to help each other through discussions. Most of the international students were smart and hard-working, say, compared with American students. Their main problem was with communication. Although they had difficulties in English, I knew they are up to their tasks, not only in experiments but also in updated literature.

When the time came for them to present their work at a departmental seminar, these students would become nervous, not so much because they would face a "big" audience, but because they were afraid of their poor English skills. The presentation itself was not generally a big problem because they rehearsed with a transcript beforehand and carried a handful of notes. It was the question-and-answer session where they stumbled. Either they did not correctly understand questions from their colleagues, or could not answer properly even when they understood a question. Albeit listening in these exchanges from afar, I clearly knew why and how my students fumbled. The most maddening part was the realization that these students knew the subject quite well but just could not express themselves. I was the fireman facing mutes, but could not blurt out a catharsis out of frustration.

What was stopping me from yelling in the seminar was not because I am a man of patience. As a matter of fact, I have always had a short fuse, especially when I come across a mediocre job. In some instances, I would step into the discussion to guide my student to formulate answers. Professors were not supposed to do so, but the frustration on my part had the upper hand here. Whenever such an occasion took place, I would afterward urge them to improve their English skills. My nagging was not justified or warranted because I had been in their situation when I arrived in this country, many decades ago. As I look back now, it was remarkable how patient and tolerant my American mentors, friends, and even total strangers on the street were, toward my poor English. Whenever I think about their kindness, I am most grateful and try to be as nice towards foreigners with limited English skills. It has little to do with my patience. It is all about empathy and compassion.

The diversity in ethnicity is something we Koreans should accommodate wholeheartedly. Unfortunately, it has been my observation that Koreans display affection only to a certain nationality. As a whole, Koreans have been mimicking the cultural trends of China in the old days, Japan and Europe in the late 19th century, and the U.S. in modern days. See more on this in Entry #27. "Another's bread looks bigger, but my child looks better." The upshot is that we seem to prefer Westerners to Asians, and show kindness and hospitality accordingly. This strange "discrimination" is patently not based on poor communication. Witness that the folks in South Korea show only lukewarm compassion to migrants from North Korea who speak the same language. It is borderline "racism." The phobia expressed by South Koreans toward asylum seekers from Islamic nations is almost identical to that of the United States towards immigrants from Latin America and of European countries towards Muslims.

Unwarranted rejection of people simply because they speak a different language, akin to yelling at deaf-mutes, is simply a matter of patience. On the other hand, our affinity toward Westerners is a reflection of our admiration of their culture, a topic to be addressed later. Suffice to say, it has little to do with a communication problem. (02/11/20)

41

211. Strike while the iron is hot.
쇠는 달았을 때 두드려라.

The blacksmith hammers red-hot iron all day on an anvil to produce objects such as gates, railings, light fixtures, furniture, sculpture, decorative items, weapons, etc. Needless to say, most of his work, such as bending, cutting, and hammering is done only when the wrought iron is heated to a bright orange color, and becomes soft. Just like any other proverb, this one also states an obvious observation to make a point. Here, it emphasizes the importance of timing in any matter. If you miss the perfect time to do a job, you may have to repeat the effort. In some cases, there may not be another opportunity. In a Dutch fable, a little boy "saves the Netherlands" by sticking a finger in a hole, to stop a seawall from leaking. See Entry #112, "Use a shovel for a job for *homee*?" Or, "A stitch in time saves nine."

Depending on what a blacksmith is making, a simple mistake can be remedied to some extent, by re-forging softened iron to a more desirable shape. But this is not always the case. Any imperfect forging, for instance, would produce an imperfect sword. Later, on a battlefield, it may become a matter of life or death. Famous Japanese samurai swords consist of a hard outer layer and a softer inner core, such that the final product can maintain a sharp cutting edge as well as absorb any shocks that can break the blade. The billet of steel is heated and hammered, split, and folded back upon itself many times, then re-welded to create a complex structure consisting of many thousands of layers. Folding not only ensures a homogeneous product but also evens the distribution of the carbon in the steel. Hammering also eliminates void volumes that can cause fractures in combat.

Human history, especially war history, is full of missed opportunities. "What-ifs" render us to imagine a variety of alternative outcomes of virtually any given event, usually accompanied by completely different consequences. Unlike ironwork by a blacksmith, any missed opportunity irreversibly fixes the course of history. There is no way to go back and re-create the historic events unless we can travel faster than light, that is.

During the 1948 - 49 Chinese Civil War between the Communists and Nationalists, North Korea supported the Communists, while suffering from their own adversities of poverty as well as political unrest. Remember that the North Korean government was barely formed when the Second World War ended in 1945. As a token of gratitude, Chinese Communists, now the clear winner of the Civil War, equipped almost 60,000 North Korean veterans, who had fought for them, with modern weapons and send them back to North Korea. These soldiers, with battle experience, were the backbone of the North Korean army. They were buoyed with a victorious spirit like their Chinese comrades.

While such "positive" progress was taking place in the North, South Koreans were in a big mess, with social unrest from in-fighting among various political factions. It was a well-prepared "meal" for the North. This is one way to look at the emergence of the Korean War in 1950. Since AD 668, when the Kingdom of *Goguryo* gave up the vast territory of Manchuria, the Korean peninsula has been the only piece of land our ancestors occupied. Korea, as a nation, has become smaller and weaker, always trying to read the intention of other stronger countries. The nation has been invaded constantly by neighboring "barbarians." See more in Entry #116, "The crayfish sides with crabs." Two major ones, which really broke the spine of national character, were *imjin-oeran* (임진왜란) during 1592 – 1598, by the Japanese; and *bungja-horan* (병자호란) by the Quing Dynasty of China, in 1627.

If there had not been any serious foreign interference in our domestic issues, what could have happened to Korea? We, all Koreans, might have been living under one nation, peacefully now and forever. How have our ancestors let other foreign peddlers come into the scene? Could we have maintained political neutrality, rather than leaning on a powerful nation? Switzerland and those Scandinavian countries come to my mind. It is not simply because Korea is a small country. It is the mindset of the people that we should re-forge, like hot irons on an anvil, for complete independence. Such opportune times will certainly come in the future. Do we have the collective willpower to grab the opportunities though? (02/18/20)

212. Promises are easier than deeds.
말은 행동보다 쉽고 약속은 실행보다 쉽다.

It is a lot easier offering a promise than delivering the promise in deeds, or "Tons of promise is lighter than a gram of act." There isn't much to add to what is said here. Unless one records a conversation, the words of promise disappear into the thin air soon after they are spoken. I suppose this may be the real reason why people keep a promissory note signed by the parties involved, often under the scrutiny of attorneys, or why nations proclaim a peace treaty in the eye of the whole world. Even a marriage entails prenuptial agreement nowadays, especially when one party is wealthy. In reflection of this proverb, I am submitting two cases I have learned during my life in this country. One involves a politician and the other a love-turned tragedy.

In 1992, Republican President George H.W. Bush lost his bid for re-election to Democratic candidate Bill Clinton in the general election. It is rather unusual that an incumbent president loses re-election. To this day, many people believe that Bush lost because he broke the promise not to raise taxes when he got elected. Four years earlier, on August 18, 1988, this is what Bush said at the Republican National Convention that chose him as the presidential candidate:

And I'm the one who will not raise taxes. My opponent now says he'll raise them as a last resort, or a third resort. But when a politician talks like that, you know that's one resort he'll be checking into. My opponent won't rule out raising taxes. But I will. And the Congress will push me to raise taxes and I'll say no. And they'll push, and I'll say no, and they'll push again, and I'll say, to them, "Read my lips: no new taxes."

Once elected, Bush found it impossible to keep his promise. He and his advisors had assumed that the high economic growth rate of the late 1980s would continue during his tenure. Instead, a recession began. By 1990, his administration just could not balance the budget: reducing the mounting federal deficit without new cuts from popular programs such as Social

Security, Medicare, or the defense budget. In the end, Bush had to increase taxes. Some newspapers called it, "Read my lips: I lied."

Jean Harris, at the age of 57, killed her 70-year old lover, Herman Tarnower, with a pistol. That was in March 1980. This murder became the fodder of news outlets because of Tarnower's fame as a cardiologist as well as the author of a best-selling diet book at that time: *The Complete Scarsdale Medical Diet*. Harris was the headmistress of a reputable school for girls in Virginia. After graduation from Smith College, a prestigious women's college in Northampton, Massachusetts, she married in her early 20s, but divorced with two sons, when she was 42 years old. Soon after, Harris and Tarnower began a 14-year relationship.

Tarnower was quite a womanizer: he maintained love affairs with various women during this period, and Harris was aware of them. On the day of the shooting, Harris made a five-hour drive from Virginia to Tarnower's home in a small, but wealthy village, about 20 miles northeast of New York City. When she arrived at the house, she noticed someone's lingerie in the bedroom. An argument ensued, and four shots were fired toward Tarnower at close range, from the revolver that Harris carried from Virginia. The court followed what Harris claimed to have happened. For instance, she said that she had planned to commit suicide after talking with Tarnower one last time, but prosecutors disputed her claim, noticing that she had placed extra ammunition in her pocket before confronting Tarnower.

In the end, after eight days of deliberations, the jury rejected her story, convicted her of second-degree murder, and the judge sentenced Harris to a minimum of 15-years-to-life. Eleven years later, in 1992, she was released, as she was about to undergo heart surgery. Harris died 10 years later of natural causes. She was 89. She lived her last 30 years of life in resentment that the fidelity she had expected from her lover had been missing. In both instances of Bush and Harris, their disappointments were from unfulfilled promises. (02/22/20)

213. An angry man pounds a pestle harder.
골 나면 보리 방아 더 잘 찧는다.

If you are a high school football coach, you do not let your players speak ill of the team you are about to play against, in public. It may inspire the other team to a fervent state of resentment, such that they could beat your team easily. Conversely, if you heard through the grapevine that they mocked your team rather personally, then by all means, tell your boys what you have heard, plus some modifications of your own (But, don't exaggerate too much, or invent a story, as honesty still matters in sports). Your players will get angry, with teeth grinding and fists showing white knuckles. You've won the game already. The above proverb speaks of a similar situation: An angry man would plunge a wooden pestle harder into a mortar full of grain.

I used to visit an IT guy in the basement quite often when I was a professor, as I was not savvy enough to solve numerous computer-related problems myself. It became particularly troublesome as I approached retirement because our teaching method began to rely heavily on the web and a variety of teaching apps. There was one particular young man assigned to my class, a very nice guy, with lots of patience with little words. Usually, he worked on my laptop while I looked around for any interesting objects for starting pleasantries. We got along quite nicely, if I may add. There was a small wooden bin sitting beside his desk, full of broken parts of the computer and cables. On this particular day, I noticed that a hammer was sitting on top of the mess in the box. Here was our conversation, as I remember:

"What is this hammer doing here?" I asked.
"I use it to break computers," he replied.
"You must be kidding," I continued, somewhat shocked.
"I'm serious. It's my way of managing anger," the IT guy stated.

He was then telling me how frustrating his work had been, tackling idiotic problems from people like me (he didn't say it but I could guess), new directives from the Dean, and dealing with mundane technical glitches in a classroom, etc. This particular approach of smashing old computers with a hammer was from what he had learned in an anger-management class. Besides, he might have had some domestic issues too (once again, it was my guess). Later, I gave him a pair of safety glasses from my lab.

A few days ago, just several yards away from the finish line, on the last lap of the Daytona 500, the leader of the race, Ryan Newman, got involved in a spectacular crash. His car was airborne, broken into pieces, and moving upside down on the track for a while dragging sparks and flame along. With the flying debris and thick smoke, he somehow completed the race and was awarded fourth place. He did so, hanging upside down, inside what appeared to be about half of his car. Miraculously, he survived. Then I remember what we learned in a high school physics class: one best way to dissipate the destructive energy from such collisions is to induce as much disintegration as possible. The IT guy was somehow taking advantage of the increase in entropy to mitigate his frustration.

It is quite common, and much more frequent than we may acknowledge, to utilize "negative" energy gained from anger and hatred, for one's shrewd purpose. The current modus operandi of Trump and his cronies, "divide and conquer," would be an example. As discussed also in Entry #175, "Oil droplets on water," Hitler was able to consolidate political power by establishing a collective enemy in Jews. Likewise, we could have permanent peace on this planet if we discover life on Mars and fool the entire humankind with propaganda that they are our common enemy.

During the Cold War era, anti-communism served the free world very well in uniting the nations of Europe and the United States. Anti-communism has also been the main political backbone of South Korea. Anti-capitalism has evolved from the democratic socialism of Scandinavian countries and has now brought about a powerful Democratic presidential candidate, Bernie Sanders. Any strong opinion against something well established and observed often leads to a state of frustration, anger, and even hatred. How we dissipate such negative emotions has often led to revolutions in human history. Now I see the wisdom of the IT guys who used to bang the computer parts with a hammer. (02/24/20)

214. No fault in the lovely, no courtesy to the homely.
고운사람 미운데 없고 미운사람 고운데 없다.

All things being equal, we prefer interacting with attractive people to homely ones, especially when people meet for the first time. This is as true as the sun rising in the east. It's just human nature. "There are few things to dislike about a beautiful person, while there is little to like in an unattractive person," is the direct translation of the above proverb. As I look back on my own, I will have to agree with this old saying. Men often bend backward to accommodate a plea from a beautiful woman who is seeking some kind of favor or help. An act of chivalry may include throwing a jacket over a puddle of water on the street so that a lady can walk over without soiling her shoes. Or, going out of his way, a young man may walk all the way along with an attractive lady, who is asking for a direction. I do not know for sure, but my hunch is that it is also true for women in dealing with men.

A boss may overlook a simple mistake made by an attractive assistant, but may easily get upset by the same mistake made by another homely assistant. For the former, forgiveness comes out easily, along with some comforting and encouraging words towards the despondent. For the latter, the boss may blurt out in a heartbeat harsh words as a reprimand. Such a double standard shown by a supervisor is pathetic, but happens quite often at an office. It is patently an act of sexism at its worst.

If we assume that the female subject of an old painting represents a beautiful woman at that particular period of time, we can safely say that men's perspective of the physical beauty in women varies with time. I don't know if this is just my illusion, but the women illustrated in pre-renaissance Middle Ages paintings were invariably plumper with rounder faces than those appearing in modern drawings. In the world of contemporary fashion, the thinner the better: it has gotten to a point where a female runway model died of starvation-related complications several years ago. Some countries have recently begun to legally prohibit designers and agents from employing models with a body mass index below 18. How have we begun to equate malnourished models to the benchmark of beauty?

As they say, "Beauty is in the eye of the beholder," and the concept of female beauty varies from one man to another. Many good looking friends of mine ended up marrying a "cow," a prevailing consensus among friends when they were dating. These opinions would, of course, immediately disappear upon learning they were getting married. And as I see now, several decades later, they are the ones who appeared to have lived a happy life. On the other hand, once a man gets to know a beautiful woman after a maddening crush, he may find her to be selfish, shallow, mean, demanding, and cruel. Thus, people also assert, "Beauty is only skin deep."

Although the above proverb implies otherwise, some people are not only physically appealing, but are also beautiful in heart: loyal, kind, honest, selfless, forgiving, and fun. These women can make the best wife, friend, companion, and lover. In Victor Hugo's classic, *The Hunchback of Norte-Dame*, we see the beautiful gypsy Esmeraldo capture the attention of virtually every man, including the hunchback Quasimodo and his guardian, Deacon of the cathedral. The latter is constantly tormented by the lust for the gypsy but also found a rival in a King's man. Amid the messy love triangle, Esmeraldo was hanged, and Quasimodo follows her with his own death. That was the way Quasimodo paid back the gypsy's kind and compassionate acts when both were alive.

I do not remember exactly when I watched the 1956 version of the French film, starring Anthony Quinn and Gina Lollobrigida as the hunchback and the gypsy, but what impressed me most was Quinn's disfigured transformation to the hunchback and sexual appeal of Lollobrigida. Speaking of a stark difference in appearance, this was it. Her tender treatment of Quasimodo, compared with the treatment he received from other people of power and authority, wasn't exactly based on love as we know nowadays, but more on compassion to the seemingly poor soul with a hunched back.

As a footnote, Victor Hugo wrote the novel apparently to preserve the value of the Gothic architecture, which had been neglected and often destroyed. Had they made a movie with this theme, it might not have been a commercial success. (03/03/2020)

215. Stealing the doorknob of a police station.
포도청 문고리를 빼겠다.

"I will steal the doorknob of the police station!" declares a man. It is quite a boastful audacity of arrogance and self-confidence because *po-do-cheong* (포도청), of the old Joseon Dynasty of Korea, was not just a local or provincial police station where a few flies idly moved about in a dog-day afternoon of summer. It would be equivalent to an imaginary law enforcement agency that combines the security functions of our current CIA, FBI, NSC, ICE, DEA, and other some such fearsome outfits. Once you enter the place as a suspect of a crime, you may not see the daylight not to mention unobstructed blue sky, for the remainder of your life. Even if you are a law-abiding citizen with an impeccable record of civil duties, when you pass by a huge *po-do-cheong* building, you would feel a cool breeze from the open gate, manned by two sentries, each holding a long javelin. You would also realize that your hair is standing at the back of your neck and there are goosebumps all over the body, for no obvious reason.

  The immediate thoughts about this blow-hard man from startled listeners may include why, how, and when. Is he planning to rescue his kid brother, who was put into jail this afternoon, for what he thinks is a very trivial offense? For crying out loud, the kid just whistled at a girl walking across the street! Is he going to pick the door lock during the wee hours of the darkest night? How? Does he have some kind of special tool? Or does this man just want to demonstrate how brave he is to everyone listening? It is also possible that he has been cultivating a great deal of resentment against the law of the nation, for some reason that nobody can fathom. No matter, his daring plan holds the breath of listeners and stirs a kind of admiration among the cowards.

  We can find a good example of bravery in the independent movement of our forefathers during the unlawful occupation by Imperial Japan that began in 1910. The Declaration of Independence, commonly observed as 3·1 Movement, or 삼일절 (*sam-il-jeol*), took place on March 1, 1919. The anger and frustration of Koreans from suppressed freedom by militant Japan had reached a point of explosion. About a year earlier, at the

50

Paris Peace Conference in 1918, Woodrow Wilson, the 28th President of the United States, called for the establishment of the League of Nations, to guarantee the independence and territorial integrity of all nations in this world.

On March 1, at 2 PM, leading Korean patriots proclaimed Korea as an independent nation, at a restaurant named *Myung-wol-gwan* (명월관), in *In-sa-dong*, Seoul. The decree was signed by 33 prominent revolutionaries, many Christians. After the brief celebration, the leaders asked the owner of the restaurant to inform the Japanese police that they were having a peaceful gathering. The keyword here is "peaceful," as they surrendered themselves voluntarily to avoid unnecessary confrontation with the notoriously brutal Japanese police. In January of 1919, the penultimate king of the Joseon dynasty, *Go-jong* (고종), died under a suspicious circumstance and a large mourning crowd was expected at his state funeral, slated on March 3. Thus, the signatories of the decree wanted to have a gathering two days earlier to avoid any violent confrontations with the Japanese police. Despite their effort, there was a gathering of tens of thousands, in nearby Pagoda Garden, at exactly 2 PM. After declaring independence, they marched on the major streets of Seoul, many waving the national flag. *Gwan-soon Yoo* (유관순), a Korean Joan of Arc, deserves particular recognition for her courage. Not only were her parents killed by Japanese police, but she also died in jail at the tender age of 17.

Subsequently, numerous patriotic leaders established satellite nations in Shanghai, Russia, and even in the United States. Historic records later showed that as many as 590,000 citizens participated in the campaign, 12,175 were arrested, 553 people killed, and over 1,400 injured. On another political front, the movement rendered a swerve in Japanese administration policy in Korea, from iron-fisted outright suppression to persuasive control via a cultural influence. Indeed, I was born with a Japanese name along with a Korean name. It sounds and reads so awkwardly, I have been using it as a password on many of my PC-related accounts. (03/08/20)

216. The picnic basket overturns with lunch in it.
광주리에 담은 밥도 엎어질 수 있다.

No matter who says what, the main staple of a Korean meal is *bob* (밥), steamed rice. Broadly, the word *bob* can also mean a meal in general, inclusive of all types of cuisine, at any time of the day or night. Another word for the same connotation is *jinji* (진지); however, this word is used only when you address an elderly person, as in an inquiry, "Have you already taken dinner?" See more in Entry #1, "Be careful what you say, even inside a coffin." The above proverb invokes *bob* in a basket, not on a dining table, implying something like lunch for a picnic: "You can lose your meal, or *bob* (밥), that has been packed safely in your wicker basket, as it can still tip over."

In a formal setting, steamed rice is offered while still warm in a round bowl with a lid, usually made of glazed porcelain or silver. It would be hardly suitable for a lunch bag though. A most common lunch box for a field trip or a picnic, that school children used to take, consisted of Korean rolls of steamed rice, wrapped in dried seaweed, commonly known as *gym-bob* (김밥), along with an apple, some sweets, chewing gum, a bottle of cider, and of course a pair of chopsticks, which we always managed to forget to pack at the last minute of the exciting morning of an excursion. It is not easy to prepared *gym-bob* (김밥).

Every mother would have her own method, but the gist is the taste and texture of the final product in the mouth. Just like any other meal a mother prepares for her children, the adopted taste would last for the child's lifetime, and render a grown man yearning for the original taste of his mother's *gym-bob*.

This is how my mother used to prepare it. The first necessary "equipment" is a roller: thin bamboo strips woven together by a few strings to form a kind of small mat, about 10-inch square. It looks like a miniature bamboo screen. On this, place a sheet of dried seaweed, *gym* or 김. Spread steamed rice, adequately salted, and mixed well with a small quantity of sesame oil, on top of the *gym*, evenly pressing it down with the flat side of a wet spoon. It is a lot easier to do this while the rice is still warm and soft.

Now comes the creative part of the preparation. In the middle of the rice, place a row of sliced pan-fried egg, seasoned spinach, and a thin strip of radish, called *da-kuang*. Optional items may be carrot strip, sliced cucumber, and diced Korean *bulgogi,* or spam. *Da-kuang* is a Japanese pickled radish that tastes a bit salty and sweet. Since the word is Japanese, and since Koreans try to avoid any Japanese words – just remember the 35-year occupation of the Korean Peninsula before the Second World War – the word is no longer used and has been replaced with *dan-moo-ji* (단무지).

Once all is placed on the steamed rice, beginning from one side of the bamboo mat, the whole thing is lifted and rolled slowly, but firmly, to the other end. This is the most critical and difficult operation that will test how dexterous you are. A few failed rolls are always welcomed by hungry younger siblings. Finally, the mother would slice the rolled *gym-bob* with a sharp knife, after its blade is dipped in sesame oil, into pieces about one-centimeter in thickness. It is like cutting a sausage. The cross-section is multi-colored with all the ingredients: yellow from *da-kuang*, green from spinach, brown from cooked beef, white from the egg, etc. Some ambitious and young mothers would go for the seven colors of a rainbow, imagining how proud their child would be at the school picnic.

Going back to the proverb, how would a schoolboy feel if the lunchbox that *their* (see the foot-note of #207) mother made with such care and love, for *their* picnic, was dropped to the ground by a silly mistake or carelessness, and the *gym-bob* is now all spoiled, just before the lunch break? The boy might have been too excited about the prospect of a delicious lunch.

In all, the proverb is similar to "The way to be safe is never to feel secure." Or, the most vulnerable time is when you are off guard. We have also come across a similar one in Entry #174, "My ax injures my foot." The proverb should not be interpreted as one cannot be at ease and must be on alert all the time. Rather, it reads like simple advice that we ought to maintain a reasonable level of mindfulness to what we routinely do in any daily life. Oftentimes we still encounter an unexpected, inevitable disaster though. (03/20/2020)

217. Blame the painter for a picture hung upside-down.
문비를 거꾸러 붙이고 환쟁이만 나무린다

On the first day of a new year, Korean folks used to hang a huge painting of fearsome-looking guards on the main front door of a palace or even a private dwelling. It was to protect the resident, throughout the year, from unwelcome ghosts who may bring in diseases, unhappiness, or misfortunes. The painting, mainly drawn in a bright red color, usually depicted armed warriors carrying such weapons as an ax, spear, javelin, etc.: perfect hunters of evil. This tradition, certainly imported from China, had been observed for many centuries, beginning in the early days of the Joseon Dynasty (1393 – 1897), till the mid 19th century. The practice is certainly in the realm of superstition; but, then, who am I to say what is good or bad. It must have offered our ancestors some sense of security. That is perfectly fine with me.

The painting of guards is referred to as *moon-bi* (문비) in the above proverb, which I just call a picture. As I implied, the drawing is complicated, crowded with many doohickeys, often animals, and quite "noisy," but one should be able to discern at least which side is up. This man, presumably the head of a well-to-do household, has just learned from a better-educated man, that he hung the drawing upside down. More or less out of embarrassment, he curses the man who drew the painting, *hwan-jaeng-y* (환쟁이), as the scapegoat for his ignorance. Sounds very much like our President Donald Trump. Who can beat him in a blame game? His pathological lies and blaming others for his benefit are so numerous, even the biggest tome may find itself too small in space.

As of this writing, the United States has reported nearly as many cases of coronavirus infection as any other country: We're in third place, after China and Italy, followed by Spain and Germany. In hindsight, the pandemic in this country could and should have been much less severe, had the federal government (Donald Trump, that is) reacted promptly and decidedly. On Friday, March 13, the day he declared a National Emergency, his tweets spoke volumes on the subject relevant to the present topic.

"For decades, the CDC (Centers for Disease Control and Prevention) looked at, studied its testing system but did nothing about it. It would always be inadequate and slow for a large scale pandemic, but a pandemic would never happen, they hoped. President Obama made changes that only complicated things further."

As a follow-up: "Their response to H1N1 Swine flu was a full-scale disaster, with thousands dying, and nothing meaningful done to fix the testing problem, until now. The changes have been made and testing will soon happen on a very large scale basis. All Red Tape has been cut, ready to go!" During a news conference he declared: "No, I don't take responsibility at all, because we were given a set of circumstances." The next day, another tweet said, "Sleepy Joe Biden was in charge of the H1N1 epidemic which killed thousands of people. The response was one of the worst on record."

The man, who hung the *moon-bi* (문비) upside down, did not commit any harm to others. He just made himself a laughing stock, perhaps a good deed, as he at least entertained others. The case of Trump blaming others for his inadequacy leads us to only two interpretations. If he is conscious about his excuse and blaming, he is simply deceiving the nation and its citizens, hiding underneath his stainless, and not just thick, skin. If he doesn't, his head must be examined to confirm the big empty space between his two ears. All said, have you ever seen a captain blaming his subordinates when a disaster strikes his ship? What happened to the presidential motto, "The buck stops here," by Harry Truman?

The temptation to blame others for an unexpected failure or disaster is simply human nature, perhaps deeply embedded somewhere in our DNA. That's what we cowardly do first, at the spur of the moment. On the other hand, claiming credit for an unexpected success or fortune always tempts us into wanting a share of the outcome.

Truly brave men are those who readily admit their own mistakes and yet can maintain a peaceful mind within. Likewise, truly humble men do not advertise their good work, as Mathew 6:3 reads: "But when you do merciful deeds, don't let your left hand know what your right hand does." And think about those thousands of medical professionals who are now on the front line, in defense against the coronavirus. (03/22/2020)

218. A needle beats an ax.
도끼 가진 놈이 바늘 가진 놈을 못 당한다.

I am an unabashed and proud minimalist. This has sometimes led me to a quarrelsome moment with my wife, who often behaves as if plentifulness is a requirement of happiness. For her, the feeling of security and thus happiness is from the excess of everything; say, overflowing stuff in our refrigerator and freezer, clothes and shoes in the closet, stationary in her room, boxes of Kleenex in every room, bottles of distilled water for humidifiers, and of course a large sum of cash in our checking account all the time. Just plain silly, if you ask me. I am not complaining about the variety of items she keeps, but what bothers me is the large quantity of nearly everything we maintain, at a steady-state. I remind her that we have a grocery store around the corner but to no avail.

Whenever an occasion deems warranted, she confesses her anxiety about money when we married decades ago. "You had only a few hundred dollars in your checking account. Many nights I couldn't sleep, worrying about where our next meal would come from." Whenever I hear her past anxiety about money, I become dumbfounded, not only because it was a long time ago, but also because I have never felt the same way about the finances of this household as she did. In the end, I belatedly apologized for my inability to erase her past anxiety. People may say, "Ah-ha, she must have been raised in poverty!" That's hardly the case. I don't understand her logic because I know for sure that we cannot carry the leftovers to the next world when we depart this world. Truth be told, we have never lived "poorly" on my watch. She should see a shrink, period.

"A man with an ax can be beaten by a man with a needle," is what the above proverb says. Is it the same as, "the pen is mightier than the sword?" Can a colossal criminal be neutralized by a micro-gram dose of the plant toxin, ricin? Why were the almighty American military forces, with $50-billion B-2 bombers and $80-billion F-35 fighters, unable to stop the 9·11 attack by a handful of al-Qaida terrorists in 2001? Doesn't a small measure in time save more for later? See more in Entry #113, "Use a shovel for a job for

56

homee," where I introduced the Dutch fable, "A boy who saved the Netherlands."

How was it possible that an unknown, poorly-funded congressman candidate, Alexandria Ocasio-Cortez, beat a well-oiled incumbent for the 2018 Democratic nomination and eventually became a House representative? See Entry #110, "No one can go to the bathroom or heaven's gate on your behalf."

In the mid 19th century, there lived a legendary poet named Kim Saat-gat (김삿갓). He was born to a well-established *yang-ban* family, but when he was six years old, he had to flee home as his grandfather was condemned as a traitor. More than a decade later, his family received clemency and he, now at the age of 20-something, was able to pass the prestigious national exam, 과거 (*gwa-go*). During the test, he submitted an essay that severely criticized a particular traitor.

He did not know that the traitor was in fact his grandfather until he was appointed to a government post. After resigning from the position out of shame and self-pity, he began a life-long journey as a perpetual traveler, until he died in 1863. He was 56 years old. Having accepted his tragic fate and irony, he felt that he could not face the sky, and thus he always wore a wide-brim bamboo hat, or *saat-gat* (삿갓). His open-ended journey, mainly on foot, from one village to another, was accompanied by poems that often tried to define a life. His eccentricity likened Don Quixote and his simple life represented the best of a minimalist. So many centuries later, in this foreign land, I find myself humming a Choi Hee-Joon's pop song of the 1960s, called *A Student Boarder*.

인생은나그네길,	Life is a journey,
어디서왔다가어디로가는가?	Where is it from and to go?
구름이흘러가듯떠돌다가는길에,	Wanders like a cloud,
정일랑두지말자미련일랑두지말자	Never leave love nor sorrow.
인생은나그네길,	Life is a journey,
구름이흘러가듯정처없이흘러서간다.	It passes like a cloud.

(03/24/2020)

219. The diligent beggar receives warm meals.
거지도 부지런하면 더운 밥을 얻어먹는다.

In the good old days, when all was innocent, a wandering beggar or two used to visit our home in the morning, asking for a meal. Our kitchen-maid would open the door to offer some leftovers from breakfast, into a tin can they carried. She used to do the same, along with some alms, to a few young boys who were to become monks at a local Buddhist temple. The memory was so old, now it could well be just a phantom image, rather than a recollection of what actually happened. If such instances did happen, it must have been when I was just a toddler and my parents lived a comfortable life in Hamheung, North Korea. My father was a wealthy man then, as he had literally struck gold, and immediately sold the mining rights to Japanese investors.

If a beggar or a young Buddhist disciple was diligent enough to get up early in the morning, and knock on the front gate of our house, he must have received a warm meal from our housemaid, not just the leftovers, but the same meal our family was having at nearly the same time. The housemaid, who would become one of my many sisters as she was officially adopted years later, was a woman of warm heart and boundless kindness. This scenario is essentially what the above proverb was saying. It is thus equivalent to, "The early bird catches the worm." The merit of diligence has been the subject of many proverbs in the past; for instance, see Entry #99, "All fields are fertile to diligent farmers."

A brief comment is warranted regarding the significance of "warm" rice. Steamed rice, the main component of Korean meals, is best served when it is warm, in a silver bowl with a lid. At the beginning of every dinner, my father would lift the lid and pour sake onto it. It held just the right volume of the liquor to be appetizing. Only then, the whole family would start the dinner, beginning with the first spoonful of warm rice.

I don't know if there is any significant difference in taste between warm and cold rice, but cold rice is bad news to anyone. Some cantankerous siblings in a bad mood may formally complain about it, kicking the leg of the dining table and raising a voice. Koreans were so accustomed to warm rice that receiving or offering cold rice, *chan-bob* (찬밥), was like offering or receiving an unwarranted humiliation, intentional or unintentional. If it was intentional, it would be equivalent to spitting at the feet of the other person, just before challenging a duel. When one of us was late for the family dinner, our mother used to keep the steamed rice in a silver bowl with a lid, inside the blanket so that it would remain warm. This is well before microwave ovens became available. Even a beggar wanted to be treated properly by getting warm rice. That is the gist of the proverb.

Diligence, as opposed to laziness, is one of the so-called seven heavenly virtues of Christian origin from the Middle Ages. It would be an acquired trait, likely little to do with genetic inheritance, as we see many lazy sons and daughters from diligent parents. In fact, we witness many opposite cases: hard-working parents with a prodigal son. See Rembrandt's painting of the same title, depicting Luke 15: 11 - 32. Diligence is ultimately from a belief that work is good in itself and that we have to work hard to respect the work. Besides, hard work usually yields a sweet success that no one can take away from us. Even if it fails to satisfy you, it will never bring you regret.

The other six virtues are chastity, temperance, charity, patience, kindness, and humility; as opposed to lust, excessiveness, greed, wrath, cruelty, and pride, respectively. These distinctions have helped the human battle between good virtues and evil vices throughout history. In modern living, however, some of these elements seem to have lost their persuasive powers. In some decadent social circles, hedonism and greed seem to have the upper hand, while cruelty has become an effective tool for controlling the masses. Witness the currently rampant, so-called cancel culture, or shame culture. They are hardly based on any of the above seven virtues.

According to the above proverb, the constant reminder and practice of the seven virtues would guarantee not only a bowl of warm rice but also a glass of warm sake on your dinner table. Why, then, do I feel these words sound so hollow in this day and age? (03/26/2020)

220. Weeds in a flowerpot are flowers.
분에 심어 놓으면 못된 풀도 화초라 한다.

This proverb reminds me of an episode that happened about eight years ago. In our living room, we had two good-sized plants, each in a pot, and occupying the right and left side corners of the room. The one at the left was some kind of rubber plant and the other one looked vaguely familiar, but I wasn't quite sure what it was. Both had been with us for a while, most likely gifts from friends.

One day, the plant on the right began to bloom after all those dormant years. It was quite an excitement. I thus took pictures and described the fragrance as best as I could for my wife, who had been living in Birmingham, Alabama at that time. If I recall, the flowers lasted for a long time, at least a month, and so did the aroma. A few months later, after the flowers were all gone, I downloaded an App called PlantNet. It identified a plant when you took a picture of it. It said I had corn! To this day, I still don't know what I had, but I have never used the App again since then.

The above proverb says that a weed becomes, or is, a flower when planted in a fancy flower pot. It implies how easily appearance can deceive people. Here, there are three parties involved: the cheater, the fooled, and the third-party observer. People who commit fraud must have a reason to justify their behavior, most likely it's for monetary reasons, or out of greed. However, they cannot succeed without victims. These are the vulnerable, often innocent, people. Then, some bystanders may learn something, from just watching what has occurred. Blindly trusting any strangers is part of me that has frequently made me appear as a fool in the eyes of my wife. Here, I would like to introduce a few episodes, all of which have happened within the past year.

The Wi-Fi signal was once so weak that I was not able to get it, even in our stamp-sized backyard. Then I came across an ad for a Wi-Fi booster in a reputable newspaper. Hurriedly, I ordered one, but it was a big disappointment: the signal was still weak and the download speed was actually slowed from about 90 MBPS to 60. When I returned it, they said that the package was compromised, and thus I would not get any refund.

With this rapidly advancing age, what irritates me most nowadays is finding that I cannot cut my toenails as easily as before. Instead of accepting the somber reality, I had been blaming the clipper I have had for many years. I was thus most glad to see an ad for a high-tech, "modern" nail clipper in the same national newspaper. When I ordered the item, what I saw in their acknowledgment email were some additional accessories that I did not want. The total price was more than double the price of the clipper. Out of principle, I canceled the whole order. I was proud of myself for not having lost money this time. Similarly, I canceled the contract with a local Internet/TV/phone provider. Even when one deletes an item, say phone service, there are no savings in this so-called "bundle" product.

Just last month, I noticed in my monthly Visa card statement, an item for $39.99, which I couldn't recognize. As I later found out from my bank, an outfit called Lenosity had been withdrawing $1 every month. This time they became bold and tried $39.99. A phone call to their 800 number told me that it was something to do with a magazine subscription. It was a lie. My bank had to issue a new card after my account received the reimbursement of $39.99.

The trust between consumers and suppliers used to be the backbone of any commercial transaction, not only here but also in Korea even when we were dirt poor. This issue becomes more important nowadays, as we order items online more frequently, primarily based on advertisements and reviews by other users.

According to my experience, neither review nor ad seems to be reliable. What I have to do from now on are a thorough investigation and serious vigilance. As they say, it is a new norm.

This would be my conclusion, as a third person looking at the current trend of trust, not only in commerce but also among ordinary citizens. What you see is one thing, but what it really is could be a completely different matter altogether. Not all plants in a fancy pot are exotic flowers. It can be corn if you follow a fancy new app on the cell phone. (03/29/20)

221. Young beggars are more troublesome than the old ones.
묵은 거지보다 햇거지가 더 어렵다.

One of the best American films ever made, *One Flew over the Cuckoo's Nest*, released in 1975, begins with a scene of Randle McMurphy (played by Jack Nicholson) being admitted to a mental institution. This is after serving a short sentence on a prison farm for several charges of assault and statutory rape of a 15-year-old girl. He was not mentally ill but hoped to avoid hard labor and serve the rest of his sentence in a "relaxed" environment. He immediately noticed that the place was run by a cold, passive-aggressive nurse, named Mildred Ratched (played by Louise Fletcher). She used her rules and authority to intimidate her patients into a restrictive, joyless existence. In the movie, one could see everyone, except this new inmate McMurphy, hated her but was helpless about her tyranny.

The all-male patient community consisted of an anxious stutter named Billy, a well-educated but paranoid individual with childish tantrums, and delusional but harmless; an aggressive and profane guy named Max Taber; two epileptics; a quiet and yet violent-minded man; a giant Native American deaf-mute called "Chief," and several others with chronic conditions. As the story develops, we begin to see an antagonistic relationship between Nurse Ratched and McMurphy. The nurse, who sees McMurphy's lively and rebellious presence as a threat to her authority, begins cigarette rationing and curtails their card-playing privileges. McMurphy, on the other hand, keeps testing her will by continuously violating rules. One day he even steals a hospital bus, escaping with several patients to go on a fishing trip, encouraging his friends to discover their abilities and find self-confidence.

Now, he finally realizes that he won't be able to complete the jail time in the mental hospital and that he could remain there indefinitely. McMurphy makes plans to escape with help from Chief. It is also revealed that McMurphy, Chief, and Taber are the only non-chronic patients sentenced to staying at the institution. All others are self-committed and could voluntarily check-out at any time. After a fight with the orderlies over his confiscated cigarettes, Ratched sends McMurphy and Chief to the "shock shop," where McMurphy discovers Chief can actually speak and hear, having feigned his deaf-muteness just to avoid engaging with anyone. After being subjected to electroconvulsive therapy, McMurphy returns to the ward pretending to have brain-damage, the incident making him even more determined to escape the ordeal. First, they decide to throw a secret Christmas party for their friends, after Ratched leaves for the night.

McMurphy sneaks two women into the ward. After a night of partying, McMurphy and Chief prepare to escape, while arranging for one woman to have sex with Billy, the stutter. Ratched arrives in the morning to find the ward in disarray and most of the patients passed out drunk. She also discovers the dalliance and embarrasses Billy in front of everyone. Billy manages to overcome his stutter and stands up to Ratched until she threatens to inform his mother about his escapade. Billy's stutter returns and he cracks under the pressure. In the end, Billy commits suicide.

McMurphy attacks the nurse and gets a prefrontal lobotomy as a punishment. Some level of normalcy returns to the ward, but rumors spread that McMurphy has escaped, avoiding the lobotomy. Later that night, Chief sees McMurphy being returned to his bed. When McMurphy is utterly unresponsive and physically limp, Chief discovers lobotomy scars on his forehead. In an act of mercy, Chief smothers his friend to death with a pillow. After breaking windows, he is then finally able to escape into the night while others cheer him on.

A young man could become a beggar for a variety of reasons: he might have been abruptly disowned by his rich parents, for his bad behaviors or his investments might have gone south via a bad strategy. This new beggar understandably has more displeasures and complaints than an old beggar who, over time, has become acclimated to a beggar's life. This is the essence of the above proverb. As a metaphor, I introduced McMurphy in *One Flew over the Cuckoo's Nest*. He was a new member of the mental institution. His rebellious acts out of the will to survive are the last things that Nurse Ratched could tolerate in her otherwise uneventful work. Also, don't forget that it is always the new kid on the block who brings along a new game into the neighborhood. (03/31/2020)

222. Stealing bells with ears plugged.
귀 막고 방울 도둑질한다.

Absurdity and irony are often an essential part of a proverb. We see another example here: "When you try to steal a bell, make sure you close off your ears, lest you hear the bell ringing." The logic behind the advice appears to be that no one hears the noise if you don't hear it. That is to say, "hear no evil" or "blind men describing an elephant." Such a superficial approach to an easy way out of a given problem seems more popular in contemporary medical practice. A few cases in point are given below.

The medical practice mainly consists of diagnosis and treatment, with a wrong diagnosis leading to various irrelevant treatments and sometimes even wrongful death. That much everyone would agree. However, some physicians seem too anxious to jump into treatment without due process through pathological etiology. This trend, perceived by this old man, was undoubtedly aided by the rich literature of drugs and various "educational" sales pitches by pharmaceutical firms. My wife had been suffering from common bursitis in the hip bone for a while and complained about a low-grade pain when we would take a walk. Her primary care physician suggested the Salonpas patch. I had to drag her to see an orthopedic to confirm what we had been suspecting.

As far as I could tell, I was the only one among my contemporaries who had not been taking blood pressure-lowering or cholesterol-lowering drugs. This is a reflection of my stubborn dislike of oral medicine. I know a lot more than my friends about both what medicine does to our body and what our body does to the xenobiotic. The knowledge is from my previous profession. About a month ago, a nurse at the allergy clinic I visit for an injection every other week, discovered that my systolic blood pressure was over 160. She was alarmed and so was I. As it happened, a few days later, I had a bi-annual physical with my primary care physician. Once again, the blood pressure was close to 160 and my doctor recommended a calcium channel blocker, amlodipine (same as Norvasc®), the same medicine my wife has been taking against my wishes.

Drugs for managing hypertension are not like medicines for managing transient medical issues such as antibiotics for bacterial infection or Tylenol for toothache, in that you will have to take them, pretty much continuously, until you die. Since the remaining days of my life are, more or less, "numbered," any reasonable old man would have agreed to the recommendation. But, that is not me. I immediately bought a blood pressure monitor, the same model the nurse at the clinic was using, a Welch Allyn 1500 Series. Every day, three times a day, I measured my blood pressure for one month: morning, mid-afternoon, and night time. The raw data indicated that the pressure in the morning is significantly lower than the other two measurements. The numbers are also tightest, ranging from 125 to 145. The afternoon pressure is highest, in the range of 140 to 160. At nighttime, the pressure is in the middle, from 130 to 150. What surprised me most was finding that the data are scattered all over the place, as low as 120 and as high as 170.

I understand that resting blood pressure above 130 (80 for diastolic pressure) is considered a borderline between normal and hypertension. Mine is certainly above the threshold, but I am not completely persuaded by the medical intervention. I asked my wife how many times her physician measured her blood pressure before she accepted the physician's advice and started taking amlodipine. She didn't remember. Would it be possible that the measurement(s) that led to the decision might have been an outlier? Superimpose this question onto another question regarding the physician's stand: Why would a physician not prescribe a blood-pressure-lowering medicine for a patient at the borderline like me? There is no reason for him not to, right?

One phone call to a local pharmacy from the physician's office would be all that is needed for you to take a drug for the rest of your life. The shaky diagnosis, based on erratic blood pressure measurements in this sequence of events, appears to be an after-thought. What bothers me most is the fact that my wife's physician had never taken her condition seriously enough to repeatedly monitor the blood pressure. This is as bad as a guy who plugs his ears when trying to steal a bell. (04/01/2020)

223. Putting off a promised visit till three births later.
간다 간다 하면서 아이 셋 낳고 간다.

Let us imagine a hypothetical, but quite plausible, situation that a young woman is facing. She has just married. Before her marriage, she and her fiancé used to visit the gravesite of her future father-in-law quite often. In many ways, it was akin to date: on a sunny and beautiful fall day, at a quiet cemetery, offering soju to the dead, trimming the weeds around the tomb, lying side by side, and staring upward into the blue sky. They learn more about his family, especially the father, and map out the future family plans, etc.

With the whirlwind wedding ceremony itself and the usual bliss of the newlyweds, visiting the tomb has been placed on the long to-do list. Now that they have their first child, the situation has become more hectic, and the visit she had promised her father-in-law inevitably gets delayed: with the unstoppable time flying by, it is postponed until they have two more children. So said is the above proverb. I cannot tell you why specifically after three births, not four or even six births later, but I suppose it's just a manner of speech to mean a long time.

The somber truth may be that visiting the tomb of the late father-in-law has never been a top priority. The delayed visit could be less than enjoyable, were she ever to feel it an obligation. Or she could say aloud, in a belated justification, "Being late is much better than never." Either way, the next visit may well be after another three births. "Oh, I meant to call you but…" says a man to his friend, whom he has not seen for a while when they come across each other by chance on the street. The truth is, his friend is not that important at present. That is usually how a casual acquaintance fades away.

In one's life, however, there are a few visits you should not postpone. One such case would be visiting ailing parents or old friends: See Entry #66, "I have few invites, but many places to visit." My father passed away in 1984, the year my favorite baseball team, the Detroit Tigers, won the World Series. I arrived in Seoul for his funeral, having missed a few chances to see him alive earlier. It was such a long trip and physically exhausting, I was not fully aware of its significance right then. A dozen years prior, my mother died without me being informed. I was then a graduate student in Kansas. How I was not aware of her death was explained in Entry #140, "Parents can take care of their ten children, but not vice versa." Then, moving forward, in the bitterly cold winter of 2013, I visited a dear friend of mine on his death bed. Everybody said that it would be more meaningful to visit him while he was still alive than just attending his memorial. I guess I could have done both, but did not. When we sat together, if I remember correctly, there were no serious, soul-searching conversations. I just took him in a wheelchair, out to a restaurant near the hospital, and had him enjoy smoking outside on a cold day after lunch. We just reminisced what "evil" things we did together in the good old days, so-to-speak.

In a completely different context, I strongly believe that President Trump and his cronies should have visited the issues involving COVID-19 much earlier. A brief chronology may justify my complaint. On December 31, 2019, Chinese health officials in Wuhan reported dozens of pneumonia cases of unknown cause. This date is considered Day 1 of COVID-19. Approximately 10 days later, a 61-year-old man died, becoming the first casualty. On January 20 this year, the first confirmed cases were reported in Korea, Thailand, and Japan. The very next day, the U.S. announced its first confirmed COVID-19 case in Washington State. On February 20, Korea reported its first death from COVID-19.

Both the U.S. and Korea discovered their first patients nearly at the same time, but see where they are now, on April 4, 2020. Instead of moving quickly and decidedly before it became an unprecedented disaster, this President, utterly incapable of really anything, was in denial mode, fashioned by his know-all attitude and did not do anything. His inaction during the critical early phase of the coronavirus pandemic was "deadly" and cost American lives.

Just yesterday, when a reporter reminded him of his statement that the problem would disappear in April, he flatly denied having made such a declaration. As far as I can tell, all he did yesterday in the White House was to determine if wearing masks should be mandatory in public places. His recommendation was, "You can if you wish but you don't have to." That's the conclusion from hours of discussion? Duh... (04/04/2020)

224. A small blow to start a fire, a gale to quench the fire.
작은 바람은 불을 붙이고, 큰 바람은 불을 끈다.

Starting a fire, say with wood, first requires heat which would produce gaseous fuels. It is the gas, upon ignition with a match, which produces more heat when burned and sustain the fire. If we borrow chemical jargon, the reaction with oxygen in the atmosphere for the start of a fire is endothermic, while the burning itself is exothermic. Heat is absorbed and is emitted by a given "system," respectively. In short, it is analogous to saying, "You will need money to make money."

One product of combustion is invariably carbon dioxide (CO_2), and other gaseous materials including smoke. When accumulated at the burning site, they prevent the continuous supply of fresh oxygen from being taken from the air, smoldering and eventually extinguishing the young fire. To continuously remove CO_2, we blow at the twigs with a ball of fire on paper or dry leaves. That is what we see kids practice at a campsite, with knees bent down and eyes teary from smoke, without analyzing the above microscopic processes. On the other hand, any open flame can be blown away with a gust of wind. This proverb thus says that a gentle blow helps fire get started, but a violent wind can quench it.

Of the many ramifications that can be derived from the proverb, an immediate and obvious one must be that anything excessive can be harmful. A gust of wind may interfere with one's effort to start a campfire, but it can also create the havoc of an uncontrollable wildfire. It is all a matter of circumstance, in a relative sense, such as the purpose of a certain act.

Over-indulging in anything that gives *them* instant gratification, defines addiction, as *they* succumb to the same action repeatedly (as to *they* and *them*, see the footnote of #207). It can be an addiction to drugs, alcohol, sex, gambling, porn, social network service, work, smoking, food, video game, etc. The word addiction usually carries a negative connotation, but food addiction would be only marginally harmful. A workaholic can lead to so-called *karoshi,* as presented in Entry #96, "Drinking can be medicinal with proper consumption, but..." Truth be told, over-indulging in anything innocuous, like love, can be just as harmful when it becomes a dotage.

Younger generations seem to spend much time on social networking nowadays. Should it be our concern? An excessive administrative structure in any organization, albeit pleasing to onlookers, can spell a disaster due to heavy bureaucracy and can result in "a dozen chiefs with one Indian." Too many options may mean no outstanding choice. Too much idling time may render people lethargic. Too much money could make its owner greedier. In a similar vein, a religious fanatic can easily become a terrorist with twisted idealisms, defeating the very meaning of religion. The list in the same vein can go on for a while.

The Buddha defined his teaching as "the middle way" between one extreme of austerity along with bodily denial and the other extreme of sensual hedonism or indulgence. The former is also practiced by the Catholic, while the latter may be by some wealthy sectors of modern societies. The Buddha subscribed to the notion of "a sound mind in a sound body," not with luxury or poverty, but with the human response to circumstances. Too small a fire is of little use for anything, while a bonfire can yield to an inferno of a whole town.

As explained in Entry #96, in an ideal pharmacokinetic scenario, after we take medicine, the drug concentration in the bloodstream remains above the therapeutically effective minimal level, while it never reaches and goes beyond the maximum tolerable level. This can be readily obtained if one receives the drug following an infusion protocol: lying in a hospital bed and intravenously receiving a solution containing the drug at a constant rate.

Because of the hospital overhead cost and because not all agents are water-soluble, the practice is severely limited to some serious cases only, say, chemotherapy for cancer with some nasty side effects. If a patient takes a chemotherapeutic agent orally, with infinitesimally small doses and as frequently as possible, the net effect should mimic the pharmacokinetics of infusion protocol. This practice is known as metronomic chemotherapy and has recently become an important armament in cancer therapy. It is a long way from the above proverb, but the crux remains the same in both cases. (04/05/2020)

225. Pots in the kitchen, a hoe in the barn.
솥은 부엌에 걸고 절구는 헛간에 놓아라 한다.

You are to keep all cooking utensils in the kitchen, while other household items like a mortar, wheel barrel, shovel, ax, ladder, saw, etc. are in a barn or shed. In a modern house, most of the man's tools are kept in a garage, where you may occasionally find an automobile. Putting things away in a proper place, where they belong, serves several purposes. First, such practice keeps a house in good order without much clutter. That, plus regular dusting, would make a house appealing for living in. Secondly, such a practice always helps find what one is looking for. As said in the above proverb, the stuff has been kept in a place based on a reasonable judgment of its function. Thus it would render a quick finding possible, avoiding the unnecessary frustration of looking around endlessly.

I have my own way of filing important documents on my laptop as well as the actual filing cabinet. It is in a simple alphabetical order based on headings, starting from AARP (American Association of Retired Persons) to United Health Care, Vegas Home, and Will & Trust. It is far from water-tight. Medical records are kept under "Medical," while medical bills are in the "Insurance" folder. And yet, car insurance-related documents go to the "BMW" folder. When I put a new document in a hanging folder, it goes at the back. Americans seem to place recent ones at the front. I guess both cases have their own merits as well as disadvantages.

My wife is not as well organized as I am, but she finds what she is looking for much better than I do. The office of my old professor, T. Higuchi, was one of the most chaotic ones I have witnessed: books, papers, awards, and all sorts of nick-nacks would be sitting precariously on his desk, window sill, chairs, and any other surfaces available. But, he never seemed to have any difficulty when he had to find a particular something.

In my case, when I fail to find what I am looking for in the first few places I choose to look, I get completely lost. This is the dilemma of a person too well-organized. Indices in those two books I published earlier are useless in locating an essay very similar to what I am writing. It is both maddening and frustrating, but what can I do? Is my memory power getting dimmer every day? Maybe I rely on my computer and smartphone too much.

Many years ago - nowadays, everything seems to have happened many years ago - a colleague of mine declared, "a clean desk, a sick mind," when he saw how clean my desk was. I think he meant to say "closed" mind. The point is well taken, as I also believe that creativity thrives out of chaos. We, Koreans, grow up under a very rigid set of environments including home, school, job, and society, to become conformists. When does one have a chance to truly become oneself? We were not exposed to the concept of diversity. It's like, "my way or no way!" When different opinions emerge, the whole population arises to shut them down or fight like cats and dogs. Just look at the current political scenery in Korea. In many instances, Koreans run first and later ask themselves "why did I run?"

If left alone, all things in the universe become disorganized to chaos. The driving force is entropy, a conceptually elusive and intangible quantity from thermodynamics. It could be said that the effort to fold dried laundry into a nice pile of clean clothes is the energy required in overcoming the entropy involved. An entropy-driven spontaneity is what is lacking in a society of conformists like old Korea. See more in Entry #177, "Get the land, then build a house." If you leave a shovel, for instance, in the middle of tall grass during hectic hours of ending a day, you may have a very difficult time finding it again the next day. This is the crux of the above proverb. Even when you are in a hurry, there are things you will have to take care of first.

In human terms, this old saying seems to emphasize the importance of placing a person in a position that is best suited for *their* (a gender-neutral, third-person pronoun: see the footnote of #207) qualifications and experience. No one with a reasonable mind would ask an artist to lead a chemistry lab. It could lead to a dangerous consequence, like an explosion. When we elect an idiotic man as president, we all suffer from its consequences. As my wife says, "When you have a poor brain, your body suffers." All of us could have learned a thing or two from the proverb. (04/08/2020)

226. No bugs in the sanctuary with carnivorous Buddhists.
중이 고기맛을 알면 법당에 빈대가 안 남아난다.

Like Roman Catholic priests, Buddhist monks also observe celibacy. But there are some additional challenges in testing the willpower of a monk. Unlike Catholic priests, they are supposed to stay away from any meat and alcoholic beverages: no hamburger, no chicken salad, no broiled fish, no scrambled egg, and no Johnnie Walker, soju, or sake. As is the case for almost everything involving humans, Buddhist monks are not perfect either. Some succumb to various temptations and become compromised in distancing from either women, meat, or both. Here, the proverb says, "Once a Buddhist acquires the taste of meat, he will eat anything with flesh, including bedbugs and flies, so that their sanctuary hall is completely devoid of any bugs."

Corruption tends to beget more of the same or other similar corruptions, as it is easier to abandon the integrity than to right the wrong with a renewed determination and effort. For example, a person who has already committed an illicit love affair may repeat the same act with less mental struggle than the first time. The first-timers may agonize with moral questions, in addition to scheming. Shall I ask this woman out to a restaurant first and later to a motel? How can I lure her to follow me? Then, how am I going to face my wife and kids later?

To be fair, the Buddhist monk might have gone for *bulgogi* for the first time, just out of curiosity, as he must have heard quite often about how delicious the dish is, especially with a glass of soju. Certainly, there must be a component of thrill associated with committing the forbidden act, like adultery by the first time offender. It would be the excitement of trying something new, rather than having the same vegetarian meals day in day out. Let's say, he did so more or less out of boredom. But still, it is quite an exaggeration to say that a monk, once exposed to a delicious dish of meat, would go after anything like flies and bugs to such a length that he devours all bugs in the sanctuary, making it devoid of any bugs. How much meat is there in such a bug?

The American film *Spotlight* won the Academy Award for Best Picture in 2015. It was about a group of investigative journalists who had doggedly pursued and finally exposed the numerous cases of widespread and systemic child sex abuse in the Boston area by Catholic priests. For their investigations, the team of reporters known as "Spotlight," earned the *Boston Globe*, the 2003 Pulitzer Prize for Public Service. The movie begins with interference by an Assistant District Attorney in 1976 with the arrest of a priest for child molestation by two policemen. In no uncertain terms, the policemen were told not to let the press get wind of what had happened. The arrest was hushed up and the priest was released.

Upon learning that Cardinal Bernard Law knew that the priest was sexually abusing children and did nothing to stop him, a news editor of the *Globe* urged the Spotlight team to investigate further. Initially, they believed that they were following the story of one priest, but soon the Spotlight team began to uncover a pattern of sexual abuse of children by Catholic priests and an ongoing cover-up by the Boston Archdiocese. Soon the team widened their search to 13 priests and learned that as much as 50% of priests were not celibate. Eventually, they developed a list of 87 names and began to find their victims to back up their suspicions. The Spotlight team finally began to write the story and planned to publish their findings in early 2002.

The movie *Spotlight* opened the floodgate of similar scandals, not only in the U.S. but also all over the world, tarnishing the image of Roman Catholics for many subsequent years. Cardinal Law resigned in disgrace in December 2002 but, to the surprise of many, was promoted to the Basilica di Santa Maria, the largest Catholic Church in Rome. In due time, a list of places in the United States and around the world, where major scandals involving abuse by priests took place, became public.

Late in 2015, the parishioners of our church received a letter from our local Bishop, which belittled the newly-released *Spotlight*. The letter pointed out that the movie conveyed many wrong pieces of information. The Bishop's letter strongly discouraged us from watching the movie. That certainly piqued my curiosity, and I saw the movie. (04/08/2020)

227. No new birds in old nests.
작년 둥우리에 새가 없다.

Come spring, birds of a new generation come back to build a fresh nest. They are not interested in staying in the nests their parents built last year, although it could save them a lot of time and effort. A new home for a new family is what they are telling us. If it requires a lot of effort, much more than fixing an old nest, so be it. What is more important than building a new dwelling place for my babies? Without a brand new and appealing nest, how can I lure a mate? But, wait; there is already a nest at a perfect height, with an excellent entry and roof. There is no way a squirrel can come in either. It's good looking too, just like a Swiss chalet. All I need is to bring some twigs for the babies coming later. This is a male chickadee talking to his female date.

The first two houses I purchased in Michigan were old ones: especially the first one, located in an old neighborhood of the town, well established and very quiet. It was built in the 1950s. I was a bachelor then and did many renovations myself, learning how a house was built. Unavoidably, what I thought was an improvement wasn't so at all. The second one was on a nice lake and more expensive. Still a bachelor, I threw my share of parties and sailed a catamaran almost every day in the summer afternoons. My renovation skills improved significantly, but later on, it became a task to do rather than a hobby to enjoy. During the winter, it was tough going, as the wind blew from the north across the lake. In the night time, I could hear the cracking noise from the expansion of the frozen lake.

The last three houses we lived in, two in North Carolina and one in Las Vegas, were all new ones. Not having to work on the house was indeed a relief, but yard work remained a chore, as I was suffering from allergies all year round. As I look back, living in a new house was much more agreeable, not so much because I didn't have to repair here and there, but because we began to enjoy living without the "ghosts" of previous owners. I am too old to do any major mends anyway. The stamp-sized backyard of the current home requires only a few hours to complete a garden project, like planting seasonal annuals. Even this, I do just to avoid unnecessary nagging from my wife.

In late fall if I feel ambitious, or in early spring out of necessity, I empty and clean the birdhouses that were occupied by chickadees or bluebirds, to prepare for the arrival of their next generation. The entrance area is invariably smeared with dried saliva. It is from drooling during feeding. It is ugly, white and grey, and scrubbed off with a steel brush. The nest inside is more pathetic: twigs and sticks are all flatted down by the babies and their mother. They can be removed easily in one piece. In between those sticks, there is what appears to be dried feces and saliva, again greyish white. As much as I love those birds, I cannot stand the dirty-looking remnant of the nest. Good thing there is no smell, as they are all dried up, just producing dust in the wind. I usually wear a mask and a pair of gloves.

Each time I clean the birdhouse, I cannot stop asking myself, how in the world can one enjoy the soup from a bird's nest. The bird's nest soup is one of the most expensive Chinese delicacies. I don't know if I could handle it, if someone offered me a bowl, even along with money. Edible bird's nests are primarily from swiftlets, a small bird that dwells in a cave-like chimney swift. They are highly prized, possibly because of their rarity: high demand with limited supply. Its nutritional value is questionable, but the soup with its unique flavor and gel-like texture is said to promote good healthy skin.

According to Wikipedia, the most heavily harvested nests are from the edible-nest swiftlets. They are built during the breeding season by the male swiftlet over the course of 35 days and take the shape of a shallow cup, stuck to a cave wall. The nests are composed of interwoven strands of salivary, that serves as cement. It contains a high level of calcium, iron, potassium, and magnesium. Traditionally, the nests are harvested from the big limestone caves in Borneo, a huge island in Southeast Asia's Malay Archipelago. Because of the high demand and the value, nowadays, people provide a nest made of concrete (what else!), in strategic urban locations near the sea. In this case, the bird may not have any other choice, but to build a new nest every year on a concrete platform. (04/12/2020)

228. A virtue from vice.

큰 악에서 큰 선이 생긴다.

As I had expected, the words "virtue" and "vice" appear together in many idioms, old sayings, speeches, and proverbs. The following, listed at random, are what I found through a cursory survey. Some of them are only indirectly related to the above proverb: "Most desirable virtues originate from serious vices." The saying makes perfect sense since you cannot conceive one concept without the other. That is, if we do not understand and define a vice, how can we know anything about a virtue?

1. It is easier to run from virtue to vice, than from vice to virtue.
2. It is in hating of vice that we strengthen ourselves in the love of virtue.
3. The first step to virtue is to abstain from vice.
4. The virtues and vices are put in motion by interest.
5. Virtue and vice cannot dwell under the same roof.
6. Virtue and vice, wisdom and folly, are not hereditary.
7. Virtue rejoices in temptation.
8. What's vice today may be virtue tomorrow.
9. Virtues all agree, but vices fight one another.
10. Virtue would not go far if a little vanity walked not with her.
11. Virtue sometimes starves while vice is fed.
12. Virtue itself turns vice being misapplied.
13. Virtue is never aided by a vice.
14. Virtue is more persecuted by the wicked than encouraged by the good.
15. Every virtue is but halfway between two vices.
16. He that thinks too much of his virtues, bids others think of his vices.
17. It is a virtue to fly vice.
18. Most men are more willing to indulge in easy vices than to practice laborious virtues.

Of these, Chinese proverb #6 clearly states that both vice and virtue are acquired traits in life. Although we often find that the children of a man of vice tend to grow up with dubious morals, it can be just a matter of the poor environment they were exposed to. If we change "temptation" to "vice" in #7, it is close to the above Korean proverb.

In #8, how does a vice of today become a virtue tomorrow? And does #10 mean to be cynical? As said in #9, one of the virtues in virtue is that, indeed, there is no disagreement in defining a virtue. As we discussed in Entry #226, "No bugs in the sanctuary with carnivorous Buddhists," a vice always seems to maintain an upper hand over a virtue. The same is implied in #1, #11, and #18. I do not understand under what context the author of #17, presumably the Roman lyric poet Horace, used the word, "fly." Maybe "travel through?"

Even saints in the past were not perfect and made mistakes before their hearts were converted. Matthew had been a greedy tax collector, a most hated profession in ancient Israel, before being asked by Jesus to "follow him." Following Jesus closely, he recorded what he observed in the *Gospel of Matthew*.

During his time as a student, Saint Augustine (354 – 430) was like any other student: he engaged in an illicit relationship with a woman to have a son. They remained unmarried for many years, and she eventually ended the relationship. As to his famous episode of the "stealing of the pears," this is what he had to say in his *Confessions*, "We carried off a huge load of pears, not to eat ourselves, but to dump out to the hogs, after barely tasting some of them ourselves. Doing this pleased us all the more because it was forbidden. Such was my heart, O God, such was my heart, thou didst pity even in that bottomless pit. Behold, now let my heart confess to thee what it was seeking there, when I was being gratuitously wanton, having no inducement to evil but the evil itself."

We cannot and should not judge someone's behaviors before becoming a saint with the current moral standard. But, they acknowledged that their lives had been in vice. Their change in heart agrees with the above proverb. Their virtue remains time-independent. (04/13/2020)

229. A lucky family harvests watermelons from eggplant seeds.
잘되는 집은 가지에 수박이 달린다.

First, a disclaimer: Apparently, watermelon was considered more desirable and thus more valuable than eggplant, in the old days in Korea. Let's just say that the former is gold, whereas the latter is silver. "A lucky family somehow manages to harvest watermelons when they sowed eggplants." When things go well, everything is hunky-dory, and all the stars are aligned, so-to-speak. This is exactly opposite to the case presented in Entry #36, "An unlucky man breaks his note even when falling backward." Who, or which family, is then blessed with such a fortune? As said in Entry #2, "Sunny spots and shade change places," many Koreans believe that fortune and misfortune are all a matter of fate, or *un-myung* (운명). Although most of our ancestors resigned to the notion that *un-myung* is predetermined and thus there is little one can do about it, a variety of interventions have been tried to improve the odds.

One of the most prominent practices is *feng shui*, or 풍수, geomancy originating from ancient China. It claims to fully utilize invisible forces, *gi*, or 기, to harmonize individuals with their surrounding environment. As such, it is on the borderline between science and mystery. Some practices are perhaps retrospectively explainable by science, while others may be considered just unfounded custom, yet to be scientifically justified: See Entry #2 also. According to a write-up in Wikipedia, "*feng shui* practice discusses architecture in terms of 'invisible forces' that bind the universe, earth, and humanity together." The practice has been widely adopted in orienting, to a most favorable direction, important structures such as dwellings, tombs, community centers, and new cities. As the letters in *feng shui* (風水 in Chinese) stands for wind and water, an auspicious site could be found by reference to local features such as bodies of water, mountains, or the compass. I learned from Chinese friends, when I lived in Vancouver, that the appeal of the town to wealthy Chinese expatriates is indeed based on the harmoniously located water of the Pacific Ocean in the southeast and Whistler Mountain in the north.

A good friend of mine is one of the leading architects in Korea. His professional achievements cover not only architectural work, but also environmental protection, furniture design, and conservation of Korean traditional structures. He is currently chairing a committee for a major renovation of Gang-haw-mun Plaza, at the center of Seoul. He is a firm believer in *feng shui* and had some of his students write dissertations on the topic. In 1983, he was in charge of locating an ideal site for Korea's National Independence Hall. He shared with friends a reminiscence of the time he spent on a helicopter for an aerial view of potential sites. His criteria were largely based on *feng shui*. A decade later, the project utilizing land of over 1,000 acres was completed and every visitor seems to be happy with it.

Getting watermelons, instead of expected eggplants, is surely a miraculous event, as expressed by envious neighbors, friends, relatives, and even strangers. Rumors and gossip would be rampant with unsolicited speculation. Here, "unexpected" could well be by their guess rather than fact. For their fortune, there could have been a tremendous amount of hard work and sacrifice, but the bystanders do not seem to care. All they know is that this family was unbelievably lucky. They may attribute their own lack of fortune to the wrong orientation of their home or the tomb of their parents.

Many nations are envious of the social, health, political, educational, and welfare systems of Finland and the Scandinavian countries. Is it simply because they subscribe to a social democracy entailing high taxes? I do not know what sets of criteria they used, but the Finnish, with a population of 5.5 million, is said to live the happiest life on this planet.

Out of curiosity, I briefly went over their modern history to learn that they were not exactly given a "gold mine or watermelon" when they went after "silver or eggplants." The chaos that the Finnish had to endure after the declaration of independence from Russia, just after the October Revolution in 1917, and the bitter civil war between the factions backed by Imperial Germany and by Russia, were quite similar to what the Jo-Seon Dynasty had to go through just before the annexation of the Korean Peninsula by Imperial Japanese in 1910. And yet, in 2020, we see two quite different nations. Why? (04/15/2020)

230. A groom goes on a honeymoon leaving the penis behind.
장가 가는놈 불알 나두고 간다.

This proverb is all about forgetfulness. What kind of man would forget to bring his penis on a honeymoon trip? "Where is my baby!" What kind of mother would desperately look for the baby who is strapped on her back and sleeping peacefully? People look for the pencil lodged on their earlobe. A funeral director goes to the memorial service he is to take care of, but forgets to bring the casket of the deceased: "장사지내려가는놈이영장 (시체) 두고간다."

A student forgets to bring his seating number to the national testing place for entry into college. You may know someone who realizes *they* (see the footnote of #207) did not bring their passport, only at the boarding gate. One morning, when we lived in North Carolina, we left the electric range in the kitchen on and went to work. The smoke alarm alerted a nearby fire station, who summoned me from work, in time to find a smoke-filled home.

Then, of course, there was a memorable episode involving the University of Michigan men's basketball team, commonly referred to as the Fab Five (fab as in fabulous). They were the first team in NCAA (National Collegiate Athletic Association) history to compete in the championship game with all-freshman starters. They lost the 1993 championship game to the University of North Carolina, in which one of Fab Five called a time-out in the final moments of the game. It resulted in a costly penalty, since they did not have any timeouts left.

A variety of distractions can divert your attention to other interesting stuff, away from what you are looking for. In my chemistry research lab, we used to have a drawer full of silly knick-knacks such as a lighter, screwdriver, magnifying glass, keys, pens, tapes, labels, hammer, scissors, etc., along with accumulated dust. As soon as you open the drawer, you forget why you have just opened the draw. My assistant would then lend me a small flashlight, attached to his key chain. It helped me find what I was looking for. Even Albert Einstein couldn't find the way to his own home: see Entry #38, "Each and every finger would feel pain if bitten."

The U.S. Senator from Utah, Orrin Hatch, tried to remove his glasses several times at a Judiciary Hearing that he chaired. The only problem was that he was not wearing any glasses. Earlier he must have taken them off. A short video showing this honest mistake went viral in January 2018, with the following comments from the denizens.

- He didn't see that coming.
- We are all wrong, those are next-generation glasses, we just cannot see them, advanced technology, too advanced for us to recognize.
- Wow, those invisible bifocal lenses are great in invisible frames!
- I think Mr. Hatch needs to take that test that Trump just took...
- Says a lot about the people of Utah for voting him in for 40 years straight. Then again it also says a lot about NY for voting in Chucky boy (Chuck Schumer).
- And people are worried about Trump?
- To all my fellow glasses-wearing people out there, you can't lie to me and say in your entire life this has not happened to you at least once LOL (laughing out loud).

A year later, the Senator retired at the age of 85 after having continuously served for 42 years.

Without memory, be it short-term or long-term, we humans as well as all living things on this planet, including plants, cannot exist as we do now. We simply cannot develop any firm relationships since we cannot establish any personal identities. Just visit with an Alzheimer patient for a few minutes, and you will come to the same conclusion.

As Lady Macbeth declared, memory is "the warder of the brain." Indeed, the brain without memories is not the brain we take for granted. Of the many factors affecting memory loss, stress and sleep are supposed to be the major ones, with a negative and positive impact, respectively. All said, the capacity and the ability to memorize events appear to be completely different from one person to another; some have a photographic memory, while others, like me, have a short memory. (04/16/2020)

231. The grandson from a son walks; the grandson from a daughter is carried in arms.
친손자는 걸리고 외손자는 업고 간다.

Here is a grandmother with a pair of two-year-old grandsons, one from her son and the other from her daughter. They are leisurely strolling toward a sandbox in the neighborhood park. Most likely, this grandma would let the grandson from her son (친손자) follow her in unsteady steps, but carry the grandson from her daughter (외손자) in her arms. The proverb says that a grandma tends to dote on her grandson from her daughter, with more care and attention, than the other grandson. I have also noticed that my nieces and nephews from my sisters invariably prefer being with us to their aunts and uncles from their father's side. Of course, there would be many exceptions to this generalization, but the trend appears to exist even among the families of my American friends. Why?

My wife, always the wiser one, explains that, in the case of grandchildren, a grandma has another generation in the middle from another family to deal with: that is, daughter-in-law or son-in-law. As we have seen in Entry #80, "A mother dislikes her daughter-in-law's heel," her relationship with her daughter-in-law (며느리) is more subtle and delicate than that with her son-in-law (사위).

Since they are of the same sex, they must feel quite close, and yet there always seems to exist a certain degree of tension. Are they unconsciously competing with each other, for the son-turned-husband as well as their children? On the other hand, the grandmother has raised her daughter throughout her life, up to the point of her marriage. She knows about her daughter better than anyone in this world. This intimacy and mutual affection must be carried over to her children. As far as the grandma is concerned, her son-in-law may well be just a second thought.

To the son of my oldest sister, for instance, my sister in Phoenix had been his second, but a younger mother, who seemed to understand him better than his mother. His aunts and uncles from his father's side were involved very little in my nephew's life. My nieces, now all grown up and with their own families, were once our "toys" when they were just toddlers. My brothers and I used to pass through the air, the youngest infant niece as if she were a football. So, what is all about their seemingly preferred relationship with uncle and aunt from the mother's side? Why? My wife submitted a lengthy explanation, but I just closed off my ears and let her babble on. She was even mumbling about the so-called positive Oedipus complex.

One more generalization I would like to present is that a mother's influence on her son-in-law through her daughter appears to be much more significant than on her daughter-in-law through her son. This may be because a man is generally less attentive and less clever than a woman in "scheming" and "conspiring." (Quickly, I am not using these words in any deleterious ways against women.) In many aspects, I will have to admit that women are superior to men in making rational judgments. Just yesterday, CNN News carried an article by Leta Hong Fincher, on comparative studies among the U.S. and other countries, dealing with the COVID-19 pandemic.

In Taiwan, early intervention measures have controlled the coronavirus pandemic so successfully that it is now exporting millions of face masks to help the European Union and others. Germany has overseen the largest-scale coronavirus testing program in Europe, conducting 350,000 tests each week, detecting the virus early enough to isolate and treat patients effectively.

In New Zealand, the prime minister took early action to shut down tourism and impose a month-long lockdown on the entire country, limiting coronavirus casualties to just nine deaths. All three places have received accolades for their impressive handling of the coronavirus pandemic. They are scattered across the globe: one is in the heart of Europe, one is in Asia and the other is in the South Pacific.

But they have one thing in common: they're all led by women.
(04/17/2020)

232. Don't want to be the governor of Pyung-yang.
평양 감사도 제가싫으면 그만이다.

Pyung-yang (평양) has been the second-largest city in the Korean Peninsula throughout the history of the Joseon Dynasty, second only to Han-yang, the current Seoul. At present, the town is the capital city of North Korea, or the Democratic People's Republic of Korea. Now, you are appointed as the governor of Pyung-yang by no other than the King himself, but you don't have to go there if you don't like the offer, for whatever reason you may have. But first, we ask ourselves who would refuse to become the governor of that big city? It is like refusing to become the governor of the State of New York, or California. But you can. The proverb is thus equivalent to: "A man may lead his horse to water, but cannot make him drink." What you wish to do with your life is all up to you, not by other's design.

Such was the case of the abdication in 1936 of King Edward VIII from the British throne so that he could marry a divorcee from Baltimore, Maryland, named Wallis Simpson. No longer a king, he became just the Duke of Windsor and entered into a life-long retreat into various parts of Europe, largely a life of decadent mooching. Love did it.

The Buddha was born, almost three millennia ago, into an aristocratic family, but eventually renounced an idling life for years of meditation. He awakened to understand the cycle of rebirth, to which he devoted his entire life to teaching. His unwavering desire to understand the meaning and purpose of life rendered him to sacrifice an easy life. Likewise, Francis of Assisi (1181 – 1226), the founder of the Franciscan Order, was born into a wealthy family of a prosperous silk merchant. In his youth, he was handsome in fine clothes and spent money lavishly. But, then, his compassion towards the poor took the upper hand, and eventually led him to spiritual conversion, effectively abandoning his previous lavish lifestyle. He is one of the most revered Saints in Christian history. These are just a few examples of great lives we know of, but there must have been an astronomical number of people unknown to us, who have pursued what they want out of their lives. They are our heroes, just like unknown soldiers.

Just last year the Duke and Duchess of Sussex, Prince Harry, and his wife of one year, Meghan Markle, decided to depart the royal life of the British Kingdom. Many people, certainly including me, were surprised by the seemingly sudden announcement, but fully understood in empathy their thought process through which the decision was derived. Before their wedding, Prince Harry had been a constant subject of tabloid journalism. He had been in a few long-term relationships, but he wasn't sure if he would ever be able to find a soul mate. Then much gossip emerged involving Markle, just before the wedding itself. Her sister Samantha Markle, for instance, claimed in a poisonous tongue that Meghan did not care for her or their father. It was an embarrassing display of an ugly relationship between siblings. In a recent article in the April 20, 2020 issue of *The New Yorker*, Rebecca Mead wrote:

The question of who, or what, was to blame for the rupture has yet to be conclusively answered. Were Harry and Meghan millennial weaklings retreating into self-care and self-pity, unwilling to withstand the scrutiny of their public life in exchange for the material luxury of their private one? Were they pampered hypocrites, lecturing others about climate change while cheerfully leaping aboard private jets belonging to celebrity friends? Were they just bored or burned out? Were they fatally undermined by the royal establishment? Were they too ambitions for their second-fiddle roles? Or were they, despite all their privilege, victims – he the target of relentless attention since birth, and she the object of barely concealed racism?

No one will be able to answer these questions. Even they won't be able to pinpoint one, if not a few, causes for their decision to leave the dukedom. Perhaps a combination of all the listed above might have triggered the night-long, soul-searching discussion of the newly married. I cannot stop admiring their courage and determination in believing that their lives together are their own.

No matter how impressive the governor of Pyung-yang may appear to you, it is you who decides to take up the offer or not. Just remember that nobody would force you to do something you do not wish to do, in and with, your life. (04/18/2020)

233. The bird high in the sky still feeds on the ground.
하늘을 높이나는 새도 먹이는 땅에서 얻는다.

Even high-flying, powerful, and fearsome birds of prey, feed on the ground. The list includes a variety of vultures such as California condors. They are the largest flying land birds in the Western Hemisphere, with a wingspan of at least 10 feet, and weighing as much as 20 to 30 pounds. They are known to fly as high as 35,000 feet in altitude. Also belonging to this category is what we casually call buzzards. Albeit smaller than vultures, powerfully built eagles and various hawks can fly fast and possess relatively longer and broader wings.

The albatross is an expert glider, with the largest wingspan, capable of remaining in the air without beating its wings for several hours at a time. They spend as much as 80% of their lives at sea and feed on surface shoaling fish and squid. Here, consider the sea surface as the ground also. Some falcons, well known for their acute eyes, are known to be the fastest living creatures, reaching as much as 150 mph, when swooping from great heights during territorial displays, or while catching prey birds in midair (but they also take care of their prey on the ground).

One commonality of these almighty birds is that, however they may catch their prey, they feed on the ground or at their nests feeding their babies. What does the above proverb then imply? An immediate interpretation would be that no matter who or what you are, there are many things you do, just like any other human being. I am not merely speaking of basic physiological needs common to all of us, such as eating, breathing, sleeping, and emptying our bowels and bladder. We also share mental aspects of life: love, hatred, envy, jealousy, etc.

A subtler example could be that even Bill Gates "puts his pants on one leg at a time," just like a homeless guy down the street. The ultimate point of emphasis must be the humbleness and humility, which we ought to live with. You may be a very powerful man, or famous like the president of this country, a billionaire like Bill Gates and Jeff Bozos, a Novel Laureate, or any successful man, in any field of professions, but you should not abandon the basic truth that each and every man lives on the same planet, carrying "the same size of the sky" over his head.

Arrogance, based on self-importance, often appears in some successful people, especially men of power like politicians. Take President Trump as an example. This ego-centric man is blind enough that he cannot distinguish truth from fraud. Repeated lies and false or exaggerated claims, along with blaming others, were the main contents of rally-like daily briefings on the COVID-19 pandemic. It was so pathetic, I have not bothered to watch the TV replay, just after the first few sessions. I understand now he "forces" others to "waste" their valuable time, as much as two hours; time that can be otherwise used in a productive and meaningful manner. Remember that those standing behind him, upright like school children, are the very powers that be in the nation, who are supposed to devise ways to fight off the crisis. What about the time wasted by the very citizens who are desperately and anxiously waiting for any good news or promising guidelines from him? We are simply drowning people who would grab any floating straws at this unsettling and frustrating time.

Thus far, as many as 25-million Americans have lost their jobs. More than two trillion dollars of stimulus aid has passed the U.S. Congress to shore up the collapsing national economy. Checks to the unemployed are being directly deposited in their bank account, each with Trump's signature. The federal and most state governments have to dole out more funds to barely survive the pandemic crisis. We simply do not see how and when it will end. Besides these gloomy economic pictures, human tolls are adding up: more than 40,000 fatalities with 650,000 active cases, as of 4 PM, Sunday, April 19.

Admittedly, Trump and his lieutenants were caught between a rock and a hard place: that is, the economy or human life. Citizens understood the difficulties involved and wished to help them develop a united front to overcome it together. Just like Americans did during the crises dealt by Franklin Delano Roosevelt, namely the Great Depression and World War II of the early 1930s and 1940s. What is brazenly missing in the current Trump administration is simply candor and transparency. This is, in turn, from a lack of humility or realization of the limited ability of a leader. He is trying to feed himself, high-up in the sky a futile exercise. (04/19/2020)

234. A hole gets bigger whenever you work on it.
구멍은깎을수록커진다.

Sometimes it is best if you just leave a matter at hand, as is, rather than trying to fix or improve it. This would be particularly true if the project was ill-conceived from the beginning and started in the wrong direction. Here, anything one is overdoing could backfire. This proverb says that, however careful you may be in trying to close off the hole, the surrounding often crumbles and the hole gets bigger.

In the English portion of the college entrance exam I took in 1961, a question asked where the accent was in the word "academy." This was one of the questions I wanted to revisit later, in my spare time, once I completed the test. I pronounced the word in silence several times and changed my originally correct answer to a wrong one: a big mistake. I had too much time to tinker with the answer. On the way back home, I realized the error. As an extension of this sudden realization, I also knew right there and then that I would fail the entrance exam. For a change, this time I was right with the hunch. This memory also reminds me of a Chinese idiom in which a guy drew unnecessary feet on a snake, to lose the competition for a drink: see Entry #184, "Acupuncture onto a pumpkin."

Many teenage boys suffer from acne on the face, resulting in anxiety, reduced self-esteem, and often depression: all just when they discover the opposite sex. Glued to a mirror for hours, they try to get rid of those nasty pimples with not-so-clean fingertips, finding the situation getting worse. Have you ever tried to cut four legs of a stool evenly? If you are a perfectionist, most likely you would end up with a much shorter stool. You have now learned why most stools have three legs and that a slightly wobbling chair might have been preferable to a short one. Covering only a part of an old wall with new paint leads to a big job of painting the whole wall. Out of greed, one may wait a bit too long before selling off stock to end with a big loss. And then, of course, there are lies for covering lies for most liars. The exception may be for the current President Trump: either he is not clever enough to lie again to cover other lies, or brazenly bullish enough to ignore the previous lies. You choose one.

Nixon's Watergate scandal would be another case in point, with historic significance in this country. The Watergate complex is a group of six buildings in the Foggy Bottom neighborhood of Washington, D.C., covering a total of 10 acres, adjacent to the John F. Kennedy Center for the Performing Arts. They are occupied by either offices or apartments. Its name is presumably from overlooking the "gate" that regulated the flow of water from the Potomac River into the Tidal Basin at flood tide but became notorious as the site where the scandal all began.

Sometime after midnight, on a Saturday, in June 1972, five "third-rate burglars" were arrested for breaking into the Democratic National Committee headquarters in one of the Watergate Office Buildings. A money trail connected them to the Nixon re-election campaign committee. For the ensuing two years, a series of ever-escalating cover-ups continued until Nixon resigned on August 9, 1974, in the face of almost certain impeachment.

The cover-up began with the initial denial by Nixon, "I can say categorically that...no one in the White House staff, no one in this Administration, presently employed, was involved in this very bizarre incident." This lie was followed by the resignation of two of his most influential aides, the discovery of secret taping of conversations in the Oval Office, replacement of his attorney general, the so-called "Saturday Night Massacre," and firing of the presidential counsel. Along the way, there was a "kidnap" of Martha Mitchell, the wife of John Mitchell, who was then the chair of Nixon re-election committee: quite an entertaining spectacle, if I recall. Still, Nixon emphatically stated in November 1973, "Well, I'm not a crook."

Earlier, the White House Counsel, John Dean, still believed that he, Mitchell, and the two key Nixon's aides could go to the prosecutors, tell the truth, and save the presidency. Dean wanted to protect the president and have his four closest men take the fall for telling the truth. Instead, Nixon continuously tried to "cover-up the hole with more dirt." In the end, the hole was big enough to swallow him up as well as several lieutenants of his. Had they understood the above proverb, the episode could have remained a small hiccup in the ever-turbulent political climate of Washington. (04/23/2020)

235. A country chicken gobbles up chickens from a palace.
촌 닭이 관청 닭 눈 빼 먹는다.

A cockfight is a blood sport between two gamecocks held in a cockpit, surrounded by onlookers. These chickens are specially bred and conditioned, not only for increased stamina and strength but also for aggression towards all other males. They literally fight for blood and often till one dies. Wagers are made on the outcome of the match. It is closer to gambling than a sport, which most countries have made illegal by now.

The history of raising fowl for fighting goes back 6,000 years and was popular at some point in China as well as in Japan. However, I was not able to find any literature on a cockfight in Korea. "Chicken fight" in Korea is a children's sport where a boy, while holding a leg up front with both hands, fights off the opponent in the same posture, till someone falls while jumping up and down and moving forward and back on one leg. It has nothing to do with the current topic.

The only time I was curious about this "sport" was when Atlanta Falcons quarterback, Michael Vick, made headline news in 2007, for his involvement in dogfights. After an 18-month jail time, he was again hired as the starting quarterback of the Philadelphia Eagles. The night he signed a new six-year, $100-million contract with the Eagles, he celebrated the deal in a local cockfight, the closest entertainment to dogfight. He was a damn good quarterback, especially famous for his ability in running. Why? Apparently, there are some addictive components, just like any other gambling. For people like me, who consider even bullfighting barbaric, these dog and cockfights are just too bloody and cruel. In the same token, peace-loving Koreans would not have enjoyed these sorts of violent games.

If I translate the above proverb word by word, it reads, "A chicken raised in a farmland would take out and devour eyeballs of chickens reared and nurtured by officials of government." This may sound more terrible than cockfights, but the proverb is humorous in nuance, and thus we should not interpret it literally. Instead, it implies that children who grew up in a harsh environment often outperform those from well-nourished families with ample financial means. We saw a similar essay in Entry #25, "Strong plants in strong winds."

This is a story I picked up not long ago, on April 12, 2020, in fact, from *Chosun.com*, one of the major daily newspapers in Korea. It sounds quite relevant to the above proverb. Two sisters lived with their father alone since their mother died in an accident - they did not say what kind of accident it was, but it could have been a car accident. At that time, the daughters were five and eight years old.

Their father was working as a construction laborer. As one can imagine, they barely survived with minimal resources. They couldn't afford even an eight-dollar fried chicken during big holidays like New Years Day, while they dreamt of a steak-and-lobster dinner at Outback Steakhouse restaurant. To make matters even worse, their father had an accident at the construction site.

Having abandoned any hope for further education, the older sister started to work just after a vocational school. But, she insisted that her younger one should continue her schooling and apply for college. Indeed the younger sister was an excellent student and usually top in her class. Moving forward, she passed the entrance exam to one of the most prestigious medical schools in Korea, Yonsei University Medical School. Soon, the sister was swarmed by many high school seniors who were about to write their university entrance exams and looking for a suitable private tutor.

Now, she became the breadwinner of the family. The day she learned she would be admitted to medical school, the whole family went out for a celebration at Outback Steakhouse. According to the newspaper article, which was based on a story posted on Facebook by the younger daughter, they shared tears of joy and appreciation for all the sacrifices they had endured together.

The younger daughter also confessed that she had almost accepted the path that her sister had taken. However, she remembered what her teacher in elementary school kept saying, "Your life depends on our ability." That advice always kept her studying. She sure sounds like a country chicken that pounded upon the chickens from a palace. (04/24/2020)

236. Know a weasel by the tail.
족제비는 꼬리보고 잡는다.

A weasel (족제비) belongs to the same family as badgers, otters, and wolverines. It also shares the genus with skunks, polecats, stoats (흰담비), ferrets, and mink. They are small, active predators, with long, slender bodies, and short legs. Some of them are notorious for the bad smell sprayed from their anal scent glands, which serves as their defensive weapon. Although weasels look cute and their behavior is rather entertaining, our perception of the animal is not always favorable since they can steal chickens and rabbits from farms. As a noun, the word is also used in slang for a cunning and sneaky person. As a verb, it can mean to evade an obligation, duty, and the like. Both cases are, once again, of an undesirable connotation. Similar to minks, weasel fur was once used in protecting people from the cold: Japanese soldiers used them during World War II. Call it a second-class mink.

So, how do we distinguish weasels from many of their "cousins" in the same genus? The tail of a weasel, at about 4 cm (1.6 inches), is shorter than that of the others. It can help identify them: "catch weasels after inspecting the tail." The proverb implies that a cohort of people gathered must share some common purpose that allows for a generalization. By observing one's behavior or opinion, we can accurately gauge which category the person belongs to: Republican or Democrat, Christian or Muslim, rich or poor, well educated or not, Trump supporter or not, etc. Most importantly, we can assess if a man is trustworthy or not by looking at his "tail," just like we can distinguish a weasel from a mink.

"Redneck" is a derogatory term designating a white American, perceived to be crass and unsophisticated, closely associated with rural whites of the Southern United States, perhaps someone like a Trump supporter. I may be wrong, but I thought it derived from a sun-burned, red neck, after working in the field all day. Compare it with, say, the pale neck of a stock trader on Wall Street, in New York City. Either way, we should not use the word anymore as it is "politically incorrect," albeit the word serves well as a tail.

My mother-in-law used to be a successful antique dealer who had a shop in Ginza Street of Tokyo. People would ask her to determine if a certain piece in their possession was authentic. One time, the host of a dinner party brought in an old-looking earth ware for her assessment. She gently tapped the jar near her ear, and also touched the surface with her index finger, wet with her saliva to see how quickly it disappeared. Then, of course, she examined the object this way and that way, enjoying the attention of people gathered around her for a while. Her final verdict was that the piece was a forgery. The owner was disappointed but thanked her anyway. On the way home, I suggested that she should have told them that the piece was well preserved and too close to being genuine so that she was not able to determine its authenticity. She just gave me a dirty look without saying a word.

Modern-day art specialists, with expertise in art authentication, employ various forensic methods, based on solid science, such as carbon dating, X-ray diffraction, Raman microscopy, atomic absorption spectrophotometry, etc. I took a hands-on course on these analytical methods in the 1970s, at McCrone Lab in Chicago. It was quite impressive how one can extract a vast amount of information out of a minuscule amount of sample. These are more objective, reliable, and more convincing than the spit of my mother-in-law.

According to many believers, the Shroud of Turin depicts the image of Jesus, as it was the burial shroud in which he was wrapped after the crucifixion. Extremely small fragments of the cloth were subject to several tests, to validate the claim. In 1979, Walter McCrone was not able to find any fibril from the fabric samples from 32 sections of the image: every sample was instead made up of billions of submicron pigment particles. In 1988, three radiocarbon dating tests on a corner piece of the shroud suggested that the shroud is from the Middle Ages, between the years 1260 and 1390. To this day, the Shroud of Turin remains a controversial topic as to its authenticity among historians, scientists, and the general public. Just as the owner of a stole made from a weasel wishes it is from a mink, we all wished that the Shroud of Turin was indeed authentic. (04/27/2020)

237. You will have to wade in the water to know the depth.
깊고 얕은 물은 건너 보아야 안다.

There is only so much you can do in estimating the depth of the river you are about to cross. You could approximate the shore-to-shore distance, determine how fast the water flows, check the composition of the ground, and even observe the behavior of birds above the water. However, the easiest thing to do must be just wading into the river and cautiously moving forward. This is what the proverb says. Yes, we must have a water-tight plan for a project before we embark on it. But we cannot get bogged down with the exhaustive analysis and procrastinate forever. "Just do it," Nike's ad used to say.

During a 40-year professional career, I had attended hundreds, if not thousands, of meetings on scientific matters or administrative stuff. Of those meetings, I can honestly say that only a small fraction, say 10 percent, were meaningful. With the man-hours spent, I could have run a few important experiments in the lab. Most of the time, I would leave the meeting with this feeling of having wasted time and a sour taste in the mouth, to a point that I was forced to believe these gatherings were called for basically by those who did not have anything better to do. "All talk and no action," has always bothered me. More troublesome was another meeting to discuss why there was no action. In the end, I stayed away from those who did not even lift a finger, but talked, and talked, and talked.

Why are most meetings inefficient and boring? Jeff Bezos has initiated a nontraditional meeting style at Amazon: right off the bat, no more PowerPoint presentations! Every meeting starts with each attendee sitting and silently reading a "six-page, narratively-structured memo," followed by a discussion based on fresh knowledge of the meeting agenda. He likes memos because they have "verbs and sentences and topic sentences and complete paragraphs."

Bezos further says the reason for the group reading is that "executives will bluff their way through the meeting as if they've read the memo because we're busy and so you've got to actually carve out the time for the memo to get read." Such practice would keep everyone on the same page, allowing for a meaningful outcome from the meeting. I don't know why my bosses in the past never thought of such a creative system.

Another advantage of the approach based on the "just-do-it" mentality is that the success or failure of a given strategy becomes known quickly. Hopefully, this prevents unwarranted bickering among the parties involved during the lengthy argument at the planning stage. The chance of failure could be a bit higher without thorough planning. However, we should not be terribly afraid of failure. After all, don't people say, "Failure is the mother of success?" Per a French philosopher of our older generation, Jean-Paul Sartre (1905 - 1980), "To know what life is worth you have to risk it once in a while." An Indian Hindu monk, Swami Vivekananda (1863 - 1902) declared, "Take risks: if you win, you will be happy; if you lose, you will be wise." I like these words.

As of May 3, this country recorded more than 67,000 deaths, from over a million active cases of COVID-19 infection. The government has spent approximately three trillion dollars on the economic remedy. More than 30-million people have become unemployed during a period of a few days. As we talk about "re-opening" the country, many epidemiologists indicate that what we have experienced thus far could be just the tip of the iceberg, if the second wave of pandemic takes place. While health care workers, including ambulance drivers and gravediggers, are frantically working with limited personal protective equipment and sleep deprivation, let us ask what this President has been doing at the White House, besides tweeting and playing golf?

In every-day briefings, President Trump spent almost all of the allocated time for himself with false claims and lies. This is, in itself, nothing new: "blame others when bad news arises," has been his modus operandi. Also, don't forget to take credit for any sign of imagined good news. But what bothers me most is his constant talk, with no action. Can't he at least visit a hospital just to cheer up those workers at the front line of the war? (05/03/2020)

238. Beautiful flowers lure the butterfly.
꽃이 좋아야 나비가 모인다.

The house in Birmingham, Alabama, where my wife had lived for several years because of her job at a university, had a chaste tree in the back yard. At the peak of summer, this garden tree showed clusters of fragrant, purple-colored blooms backed by aromatic green foliage. Its leaves, flowers, and fruits were rich in flavonoids and sweet nectar and thus attracted hummingbirds, bees, and butterflies: especially butterflies! Hundreds of butterflies, moving about the tree, looked chaotic on the one hand, but quite mesmerizing and peaceful on the other hand. We liked the scene so much that a chaste tree was the first tree we planted two years ago in the small backyard of our new home in Las Vegas. Last summer, we did not have many butterflies, but we are anxiously waiting for a new summer this year.

A direct translation of the above proverb may well be, "For a tree to attract butterflies, its flowers must be beautiful." It is interesting to note that it uses the word "beautiful (고아야)," when it really means "attractive" to butterflies. Why would they go for flowers that do not offer them nectar? Given a choice, we all choose what is most attractive to our taste, and we should. Why would we go with our second choice? When I was 17 years old, I failed to pass the entrance exam to my first-choice college. I was simply not competitive. Immediately, we had another round of tests, which I passed in flying colors. But it was for a college that was my second choice. I did not go for that program.

A man of virtue is always surrounded by good friends. This must have been a correct and relevant interpretation of the above proverb, to the cultural standard of the good old days. If we replace "virtue" with "money" or "power," we can also apply the saying to the contemporary world. If people are attracted to you, simply because of your fame or beauty, it may not be a good sign.

This raises a fundamental question as to the origin of attraction in human interactions. What brings a young couple together? Why do maggots crawl over decaying human flesh? What attracts metals to a magnet? What appeal was there when Americans and Koreans elected Mr. Donald J. Trump and Mr. Moon Jae-In, as presidents of the States and Korea? Those political pundits always say that they were chosen presidents, not so much because the citizens liked what they stood for as candidates, but based on dislike for other competing candidates. According to their narrative, people go for less evil. Then, we can ask what makes people dislike in human interactions?

Both my wife and I stay away from rude and noisy people, who lack etiquette and basic decency as human beings. We often come across such people on the road, in car-to-car interactions. Why can't they use the turn signal? Why does this young man bang the klaxon for no obvious reason? What would you do with a flying cigarette butt from another car, hitting the windshield of your car? As to noise pollution, what about the loud music from other cars? Does all this whining simply reflect our advanced age? I think not, as I have never been that way throughout my life, even when I was a teen-ager. It is because I was taught that such behaviors are simply a matter of comity among fellow human beings.

Etiquette is something the elders teach and the youth learn. The basic decency referred to here is, however, not necessarily anything to do with formal education per se. Imagine that I am now passing by some natives, in a remote village of a foreign country without benefit of their tongue. In those split seconds, we would invariably exchange genuine smiles, polite gestures of yielding, the body language of kindness, and eye contact with empathy and mutual respect. They do not appear to be the most sophisticated or well-educated people. These strangers, I am most attracted to, not that we will meet again at someplace and sometime in the future.

The proverb is written in such a way that being beautiful is a necessary condition for a flower to lure butterflies. Its reverse statement is not always right though: Hundreds of butterflies hovering above a tree do not make the plant beautiful. President Trump is surrounded by people, but he is hardly a "beautiful" man. This is because his cronies are, for the lack of better expression, running dogs, who are constantly intimidated by his barking order. If he told them that black is white, they would say, "Yes, Your Highness, it is snow white." Indeed, "a man is known by the company he keeps." (05/04/20)

239. A deaf hears the thunder.
뇌성 벽력은 귀머거리도 듣는다.

Try, if you can, to imagine yourself huddled inside a one-man tent, trying to get some sleep, or just to survive to be exact, during a thunder and lightning storm of biblical proportions. It happened in my youth a few times, during solo trekking on the Appalachian Trail. They are the type of incidents that I would like to avoid in the future if possible. Thunder and lightning represent sound and light. They travel at speeds of 3×10^2 and 3×10^8 m/sec, respectively. Because of the significant difference in their speeds, about 10^6-fold, we can accurately calculate the distance between where you hear the thunder and where it hits the ground, by simply multiplying the seconds elapsed by 300 m/sec. If you hear the thunder five seconds after you see the lightning, it should be approximately 1.5 km away, or a bit less than one mile. But, that is patently not how I would feel: It always *feels* only a few meters away, and the ground shakes to boot. No, I do not miss such a pitch-dark stormy night, in a deep valley of a remote mountain, with nobody around.

During such severe thunderstorms, we usually keep our eyes tightly shut, teeth clamped, fists closed, and body coiled. And yet, we see lightning, with no problem. So says this proverb: "Even a deaf can hear thunder." The crux is that there are certain things that one cannot hide from people, the truth or fact being one. Although history may be re-written later by a historian from a given perspective, there must have been witnesses of an incident and survivors from a disaster to tell others the truth. It is a fact that no one can deny.

A couple of weeks ago, somebody posted a video of Kim Jung-un's official funeral on the internet. Earlier, up to that point in time, rumors had been going around about his rapidly deteriorating health. Numerous chats dealt with some ill-fated heart surgery with his impending death. It sounded reasonable, considering he had been a heavy smoker, overweight and thus diabetic, and drank a lot. There were even political analyses on who would take over the regime once he died. Experts have kept saying that most likely his younger sister would be the one. However, major news outlets, such as CNN, as well as the South Korean government, were rather quiet. A few weeks later, he appeared in public, touring a newly built fertilizer factory. All were typical fake news.

During the 2016 United States presidential election campaign, a conspiracy theory went viral. Earlier, the email account of Hillary Clinton's campaign manager was leaked to the public via WikiLeaks. Some liars claimed on social media that in them were coded messages, associated with several prominent officials of the Democratic Party, of alleged human trafficking and child sex ring. One of the places allegedly involved in sex trafficking was a pizza restaurant in Washington, DC.

Anyone with a reasonable ability of "thinking" would have known this was typical fake news from alt-right activists. But, no, there was an idiot from North Carolina who showed up at the pizzeria and fired a rifle inside the pizza place. Now, it had all become sensational, and the incident was coined as "Pizzagate." But wait; there was more to the story: The restaurant owner and staff were continuously harassed by death threats from conspiracy theorists. What kind of world do we live in nowadays?

Only a few days ago, a Republican Congressman and the White House pressured the National Institutes of Health to terminate a research grant supporting a prominent virologist for his basic research. His grant application had received approval in the upper 3% range by peers: This range is formally termed outstanding. His colleagues and collaborators could not believe how politicians could arbitrarily decide what is good science.

As it turns out, the decision had nothing to do with scientific merit. It was made because his lab had been collaborating with researchers in the Wuhan Institute of Virology for characterizing, among others, coronaviruses from bats. Even with successful international research collaborations, it may take years before we fully understand the etiology of the current pandemic. Why are these politicians interfering with scientific research?

As far as I am concerned, the mentality of these politicians is comparable to that of the man with a rifle in Pizzagate. How in the world have we let such unjustifiable hysteria fool the public? My lament! (05/11/2020)

240. Know about where you lie down.
누울자리 봐 가며 발을 뻗어라.

This proverb says, "Before you lie down to stretch your legs all the way, assess the size of the bed." I don't remember if it is the cat or the dog that turns around in a tight circle several times, before settling down for an afternoon nap. Even a bird such as a mourning dove, chickadee, or bluebird flies by for several days, before settling onto a particular branch of a tree or birdhouse for starting a family nest. They seem to have heard of the above proverb and follow its wisdom quite well.

It also reminds me of the following story. One of my former students spent almost three years in Korea and China, after obtaining a PhD degree. He was a visiting scholar at Seoul National University, a fancy title given to him for a post-doctoral position. Then he worked for a Chinese firm in Shanghai. Before he graduated with a sheepskin on, I had urged him to have a life-long experience in Asian countries, while he could afford to do so as a non-committed young bachelor.

In all accounts, this young man from Cincinnati, Ohio seemed to have enjoyed the experience immensely, especially in terms of romance with Asian ladies and language, not to mention different cultures. The first e-mail I received from him was, however, about the small size of the bed he had to sleep on for a few months, in some kind of residence for the visitors to the University. He was a very tall man, at least six feet and a half, or close to two meters. He said he had to sleep diagonally on the bed, with knees bent. This story offers a literal interpretation of the proverb.

Tangent to the above is how a scientist selects where *they* (see the footnote of #207) would submit a research grant application. For the field of biomedical sciences, the National Institutes of Health (NIH) is by far the major funding source in the States. It has more than a dozen Institutes and Centers. The first step is determining which Institute one ought to apply to. It is easy to match the subject of the proposed research with the charter statement of each Institute. If it is about cancer biology, for instance, the applicant would most likely submit it to the National Cancer Institute.

Each Institute maintains numerous review groups, called Study Sections. Its roster, with each member usually serving for five years, is in the public domain. Once again, depending on the specialized field of research, the applicant could request from the NIH administrator, which particular Study Section should review *their* grant. The applicant may know many members of this specific Study Section through *their* professional activities. In many instances, the applicant could almost identify who will review *their* proposal, and tries to be nice by adopting some positive adjectives when *they* quote the potential reviewer's previous works. Of course, the scientific merit matters most, but doing this type of homework in advance would not hurt the standing of the pending grant. This non-technical, preliminary legwork is essentially the gist of the above proverb.

A metaphorical interpretation of the proverb may well be that one should live within *their* means and ability. See also Entry #6, "Sparrow tears legs racing a stork." Here, the proverb urges us to address how appropriate and compatible a given circumstance is when a plan is being developed. It would be pathetic for parents to blindly push their children to Harvard, regardless of *their* intelligence or studiousness. If a hole is round, a square peg won't fit.

Many years ago, my sister and her husband insisted that their son should apply for a medical school, whereas he was interested in an art program. My nephew entered a prestigious medical school, but then, two years later, he quit so that he could go to an art institute. At least he tried to accommodate his parents' wishes for a few years but then jumped to independence once he realized what he really wanted to do. The same thing happened to one of my older brothers: After two years at a medical school, he transferred himself to an engineering program, both within Seoul National University.

Here, compatibility is an important part of preparedness. In both instances, the above proverb emphasizes that one has to know in advance, where to put *their* stake in the ground for a favorable outcome. To be fair, in many cases, young people may not know what their aptitude is and what their heart tries to tell them. It will be another topic of an essay at another time. (05/12/2020)

101

241. A quick-witted man gets pickled fish at a Buddhist temple.

눈치가 빠르면 절에 가도 젓국을 얻어 먹는다.

Children acquire *nun-chi* (눈치), or perception ability, as part of maturation, not so much from school but from every-day environments. Literally, it may mean "darting eyes." It is an ability to grasp a situation, without asking anyone for any explanations. By observing someone's body language and facial expression, a child reads a person's mood and mind. An understanding of some subtler situations may require well-trained and well-practiced *nun-chi*. A person with a quick wit and perception appreciates the undercurrent of a given situation with ease and adjust *their* (see the footnote of #207) response accordingly. This ability of reading and understanding others, and thus a given surrounding, is essentially guesswork based on empathy.

My generation of Koreans has had survived numerous adversities, ranging from poverty to political corruption and social unrest, all after World War II. Besides, there was the Korean War as well as civil and military revolutions. As I look back, *nun-chi* was an essential armament for not only defending ourselves from harsh reality but also enduring adversities. It is far from being funny, as one may find in quick-witted characters like the Road Runner escaping from a hungry Wile E. Coyote. The concept of *nun-chi*, as applied to American children, may not exist. It carries more of a combined nuance of sense, tact, hunch, alertness, perceptiveness, cleverness, brilliance, smartness, etc.

The importance of *nun-chi* is well presented in the above proverb. "A man with well-developed *nun-chi* can somehow obtain (free of charge, I assume) the juice from salted fish (젓국), at a Buddhist temple." As pointed out in Entry #51, "A seller of pickled krill solicits at Buddhist temple," no animal flesh, including any fish like krill, is permitted in the premises of a Buddhist temple. Monks simply do not, or to be exact, are prohibited from eating any meat. And yet, this clever man, with exceptional *nun-chi,* can get a food item that is taboo in a Buddhist temple. This extraordinary happening amply shows what a well-versed *nun-chi* can do for us.

The practical advantage gained by *nun-chi* is knowing or understanding something significant, before anybody else. *The Night Circus*, a 2011 fantasy novel by Erin Morgenstern, introduces a fortune teller truly capable of reading the uncertain future of a young man, who later, would become a part-owner of the circus. It constitutes a major theme of the novel.

A central plot of the 1973 American film, *The Sting*, was based on wire transmissions made through Western Union. Before their contents were made public, bets were placed on a horse race which had actually finished a few minutes earlier. This con job was played on a mob boss (Robert Shaw), by two professional gambling swindlers (Paul Newman and Robert Redford). Here, their successful con job over the mob boss was not exactly based on *nun-chi*, but the ability to use a new communication tool in the 1930s.

Amazon, founded by Jeff Bezos in July 1994, started as an online marketplace for books (remember Kindle), but quickly expanded to a mammoth retailer for virtually everything under the sun, available with two-day delivery from Amazon Prime. The company now surpassed Walmart as the most valuable retailer in the United States by market capitalization. Amazon was able to make other major department stores obsolete through the brutal approach of utilizing innovative technology on a mass scale. They, with 750,000 employees around the world, changed the mode of commerce as we used to know, literally over a few years.

With the current lockdown amid the COVID-19 pandemic, Amazon is enjoying one of the best business performances in history. Bezos' *nun-chi* has become envy for everybody who couldn't stop asking "why didn't I think about e-commerce myself?" Similarly, late in the 1990s, Jack Ma, of China, "discovered" the power of Internet commerce to form the Alibaba Group. My perception has been that the company is the Chinese equivalent to Amazon.

The main risk involved in *nun-chi* would be, of course, wrong guesswork and its unfortunate consequence. In the 2016 general election in this country, who would have ever thought that Trump would defeat Clinton? Now, the whole country seems to be paying a dear price for the collective mistake. (05/15/2020)

242. A phoenix in thousands of chickens.
닭이 천이면 봉이 한 마리 있다.

The Chinese Phoenix, *bong* in Korean pronunciation (봉), is an imaginary bird found only in mythology. Per Wikipedia, "the bird is made up of the beak of a rooster, the face of a swallow, the forehead of a fowl, the neck of a snake, the breast of a goose, the back of a tortoise, the hindquarters of a stag and the tail of a fish." At one point in ancient China, this "King of Birds" symbolized the empress when paired with a dragon representing the emperor. It is an understatement to say the Phoenix is a rare and quite noble bird. And yet, you can find one among the low class of fowls such as chickens. "When there are many chickens, more than a thousand in number, surely there must be at least one Phoenix," implying a statistical odd involved in a mass.

I used to tell my graduate students to have as many ideas as they can muster - they could be good, bad, ugly, or even silly - so that we could harvest a few good ideas for further discussion. I would also emphasize that we must always accommodate all possible scientific hypotheses of a given problem, and by extension, all possible world-views on a global issue with an open mind. And express them forcefully with confidence and maintain a mental attitude such that, if people belittled your thoughts, it would be their problem.

The point is that, unless you do something for this world with the knowledge you acquired through years of education and experience, the knowledge is effectively dead and your very existence would be in question. A large number indeed has its own unique characteristics. For instance, the number of molecules in a mole of a substance is known as Avogadro's Number. It is 6×10^{23}. A tablespoonful of water contains approximately 6×10^{23} individual water molecules. A bagful of air should contain a similar number of nitrogen and oxygen gas molecules. This is such a big number that someone claimed that we still breathe a portion of the last breath of Caesar, who was assassinated more than two millennia ago. Thousands of chickens would surely have some interesting birds, like a Phoenix or a beautiful swan.

On the other hand, it could have some obnoxious or dreadful fowls too. The population of the United States is close to 330 million. Sure enough, we have Mr. Donald J. Trump as the president.

According to Albert Einstein's famous formula on the mass-energy equivalency, $E = mc^2$, an object carries intrinsic energy that is proportional to its mass (m) with a proportionality constant that is related to the speed of light (c). When the object moves the total energy gains additional kinetic energy, in addition to this potential energy. An analogy may be that when a mass of people gets agitated, say, by shared hatred, what they can collectively achieve is much more than just the sum of individual efforts. A war, instigated by a few warmongers, would exemplify the potential danger associated with thousands of stir-crazy people and nations.

The population of mainland China is currently close to 1.4 billion, approximately 4.2-fold greater than that of the United States. Many years ago, I came across the following argument in a geopolitical essay (I am afraid I cannot remember its source), but I do remember the crux of the writing. If every Chinese jumped down to the ground simultaneously, from a five-foot height at a given time, it would create a tsunami and send its devastating wave across the Pacific Ocean to the West Coast of the United States. It would cause irreparable damage along the California coast, first having wiped out Hawaii along its way.

For America to neutralize this man-made tsunami, each American citizen must jump to the ground simultaneously, at the same time the Chinese do, but the height they would have to jump from would be some 20 feet; an unachievable task, even if we are all ardently patriotic.

In modern history, China has been frequently referred to as a "Crouching Tiger, Sleeping Giant." A quote, often attributed to Napoleon Bonaparte, reads: "Let China sleep, for when she wakes she will shake the world." The above hypothetical case with a tsunami appears to attest to such a notion that China could literally shake the world. At present, the United States has a tense relationship with China, as to the origin of COVID-19 as well as ill-perceived trade practices, without any nuanced backdrop offered in this essay. (05/17/2020)

243. My mule is preferred to a neighbor's stallion.
내 집 노새가 옆집 말보다 낫다.

A stallion is an uncastrated male horse, primarily raised for breeding. Because of the male sex hormone testosterone, they are much more muscular than mares and castrated males, called geldings. They are more aggressive, and often temperamental in behavior, especially towards other stallions. Thus, it is often more difficult to train them for competition in sports. No doubt, they are spectacular to watch, especially when they are freely roaming and running as a herd, known as "bachelor bands," in the wild. The bonding between a magnificent stallion and a boy, both strayed from a shipwreck, is the storyline behind a 1979 American film, *Black Stallion.* Anyone who has watched the film cannot erase the image of this beautiful horse named *The Black,* with shiny black skin.

On the other hand, a mule is, well, a mule... To be exact, it is the offspring of a male donkey and a female horse. Just to clarify, it is different from a hinny, which is from a female donkey and a stallion. Mules are more patient, enduring, and long-lived than horses. More importantly, they are less stubborn, and yet more intelligent than donkeys. With donkey's ears, drooping eyes, and somewhat docile looking, they are no comparison, in appearance, to a broad-shouldered, shiny coat, and prominent crested stallion with seemingly restless energy. It is no wonder that a man who is regarded as having great sexual prowess is called a stallion. If I am forced to draw an analogy, a stallion is a powerful and sleek Porsche 911 Carrera, whereas a mule is a Ford pickup truck that never breaks down.

So, someone, most likely a farmer, is asked which one he prefers: a mule or a stallion. His quick answer is the above proverb. He says that his mule is of course more valued than his neighbor's stallion. He points out that, while a mule has the size and ground-covering ability of its mother (i.e., dam), it is stronger than a horse of similar size, inherits the endurance and disposition of the donkey (i.e., sire), and requires less food than a horse of the same size. Mules are more independent than most domesticated equines, other than their parental species, the donkey.

The farmer's preference is firmly established. He seems to prefer a Republican wife who can balance a checkbook and fix a delicious dinner, as opposed to a very attractive, fun-chasing, but high-maintenance Democratic wife. In short, the above proverb appears to advise us to go after substance, rather than appearance. It reminds me of the English idiom "don't judge a book by its cover." Once again, this metaphor means that one shouldn't prejudge the worth or value of something, by its outward appearance alone. Likewise, any superficial noise should be carefully assessed, as in Entry #10, "An empty wheelbarrow makes more noise."

Another equally, if not more, important message we receive from the proverb is that we should value and appreciate what we have here and now. However my home, wife, and children may appear to others, and however Korea may look to foreigners, I am irreversibly tied to them, with their warts and all. I cannot be, and I do not want to be, a separate entity from them. My mule may not be the most attractive animal in town, especially compared with the stallion next door; however, we have spent many hours together, every day in the field, sharing tears and sweat. We may not be able to communicate verbally, but mutual affection always exists. No matter what others may say, we belong to each other and the mule knows it.

After so many years of living in a "foreign" country, which has by now become "my" country, what I used to have back there, remains a mere flickering, if not unforgettable, memories. It was then, and this is now.

After a long and quite eventful trip abroad, what do we do first after we return home? The accumulated laundry is put into the washer, empty luggage bags are placed on the self where they always stay, the mail is collected, phone messages are played back, a quick lunch with long-missed kimchee is consumed, and hellos are exchanged with neighbors. We may even hum the melody "Home, Sweet Home."

Mid pleasures and palaces though we may roam. Be it ever so humble, there's no place like home. A charm from the skies seems to hallow us there. Which seek thro' the world, is ne'er met elsewhere. Home! Home! Sweet, sweet home! (05/18/2020)

244. No nation can relieve you of poverty.
가난 구제는 나라도 못한다.

On May 28, 2019, a knife-wielding man in his 50s attacked schoolgirls waiting at a suburban Tokyo bus stop, during morning rush hour. He killed at least two people and wounded 16 others before killing himself. There was no obvious reason for the tragedy, which immediately caused international outcries. Two days later, a retired top Japanese bureaucrat stabbed his 44-year-old son to death because he feared his reclusive child might be a danger to the public, just like the above incident.

Although Japan enjoys a very low crime rate, they have had their own high-profile killings: In 2016 a former employee, at a home for the disabled, stabbed 19 to death and wounded more than 20 others; in 2008, seven people were killed by a man who slammed a truck into a crowd of people in Tokyo and then went on a stabbing rampage; and in 2001, a man killed eight children and wounded 13 others in a knife attack at an elementary school in the city of Osaka.

A common thread among these attackers appears to be what the Japanese referred to as *hikikomori*, or a social recluse. A government survey showed there are an estimated 610,000 *hikikomori* between the ages of 40 to 64 in Japan, mostly men, with many still taken care of by their elderly parents, without proper support from the outside. The cause of this abnormal avoidance of social contact has not been clearly established; however, among many factors, one is the pressure on adolescents to be successful in society, if not personally.

Decades of the flat economy and a poor job market in Japan, Korea, and to some extent even this country, render adolescents to cast doubt on their competitive schooling for elite jobs. Besides, modern communication technologies such as the Internet, social media, and video games exacerbate, deepen, and nurture withdrawal. They have certainly reduced the amount of face-to-face social interactions. In short, *hikikomori* are "modern-day hermits," whose hidden frustrations can explode in a form of social violence, with even the most trivial provocation. How can one help *hikikomori*? Can a nation provide them with financial aid when they cannot find a job?

"Even the nation cannot relieve you from poverty" is a direct translation. A simple interpretation would be: It is you, who would have to rescue yourself from the dire condition you have been living in. Many people, like parents and friends, may try to help you, but in reality and for the long run, they cannot; just as in the case of *hikikomori,* for which neither a government nor his family is unable to. We have already encountered a similar proverb: See Entry #110, "No one can go to the bathroom or heaven's gate on your behalf."

It is noteworthy that a collective society like Korea has produced such a self-centered idiom as this one. If our ancestors had some kind of social welfare programs in the past, I do not know anything about it. Only after the 5·16 Military Coup in 1961, was Korean "social security" seriously considered by the Park's administration; however, the weak national economy has practically failed to offer any aid to the needy people till the year 2000, when a new law was established to prevent any long-term poverty. Its outcome has been a case of the glass being half-empty or half-full.

With the current COVID-19 pandemic in full swing, it has become quite apparent that the fatality rate among African Americans is disproportionally higher than what one would expect from the composition of the general population. Population-wise, African Americans are only one-sixths of Whites in this country, and yet their mortality rate is about three times higher than Whites. Pundits attribute the finding to the prevailing obesity and high blood pressure among Blacks. This health disparity is in turn attributed to the poor living conditions in which the Blacks reside: to be exact, the poor financial and economic situation they have been in. Then, the final question is, why and how has such a disparity in wealth existed for so long between Blacks and Whites?

Even with the Welfare Reform Act of 1996, the welfare programs in this country have been subject to constant harsh criticism, mainly for poor management, especially those programs in healthcare and medical provisions, food assistance, housing subsidies, education and childcare assistance. The above proverb tells us it may not be a bad idea to stop and restart it all over. It's something for us to think about seriously. (05/21/2020)

245. A Buddhist disciple *na-han* eats dirt.
나한에도 모래 먹는 나한 있다.

A high-ranking Buddhist disciple, called *na-han*, has already overcome every agony and passion known to human beings, such as carnal desires and power, to a point that he deserves not only offertory meals and alms from ordinary laymen but also the utmost respect from peers and Buddhist followers. He may well be equivalent to Cardinals or a Bishop of a big diocese in the Catholic Church. He is indeed, very close to an awe-inspiring saint. And yet, some *na-han* may endure the hardship of "eating sand." A standard interpretation of the proverb is that even a person in a prominent position may suffer from adversity such as consuming dirt to survive. Presumably, no one offered him due respect.

Why has he become such a figure in a dire situation, despite his official status? It implies that even a big shot, in any organization, may have a peculiar characteristic that not many people are aware of. What we see in a person may not be what *they* (see the footnote of #207) really are. In this context, the above proverb is similar to Entry #35, "You can see a fathom of water but not an inch of mind." We usually say, "Yeah, I know him quite well," but we cannot know somebody completely. The closest case may well be identical twins, but even in this instance, nurturing factors can lead to two different characters. Learn more about identical triplets in Entry #197, "None of the fingers are alike."

Let us take, for instance, *Strange Case of Dr. Jekyll and Mr. Hyde*, a short novel by Scottish author Robert Louis Stevenson, first published in 1886. If you recall, it deals with outwardly good Dr. Jekyll and shockingly evil Mr. Hyde, all in one person. Dr. Jekyll develops a potion that, when swallowed, would transform him into Mr. Hyde. Mr. Hyde is a personification of Dr. Jekyll's dark side and does terrible things, like murdering an acquaintance or attacking a young girl on a street during the spooky wee hours.

His friend, Dr. Lanyon, is the only person who witnesses the transformation, but he soon dies of its aftershock. Before his death, Dr. Lanyon leaves a letter to a lawyer friend, Mr. Utterson, but asks him to open it only after Dr. Jekyll dies. Eventually, the potion fails to work and Dr. Jekyll realizes that he would stay transformed as Mr. Hyde for the rest of his life. Dr. Jekyll then decides to confess in his suicidal letter to Utterson. "Here then, as I lay down the pen and proceed to seal up my confession, I bring the life of that unhappy Henry Jekyll to an end."

If the story of Dr. Jekyll and Mr. Hyde resonates well with readers of many generations, it is because we all recognize the duality of human nature, expressed as an inner struggle between the good and the evil. Because of morals and ethics ingrained during our upbringing, the good part in us prevails almost all the time. Social norms, further reinforced by the laws of the land, also help keep the world safe and secure. But once in a while, a hideous crime happens. We usually call the offenders a pervert, or an outlier, and tend to treat them as if they were a matter of probability in statistics. For the offenders, there must have been a justifiable cause or an insurmountable urge.

In 2018, George Pell, the former Archbishop of Sydney, was convicted of child sexual abuse that occurred in the 1990s, as well as the 1970s. They were overturned this year, by the High Court of Australia. However, he remains under a separate investigation by the Holy See's Congregation for the Doctrine of the Faith as well as by Victorian police. Amidst these scandalous court battles, we are left with a fundamental question as to the strong "pull" by the evil in us towards gruesome crimes. This is what Freud had to say: "the happiness satisfying our raw instinct such as rape and violence are restricted (only) by the law." It is surely a sad acknowledgment and we admit that it is inherent to civilization. See more in Entry #54, "A house costs less than neighbors."

If (this is a big if) Cardinal Pell indeed committed the alleged crimes, what would be going through his mind during a quiet meditation or prayer? How would his honest confession sound like? Would he offer apologies to his victims? What explanation can he submit to the public, as well as to his parishioners? What type of penance would he be willing to endure? Would it be chewing sand and trying to swallow? (05/22/2020)

246. My beans are bigger than yours.
네 콩이 크니 내 콩이 크니 한다.

Although there are currently as many as 40,000 varieties of beans in the world gene-banks, beans are all invariably small in size: for practical purpose and intention, they are all identical in size. And yet, people argue with one another about whose beans are bigger. Small-minded people tend to examine such an object with a magnifying glass, just to determine a "winner."

From a sociological perspective, there are mainly three types of political systems. In authoritarian governments, their citizens have no power and are subject to blind obedience to formal authorities. A dictatorship belongs to this category. A monarchy is a government controlled by a king or queen. In a constitutional monarchy, royalty is just a figurehead as in the United Kingdom, Spain, Belgium, Sweden, and Japan. The third type is a democracy. Here, it is ultimately the citizens that create and vote for laws. The government is "of the people, by the people, for the people." The idea of democracy stems back from ancient Greece and some serious works by ancient academics at the birth of Western Civilization. Within each of the above three systems, there are many variations.

One variant of democracy, which I have been very much intrigued by and interested in, is democratic socialism or social democracy. Although political scientists distinguish these two terms, I will use them interchangeably. Here, people believe in political democracy within a socially owned economy, and wish to eliminate the political elitism that they witness in capitalism through gradual changes, not with a violent revolution. Originally spearheaded by labor movements and as an alternative to capitalism, they seek a socialist economy with the ethical ideals of social justice as their goal. The United States has some social-democratic movements, backed by labor unions or left-leaning intellectuals, but has never been governed by a socialist party. In fact, any ideology in socialism is accompanied by the social stigma associated with authoritarian socialist states such as Stalinism.

A senator from Vermont, Bernie Sanders, who describes himself as a democratic socialist, made a bid for the 2020 Democratic Party presidential candidate. He gained considerable popular support, particularly among the younger generation and working-class Americans. Although he will not be the Democratic Presidential candidate in the general election this time around, his popularity greatly moves the party platform to the left. At the early phase of the Democratic primary, he was, in fact, the leading candidate. And yet, the anti-Trump voters, whose sole goal seems to be defeating Trump, began to worry about his candidacy, lest he would be labeled a "socialist" by Trump and his allies and lose the general election. In short, 2020 has been a historically interesting testing time for this country.

Within the existing framework of democracy, as we see now in the United States, the ideological difference between Democrats and Republicans is negligible, compared with that between the current democracy and democratic socialism. One may say that the former is like comparing beans, while the latter may well be apples versus oranges. While we constantly complain about the inequality in social justice, wealth, education, and health care, we have not shown any courage or will to change it all, by choosing a socialist ideology. We have been too complacent with "don't rock the boat."

In Korea, the political scene, as casually observed across the Pacific Ocean, is equally fascinating. Although President Moon's approval rate has been steadily going downhill, his ruling party mercilessly squashed the challenge from opposing parties in every corner of the nation in the recent 4·15 parliamentary election. Political analysts attribute their win to the spectacular success in handling the COVID-19 pandemic in Korea. But, I am not sure if that was the whole story.

Mr. Moon's long term direction for the nation has never been clear, at least to me. Every move he made was met with harsh criticism from the older generation of conservatives. His "affectionate" approach to North Korea and cautiously keeping a distance from past allies like the U.S. and Japan may indicate that he wants to bring democratic socialism to Korea, while my contemporaries may blindly resist the change. Or is it simply my naïve thought? (05/24/20)

247. Silencing citizens is more than shutting my mouth up.
백성의 입 막기는 내 입 막기보다 어렵다.

"It is a lot easier to force me to keep my mouth shut than to silence the whole nation (백성)," is the full translation of this proverb. There is nothing new in the statement. The attempt to keep people suppressed forever always gives way to a catastrophic consequence. History is full of revolutions by disgruntled people, ranging from the fall of the Roman Empire to the October Revolution of Russia.

An ideal gas law in basic physical chemistry says that the product of volume and pressure is constant, at a given temperature. As you push a piston in a cylinder further, you would feel more resistance. Conversely, a pressured piston would move backward to relieve pressure. When a given amount of water is transformed to vapor upon heating, the volume changes over 1,000-fold, which is the principle behind the steam engine in a locomotive and the origin of the First Industrial Revolution.

On April 11, 1960, a fisherman found a body of a high school student in the harbor at Masan, a southern city in Korea. He had been missing since March 15, when he participated in a city-wide protest against the corrupt government of the first President of Korea, Syngman Rhee. In contrast to an official report of drowning, his skull had been split by a tear-gas grenade, from his eyes to the back of his head. The city of Masan erupted into three days of spontaneous mass protests, which led the shocked nation to a mass movement against the corruption of Rhee's administration.

In the 1960 general election, one of the two presidential candidates was arrested for some dubious charge and swiftly executed by Rhee. The other opposition candidate, from the Democratic Party, suddenly died of a heart attack. Our high hope for replacing Rhee had quickly faded away. In a separate election for vice president, people had still believed that Chang Myon, a candidate from the Democratic Party, would defeat K.P. Lee, the running mate of Rhee. The final tally showed Lee defeating Chang by a huge margin of more than four-fold. It became quite clear to the majority of Koreans that the voting was fraudulent.

On April 18, 1960, the students of Korea University (고려대학) held a protest in front of the National Assembly. On the way back to the university campus, they were brutally attacked by gangs hired by Rhee's supporters. On April 19, over 100,000 students, not only from universities but also high schools, marched to the Blue House, calling for Rhee's resignation. Police opened fire on protestors, killing approximately 180 and wounding thousands.

On that day, the Rhee government proclaimed martial law to suppress the demonstrations. It was the climax of the student revolution. By April 25, soldiers and police refused to attack the protestors. On April 26, 1960, Rhee stepped down from power. The following day, K.P. Lee and his entire family were killed by his oldest son in a murder-suicide, as K.P. Lee was blamed for most of the corruption in the government.

Throughout his presidency, Rhee had taken advantage of the communist threat from the North as an excuse for political repression against any potential opposition. The public, on the other hand, widely perceived Rhee as a corrupt dictator, who abused his autocratic powers to maintain his power. He had faced increasing domestic discontent after the Korean War in 1953. His policies had delivered limited economic and social development, while angering citizens by amending the constitution to prolong his stay in power. In 1958, Rhee forced through the National Assembly, an amendment to the National Security Law, giving the government broad new powers to curtail freedom of the press, and prevent members of the opposition from voting. With this backdrop, the fraudulent 1960 election was the last straw that broke the camel's back.

In 1960, I was a high school sophomore. On April 19, the school principal was on a speaker in our classrooms, announcing that the class would be dismissed immediately and we were allowed to leave the school one class at a time. In a grave tone, he urged us not to get involved in the on-going anti-government demonstration and to just go home. It was a long walk on the deserted streets of Seoul. Once in a while, a motor vehicle passed by at a great speed and I heard gunshots from a distance. The eerie atmosphere, I still vividly remember. (05/25/2020)

248. Three causes of death: ruthless sun, an endless feast, and trivial worries.
사람을 죽이는 세가지: 내리쪼이는 태양, 만찬, 그리고 걱정.

This proverb says that three things can kill a person: the cruel hot summer sun upon a desert, feasts with abundant, delicious food and entertainment; and unwarranted, but never-ending silly worries. Anything in excess must be dangerous enough to kill us outright. This may include; work, money, power, sex, alcohol, etc. Why these particular three are chosen in this proverb is intriguing; I suppose it is the prerogative of a proverb. We do not have any desert in Korea, but I was imagining the Arizona Sonoran Desert sun, depicted in *American Dirt* by Jeanine Cummins:

> *The sun is lodging itself ever higher into the hot, bright shelf of the sky, and they should've made camp an hour ago. It's not safe for them to be exerting themselves beneath the burning lamp of the sun. It will sap them.* ····· *The desert sun is so bright that even here in the deep shade, Lydia finds herself squinting to block out the light. When she opens her eyes to look around, the landscape beyond this seam of shade is one wide expanse of sepia everything bleached into varying fractures of brown by the adamant sun.*

What will surely kill you would be indulging in a feast that lasts till the wee hours of the morning with a bottomless supply of delicacies, alcohol, a *gisaeng* or two on the lap, boisterous declaration of nonsenses, and noisy entertainment. You will end up with a three-day hangover, during which period you may wish you would have died, rather than suffer. Just thinking about those fancy dishes, which you thought delicious at the party, now haunt you with constant nausea. You vomit so vigorously, you can taste bile acids that usually reside in the duodenum. Then the headache, with a throbbing pain which feels like a sharp needle on each pulse, fails to surrender with Advil. Swallowing water is followed by immediate rejection. How can I take the tablet then? Regrets come much too late and it can kill any of us who have overdone it at a party of abundance.

116

Of the three causes of death, worry or anxiety is most interesting. That is because my wife often manifests such symptoms and because she should not die young. In her case, such negative thoughts are usually formed, not by a logical rationale, but by some ominous intuitions. I consider myself a generous and accommodating person, to the extent that I can listen to her dream before she makes some serious decision, but not a baseless accusation regarding my judgment capability when I offer a counter-argument. Her standard last words are usually, "You don't know what you're talking about!" Or, "No wonder why your friends laugh at you (behind your back)." Man, that's cruel.

I will have to admit this much though. She can talk, especially when she unduly worries about something she herself has devised, or fabricated, like our financial status. As to the latter, it is unjustified because we are doing just fine, with a sizable amount of cash in our bank accounts that is always available, and we are without any outstanding debts. For crying out loud, we don't even have a home mortgage and have managed the highest credit rating one could imagine.

By no means, am I a wizard in handling money, but at least I successfully maintain relativity in numbers, like Avogadro's number versus the exact length of one nanometer. As we were negotiating the sales price for a previous house in North Carolina, a few thousand dollars were moving back and forth, and yet she was quite concerned about a few bucks involved in a grocery item.

I see how anxiety or worries can lead a person to an early demise, but nonchalant behaviors are not as justified as we, my Korean generation, were once accustomed to. We were to acquire audacity, based on self-confidence and courage (배짱), as early as we could. The last thing our elders, especially my parents, wanted to see was a young man's mind swaying like a weak plant depending on the direction of the wind. Expressing our emotions to others was often frowned upon by peers, as well as our parents. How could a man shed tears in public! It was a cool thing to show a "demonstrative apathy" toward a girl I wanted anxiously to meet. If I did not initiate a casual chat with the girl, it was not entirely because I was shy, but because I was cool. (05/25/2020)

249. Pigs love mucky water.
돼지는 흐린 물을 좋아한다.

Pigs have been domesticated since ancient times, nearly everywhere in the world. They are highly social and intelligent animals. Since they share a similarity in the genome with humans, they offer various animal models of human diseases. I used to collaborate with industrial scientists who were developing genetically modified pigs, whose organs could be transplanted to humans without provoking the host's immune rejection. Likewise, their skin offered one of the best models of human skin, and my colleagues would use them in studying percutaneous absorption of drug molecules with varying physical properties.

Interestingly, because of their inherited foraging abilities and excellent sense of smell, they are trained to find truffles, fancy and very expensive mushrooms, in many European countries.

However, the concept of the pig among Koreans is quite different from that in the United States. By now, after more than 50 years of living here, I have come across many different customs and traditions from different cultures, so not many discoveries shock me any longer. However, I was surprised, when I learned for the first time, that quite a few Americans keep pigs as pets, even allowing them to roam in their living rooms. If I borrow a Korean expression, "We will never, ever, keep a company of pigs in our living room, even if you offer tons of money to plead me to do so."

An outdoor enclosure where pigs are raised, called a pigsty or pigpen, is invariably messy, filthy, and smelly, even though pigs are clean animals. Why? First, the ground is always bare, since they eat nearly everything until there is nothing left. Note that they are omnivores. Pigs cannot regulate their body temperature by sweating. They must be always provided with water or mud so that they can cool themselves through wet skin. Without access to water or mud, pigs must roll about in their own excrement. No wonder Korean farmers used to raise pigs in one of the filthiest corners of their land, and feed them almost anything, usually leftover meals.

Therefore, pigs love mucky wet mud by necessity, not so much by choice. And yet, the above proverb combines the preoccupation of our ancestors that pigs are just filthy animals and the affinity of pigs to mucky water. This old saying implies that immoral and unethical characters tend to hang around in dark, lawless environments, among people with similar inclinations. Here, however, I would like to offer a different interpretation, with a story about the lotus.

An individual lotus, also called a water lily, can live for over a thousand years and maintains a rare ability to revive into activity after prolonged stasis. It develops roots and rhizomes in the soil, under water as deep as seven feet, or two meters. While the broad leaves float on the water surface, the flowers are usually found on thick stems rising a few inches, or several centimeters, above the leaves. The leaves can be as large as 80 cm (31 inches) in diameter, while the eye-catching flowers can be up to 30 cm, or 12 inches, in diameter. Unlike pigs, the lotus has a remarkable ability to regulate the temperature of its flowers to within a narrow range, presumably thanks to insect pollinators.

Carbohydrate-rich rhizomes, which Koreans erroneously called roots, are the main stem of the plant. They are consumed as a vegetable in Asian countries, including Korea. They are like a raw potato, crunchy in texture with sweet-tangy flavors, and served in various dishes as well as a tea. On a pond, leaves not only serve as a resting and playing place for frogs but are also used as a wrapper of steamed rice after harvested. Additionally, starch from the leave is used in pharmacy, as a binder of tableting. In Korea, lotus flower tea (연꽃차, *yeon-kot-cha*) is made from the dried petals of the white lotus. It is the national flower of both India and Vietnam. The lotus is sacred to both Hindus and Buddhists. A seat, depicted by a lotus flower, symbolizes a throne for divine figures.

The water where this extraordinary plant grows is not very clean. You may not be able to see anything under the surface because it is so murky. We can say that they live in an environment similar to that of pigs. Besides, just like a pig, the plant offers every part of itself for human consumption. In short, what we see may not allows us to conclude what they actually are. (05/27/2020)

250. Words shared with a cow, but not with a wife, are safe.
소더러 한 말은 안나도, 처더러한 말은 난다.

This is another proverb telling us to be very careful with what we say: "What you have told a cow will not go anywhere, but whatever you say to your wife will find a way to others, in no time." Your cow, with blinking heavy eyes, may think it strange to hear you mumbling something, but that's about the extent of the communication. In contrast, your wife may repeat exactly what you have told her, plus her own editorial comments to her friends, sisters, and most likely her mother. On this particular day, say, you learned that your boss, Tom, is leaving his wife of many years for a young woman, his daughter's age, who also works at the firm. Who told you the rumor? Why, your mistress, that's who.

There is no incentive on your part, to transmit prematurely, a piece of what is still considered office gossip to your wife, but it so happens that she has been nagging you for several days about a long-planned, but never materialized, vacation to Europe. What could be a more powerful device in diverting her attention than telling her this juicy breaking news? One of the many questions she would ask is if you know the young woman involved? Of course, you do, but that would be revealed at another time, perhaps at a more serious occasion, like during your wife's demand for a divorce. Why give away everything right now? You need some time to map out your strategy on your own affairs. Besides, you can also get some pointers from Tom later.

This is such valuable gossip; your wife saves it for an immediate face-to-face get-together, over a cup of coffee at Starbucks, with her best friend, Felicity. Your wife tells Felicity, with an open hand going through her own throat, that if Tom finds out the source of this leak, you would get fired on the spot. Your wife thus begs Felicity not to tell anyone. But as far as Felicity is concerned, your dismissal is not a matter of significance. What matters most to Felicity now, is spending a delightful afternoon with her best friend, gossiping at a coffee shop. Together, they speculate endless scenarios of what is coming next: what is going to happen to Tom's wife, their children, house, and even their dog. The situation would be more complicated if

Felicity happens to be Tom's wife. This scenario of a greater magnitude of shock should wait for another time.

The extent to which the hearsay spreads depends on the social circles that Felicity and your wife keep. If Tom and his wife are upper-class, jet setters in this town, the story may appear in a social column of some tabloid newspapers. If a reporter somehow gets hold of some pictures of the people involved, most desirably a picture of the young woman involved, *their* (see the footnote of #207) scoop will be praised by their superior, and may even receive a pay raise. The speed at which the story spreads depends on the "weight" of people's lips. Everybody wishes to be the first person to tell others what is happening. The last thing one wishes to hear is, "Oh, yes, I also heard that rumor the other day."

In the meantime, you will receive a steady stream of updates from your mistress, who is also working for the same company. You see, she has a daily lunch with Tom's wife-to-be. She provides more information that you can use later for diverting your wife's attention whenever any inconvenient subjects appear. On the other hand, your mistress seems to be applying more subtle, but well-focused pressure, on the current state of affairs at hand. It is an attempt to establish some sort of permanent arrangement. You hear loud and clear: "If Tom can take such a bold step, why can't you?"

When you get home late, attributing the tardiness to entertaining a company client, you notice a rare visit from your mother-in-law. It is so late that your children have gone to sleep already. She was talking with your wife in a whisper, both with solemn facial expressions. Soon after a short exchange of pleasantries, the mother-in-law says that she came across an old friend of hers, at a hair salon that afternoon and learned that the friend saw you at a certain lunch place, a few days earlier. That was the place where you had a most recent rendezvous with your mistress. Then you notice white knuckles on the tightly closed hands of your wife, although she was not saying anything, just gazing down at the floor, unfocused. This sort of soap opera would not happen if you only talk with a cow (I must have watched too many soap operas on TV lately). (05/28/2020)

251. With two women, you will be safe from a tiger.
계집 둘 가진 놈의 창자는 호랑이도 안 먹는다.

The Korean word, 계집 pronounced *gye-jip*, is somewhat demeaning and deleterious when used to mean a woman. It is not as bad as a bitch, but far from a lady. Any female at any age can be a *gye-jip,* but the word is usually reserved for an unmarried young girl, a mistress, a concubine, or even a wife in a peculiar context. As is often the case, when used in jest, *gye-jip* is a counterpart of *nom* or 놈 for a man. For more on *nom*, see #118, "A thirsty man digs a well." The first reading of this proverb is based on *gye-jip,* meaning a concubine. This is a standard interpretation.

Polygamy, in the old days of the Joseon Dynasty, was quite common among wealthy *yang-ban* families, the upper echelon of the society, and fairly well accepted among ordinary people, or *seo-min* (서민). After all, most kings had a second wife called 후궁, *hoo-goong,* so "Why can't I?"

Especially when, and if, the first wife could not produce a son to continue the family name, it became a justification, or an excuse, for having another wife. In a palace or well-established *yang-ban* families, such an unwritten tradition had been firmly established. That is, there was no significant complaint from the interactions between wives, at least on the surface. Each wife would know where she belonged in the familial hierarchy.

Let us assume that you've just brought in a concubine to your family, without any advanced consultation with your wife. You are doing it simply because you can, with the sudden wealth you have recently acquired from a successful business. In this situation, those two women will have a hard time getting along.

The legitimacy of the original marriage would be a strong suit for the wife. Indulging affection that the concubine receives from the head of the family would be the strong card for the concubine. Since each side has such undeniably strong backings, neither side will bow her head toward the other without a decent fight. Sooner or later, the initial bliss of love for the concubine would have come and gone. What do you think now about the terrible mess you have created?

You will not have any single moment of peace in your life. You can see and feel, the cold stares being exchanged between those two women. They could have killed each other had you not intervened diplomatically. Remember that one time in the past you loved each of them dearly? Not any more. They are the source of this constant headache. You even entertain the thought of having another mistress, somewhere secret, so that you can hide from this miserable life. Then you immediately erase the thought saying, "Oh, I've had enough!"

The old Roman idiom, "a sound mind in a sound body," implies that your mind is always in turmoil in an aching or troubled body. In addition to headaches, you have now developed an indigestion problem: call it an ulcer! Your intestine is so corrupt by now, you as well as people close by, like your two wives, can smell a foul odor whenever you belch. And their constant complaints and nagging are pulling you apart. Ask yourself, "Why do you think a tiger would devour such a rotten gut of yours?" You are safe from a tiger. That would the silver lining of your misfortune.

The following is an alternative interpretation of the above proverb, absolutely mine, and somewhat convoluted. If you ask any parent who is more costly to raise, a son or a daughter, the answer would be resoundingly a daughter. The cost adds up quickly for piano or other music-related lessons, ballet lessons, sports gear, art classes, allowance for their clothes, cosmetics, etc. Then comes a big one: the cost involved in the wedding. Traditionally, the bride's parents will pay for not only an engagement party, but also all wedding-related costs, such as the floral arrangement, photo and video, reception party, and of course the bride's attire and the groom's ring.

So, for the parents who have a few daughters, the chances are that they are quite poor, perhaps to the point where their guts will be empty most of the time. Then, why would a tiger long for this poor man's intestine? (As an afterthought, I do not understand why a tiger would go for the intestine, when more delicious parts of a human body would be readily available. The gut with indigested foods and bile inside would taste awful, right?) (05/31/2020)

252. A summer shower keeps half of a cow's back dry.
오뉴월 소나기는 쇠 등을 두고 다툰다.

Before the modern electric refrigerator became widely available, people would use an icebox to keep perishable foodstuff. When I was an elementary school kid, a science question that appeared quite often in tests was: "Where, at the top or the bottom, would you keep a chunk of ice in the icebox?" It was a tricky question until we learned about air movement via convection: Warm air rises while cold air comes down. This knowledge, together with the differences in thermal conductivity and heat capacity between land and ocean, was used in explaining why wind tends to blow from the ocean to the beach during the daytime and in the opposite direction during the night time.

The proverb evokes a shower in May and June, or *o-nueol* (오뉴월). The months are in the lunar calendar, which corresponds to June and July, or the young summer months. As the humid air at the surface of the Earth is heated more than its surroundings, not only does evaporation occur but the air also rises rapidly, encountering colder air at altitude, forming clouds and becoming rain. When the clouds form with rapid uplifts in unstable areas, they are known as towering cumulus and are typically taller than they are wide. They are often characterized by sharp outlines and great vertical development.

This is the type of cloud that yields to short-lived showers or hail. Importantly, these clouds move with atmospheric circulation and spend little time above a point on the ground. This explains the variations in intensity, the short duration, and the well-focused area of the showers. One moment, you are driving through a violent shower under dark clouds, and another minute, you see brilliant sunshine. The border between the dry and wet ground can be well defined, literally within a few meters. Now, the above proverb is saying that, as a summer shower passes, one part of a cow's back remains dry while the other half is all wet. It is an exaggeration at best. What else can we say? But a more difficult question to deal with would be what it meant to say.

The boundary between "the haves" and "the have-nots" in a town is usually a single street, or more conveniently, a railroad or a small stream.

The distinction is often so sharp that we are forced to witness the difference in lawn care, age of the roof, peeling or fresh wall paint, windows, gutters, etc. A more abrupt change by a single thin line would be the boundary between two nations.

A few years ago, when President Trump met Kim Jong-un of North Korea, at Panmunjom, a picture was taken while they and President Moon from South Korea were straddling both Koreas. The spine of a cow, dividing a dry and a wet flank, symbolizes peripheries of the poor and the rich or two adjacent nations. Further examples would be XX and XY chromosomes defining the sex of humans, flipping a coin to determine a winner, a fact defining truth and falsehood, the moral between good and evil, differences between war and peace, etc. The dual nature of many concepts necessitates a distinction criterion.

The erratic behavior of a summer shower – spotty in terms of location, varying in intensity, and abruptly changing in duration – are all too temperamental and teasing. Together, they are a hallmark of easily agitated, cantankerous women with a tantrum. Temperamental behaviors of two opera singers, really prima donnas, come to mind. To many of her coworkers, Maria Callas (1923 – 1977) was the most difficult artist to work with. Well recorded and often spoken of were her difficult relationships with her mother, Italian opera house La Scala as well as the Metropolitan Opera in New York City, and affairs with the Greek shipping magnate Aristotle Onassis while she was still married to another man. As a footnote, the same Onassis later married Jacqueline Kennedy, the widow of President John F. Kennedy.

Likewise, Jessye Norman (1945 – 2019) was an "imposing figure, dressing dramatically and speaking with a diva's perfect diction. No one messed with her; she had a high sense of her calling that gave her justifiable pride in her achievement, but this sense of self-esteem made her no easier to deal with. Although she eschewed the indignity of tantrums and walkouts, she treated conductors, colleagues, fans, and minions with a gracious hauteur that could, on occasion, become downright patronizing." (from *Wikipedia*) (06/01/2020)

253. An idling ranger, paid by a monk.
산지기가 놀고 중이 추렴을 낸다.

Some wealthy Korean families in rural areas often own a small mountain. In the old days, it would have offered firewood, water if there was a stream, small animals for sustenance such as rabbits and deer, and plants like mushrooms or those used for herbal medicine. More importantly, a side of a hill with proper *feng shui* provided a burial ground for several generations of the family. The owner of the mountain, usually rich *yang-ban*, would hire a few forest rangers (산지기) that would continuously survey and maintain the property. As one can imagine, these employees are not equipped with much of a skill set or education to speak of. Their jobs can be quite boring. The above proverb says that this particular ranger, instead of trekking diligently throughout the premises with the keen purpose of his job, goes down to a village just to have a good time. Since his meager salary cannot afford such an idling time, someone has to pay for it. The person is a Buddhist monk.

What in the world does a monk have anything to do with a ranger, not to mention him paying for the ranger's good time of hedonism? I do not know the answer, but it may not be an intelligent question. As far as this proverb is concerned, it could have been a fisherman or a simple-minded farmer, instead of a monk. This is undoubtedly one of those Korean proverbial anecdotes that defy logic and refuses to offer an easy interpretation. But, on the other hand, that may well be the gist of the proverb: It is the ranger who had a good time in the village, but a person completely unrelated is paying for the expense. It is unfair and unexpected, but who says the world is a fair place to live?

In the first place, what is a monk doing in the village, instead of meditating and praying at his temple deep in the mountains? He is not doing what he was supposed to do: He is a slacker, just like the ranger. On top of that, he is paying for the liquor that the lazy rascal drank and the expensive meals he has consumed! Is he insane? How can he waste the offertories they have painstakingly collected from poor Buddhist parishioners? Was the monk somehow blackmailed by the ranger?

I see some resemblance between the monk paying for the good-for-nothing ranger and how the United States spends its revenues, mainly taxes collected from hard-working citizens. If the spending exceeds the income, one ends up with debt or deficit (although they differ in definition, let's use the term "national debt" and "budget deficit" interchangeably). Any reasonable person or nation would do their best to keep the expenditures within their income. When the latter is fixed, they will have to establish and follow a priority. The United States government primarily spends on healthcare, retirement, and defense programs, not necessarily in that order.

Here is a cursory review of the United States federal budget. First, in terms of revenue sharing, the corporate taxes are currently only about 6%, thanks to the Tax Cuts and Jobs Act by the Trump administration and Republican Congress: before Trump, it had been at least 10%. Secondly, our national deficit, as of 11:22 AM of June 4, 2020, is close to: $25,154,153,000,000. At present, the debt increases at a rate of $1,000,000 per every 47 seconds. The rapid change undoubtedly reflects the federal subsidiary pay for the unemployed due to the current COVID-19 pandemic. But still, it is over $25 trillion. See also Entry #144, "Buy and slaughter a cow on credit."

What are the priority items that the government sets forth for spending? For Fiscal Year 2020, the budget for the Department of Defense (DoD) is approximately $722 billion out of the projected total revenue of $3.71 trillion: i.e., about 20%. A distant second is the budget for Health and Human Services (HHS), at approximately $110 (For easier comparison, all numbers are in billions), while Education is $72, or a mere 10% of the DoD.

Federal support for my favorite agencies are as follows: National Institutes of Health, $37; National Park Service, $3; the Corporation for Public Broadcasting including National Public Radio and Public Broadcasting Service, about $0.5 (directly from Congress); and the National Endowment for the Arts, less than $0.2. In 2018, the military expenditure of the U.S. was approximately 2.5-fold greater than that of China and 10-fold greater than Russia. Did I sign up for this priority when I paid my taxes? Hell no. (06/05/2020)

254. In-laws sing my song.
나 부를 노래를 사돈 집에서 부른다.

The relationship with in-laws is usually courteous at best, but not very intimate, like with your beloved friends. By "in-laws," I mean two families who have met only through the marriage of their son or daughter. They are not getting together all the time, as they do with their close family friends. Once in a while, they meet, but it is usually a good idea to keep some respectable distance. On a rare occasion that calls for, say, a singing challenge in karaoke, this man from your in-laws' family is belting out your favorite song before your turn comes along. Now, all of their family is singing in unison. Of course, they did not know it was the song you were about to sing, but still, it irritates you.

At a gathering to honor your professional achievement with an award, the man who introduces you spends his sweet time with a long-drawn-out speech, bringing boredom to the attendees. He also states what you have planned to say in your acceptance speech. He effectively "steals your thunder." To top it all, you are to say a few words, thanking him for the wonderful and kind introduction. However nice you may want to be, it is a big-time letdown, and you've now lost all your steam and just want to go home. Every life is accompanied by such irritations and disappointments: some are mild, while others are more serious, somewhat depending on the mood you are in.

When we were leaving Chapel Hill for Las Vegas, we dropped by the Korean restaurant and the Korean grocery store we used to frequent, to say goodbye. We didn't want to make a big deal out of the move, but we couldn't just disappear either. Both places had already learned that we were leaving. Some Korean friends had already told them. We lost our moment. Other irritations may include people who speak loudly on a cell phone, never use the turn signal on the car, wear tight clothes in primary colors, empty their ashtray in a parking lot, hold up a long line of customers at a cash register, leave trash bins out on the street all day, beg for money when my pocket is empty, are overconfident of their ability, dislike the TV drama I enjoyed, vote for the candidate I don't care for, etc.

Serious disappointments come from liars. According to an article that appeared in the April 14, 2020 issue of *The Washington Post*, President Trump lied over 18,000 times over the past 1,170 days in office. That's an average of more than 15 claims a day. They also reported it had been at a rate of 23 times a day during the previous 75 days. In 2019, the average was 22 lies a day. Just this morning, former Secretary of State, Colin Powell, told CNN's Jake Tapper, "He lies all the time." What surprises me most is not simply how much he lies, but that he is still solidly supported by White Republicans. Some political pundits already murmur that he can win the general election again, later this year. This possibility is of the most horrible predicaments this country is currently facing. If the past and present predict what is coming, a big disappointment would be our future.

During the early stage of the COVID-19 pandemic, this nation failed miserably in providing adequate testing for the viral infection and ventilators for critically ill patients, not to mention simple personal protective equipment such as face masks. Although we attribute such national inadequacy to the inter-dependence of manufacturers among nations, deep in everyone's mind was the apprehension from the disproportionate wealth in service industries such as finance. We simply do not have any adequate and purposeful infrastructure for manufacturing anything tangible anymore. Gone is the almighty industrial manufacturing prowess of the 20th century. What is emerging is the ever-widening gap between the rich and the poor.

Such a Full Sea, a 2014 novel by the award-winning Korean-American writer Chang-Rae Lee, introduces a future version of the dystopian city of Baltimore, called B-Mor. Chinese descendants, brought over here many years ago from an environmentally ruined provincial China, are kept within high-walled labor colonies. They exist mainly for providing perfect produce and fish to the small, elite, satellite charter villages that surround the labor settlement. The plot depicts a feasible future we will have to acknowledge with deep sadness and disappointment. The possibility should worry parents with young children. Thank goodness, we don't have any children. (06/07/2020)

255. A new foe emerges in revenging an old one.
오랜 원수 갚으려다가 새 원수가 생겼다.

An enemy is threatening one's wellbeing. The enemy can be an individual, community, or nation. Surveying human history, it seems that we cannot live without any enemies. That much we will have to admit. Our immediate reaction to an enemy, when we identify one as such, is we either make sure we are strong enough to fend them off, should they attack us; or we preempt a sure attack from them with a declaration of war. The ultimate goal of a war is maximizing the injury to the enemy for complete annihilation in an irreversible way. We are now their genuine enemy. If one side perceives their enemy as stronger, they will seek an ally: NATO versus the Warsaw Pact in the old days, for example.

This proverb thus says that when we try to gang up on someone or a nation, that someone will invite their own ally, who will become another enemy of ours. At a national level, it is the escalation of a battle into a world war. At a local level, it could become a fight among organized gangsters.

All major religions on this planet thrive by rendering their followers to become better human beings through both the spiritual and physical practice of love. We are encouraged to treat enemies with kindness, compassion, and forgiveness. Retaliation has no place in an ideal world. The Bible is, of course, full of the ideal of forgiving enemies. "You have heard that it was said, 'You shall love your neighbor and hate your enemy.' But I say to you, Love your enemies and pray for those who persecute you." (Matthew 5:43 - 44); and "Let all bitterness and wrath and anger and clamor and slander be put away from you, along with all malice. Be kind to one another, tenderhearted, forgiving one another, as God in Christ forgave you." (Ephesians 4:31 - 32).

A passage from Talmud reads, "If a man finds both a friend and an enemy requiring assistance he should assist his enemy first in order to subdue his evil inclination," and "Who is strong? He who converts an enemy into a friend." Likewise, both Hinduism and Buddhism promote kindness and non-violence towards all living things, as they are all connected. Mahatma

Gandhi in fact advised us not to have an enemy at all, stating that "to one who follows this doctrine there is no room for an enemy."

These words of wisdom are all easy to say but quite difficult to practice. In the real world, a typical retaliation may well be like those depicted in *The Godfather* trilogy, a 1972 American crime film directed by Francis Ford Coppola. The story, spanning from 1945 to 1955, chronicles the Corleone family under patriarch Vito Corleone (played by Marlon Brando), focusing on the transformation of his youngest son, Michael Corleone (Al Pacino), from a reluctant family outsider to a ruthless mafia boss. The open warfare among the so-called Five Families was far from "forgiving enemies."

Another great gangster movie is *Goodfellas*, a 1990 film directed by Martin Scorsese. It is an adaptation of the 1985 non-fiction book *Wiseguy,* by Nicholas Pileggi. The film narrates the rise and fall of a criminal Henry Hill (played by Ray Liotta), together with his friends and family, from 1955 to 1980. The movie is widely regarded as one of the greatest films ever made, particularly in the gangster genre. In 2000, it was deemed "culturally, historically, and aesthetically significant" and was selected for preservation in the National Film Registry by the U. S. Library of Congress. Its content and style have been copied in numerous other films and television series. Once again, amongst the violent human interactions, we see hardly anything gentle, kind, or forgiving.

All said and done, the real new enemy that the above proverb is referring to could be the one from within oneself. The emotion towards an old foe, filled with "bitterness and wrath and anger and clamor and slander" (Ephesians 4:31 - 32), together with negative thoughts and wishes for one's demise, is not something *they* (see the footnote of #207) wish to live with throughout *their* lives. Besides, unless something is done in earnest, *their* self-condemnation of *their* hateful thoughts against another human being would remain outrageous mental torture for the rest of *their* lives.

I do not know if any level of confession would erase the guilty conscious once and for all. If these do not personify an enemy, what does? (06/08/2020)

131

256. The small hawk catches pheasants.
초고리는 작아도 꿩만 잡는다.

The hawk is smaller than most of its prey but it doesn't have any problem in hunting and killing pheasants, rabbits, pigeons, squirrels, and the like. In this sense, the proverb is very similar to Entry #50, "The smaller pepper is hotter." There, I mentioned that the yellow habanero is one of the smallest peppers, and yet it's hotter than the large bell peppers one eats in a salad, as a whole. They are somewhat related to another metaphoric phrase, "Don't judge a book by its cover."

As a bird of prey, hawks are well equipped with strong and powerful talons and a laser-sharp beak; perfect for killing and tearing apart fresh kill for consumption. Their excellent pair of eyes (thus the word "hawk-eyes") comes with the ability to perceive a much wider range of light including ultraviolet light. It is said that their eyes are also adapted for polarized light or magnetic fields. Some hawks are monogamous and stay with the same mating partner throughout their lives.

Hawks usually live in places like deserts and open fields, as it is easier to find prey. The red-tailed hawk is the most common in North America and easily adapts to any surrounding. In the winter of 1991, a red-tailed hawk, named Pale Male, landed in Central Park, New York City, starting a dynasty. They soared over Fifth Avenue, fascinating the imagination of New Yorkers. It was certainly the beginning of a unique New York love story that inspired a documentary film, *The Legend of Pale Male*. It was "a tribute to the magic of nature and the spirit of the greatest city in the world." One can still enjoy the three-minute trailer of their saga via Google or YouTube.

Hawks are considered one of the most intelligent birds on this planet. The art of falconry, raising and training them for hunting small wild animals in their natural state and habitat, goes back as far as the beginning of human culture, 2000 BC. Much of what I know about falconry is from *H is for Hawk*, by Helen Macdonald, one of the 2014 bestsellers. It is a story of the year she spent training a northern goshawk in the wake of her father's death. Her father was a respected photojournalist who died suddenly of a heart attack, in 2007. Having been a falconer for many years, she purchased a young goshawk to help her through the grieving process.

Then, one summer day of last year, I found an equally fascinating story in *The New York Times*, written by Kurt Streeter, "On Pigeon Patrol, Rufus the Hawk Rules the Skies Over Wimbledon."

Flocks of pigeons and their poop became a growing problem in the late 1990s, a threat to the prim fastidiousness that Wimbledon prizes above all. Pigeons could reign supreme, not just in the air, but also in the rafters, on the rooftops and across the grass courts. The place is perfect for pigeons. "All of the grass seeds, all of the nooks and crannies, and the food waste from the fans," Wayne Davis, one of Rufus's handlers, said. Without Rufus, he reckoned, pigeons would number in the hundreds.

Now, thanks to Rufus - a brown and chestnut bird of prey with keen eyes, a four-foot wingspan and bone-crushing talons - the skies over the All England Club is clear from pigeons. Every day, in the early morning, well before the matches begin, Rufus soars, on the prowl for pigeons. Although he weighs just one pound six ounces, he cuts a much larger figure with his confident bearing and cascade of feathers. He can spread his talons almost as wide as a person's hand, and he can see 10 times better than any human. He can focus on a pigeon from a mile away. Without him, Wimbledon just might descend into aviary chaos. Davis and his daughter, Imogen, feed him by hand because his weight is important. At less than a pound and a half, he can become too hungry and might have a pigeon for lunch. Maybe in front of the royal box. They have taught him to come when they whistle. Most often, he does.

So, even a small bird can rule the sky, the above proverb is declaring. Its inspirational statement implies that one can be anyone or someone to reckon with, once a determination takes hold of *them* (see the footnote of #207.) (06/10/2020)

257. The eye of a needle is too wide for loved ones, the world too small for distant ones.
친한 사이는 바늘귀도 넓고, 친하지 않은 사이는 세계도 좁다.

This proverb is concerned with the distance and space involved in human interaction. For a certain relationship, even the tiny eye of a needle is too big and wide. For a relationship, where two parties involved wish to be as far away from each other as physically possible, even the whole world is too small. The former is applicable in the case of loved ones, while the latter may involve two unbearable enemies. Both cases are at the extreme in human interactions.

For ordinary relationships, we somehow get to learn, and try to maintain, an optimal distance. Earlier, I used the principle of the Lennard-Jones Potential in physical chemistry in developing an essay on a similar topic: See #34, "A man in love salutes his in-laws' horse post," and #86, "The squabble of a married couple is like cutting water with a knife." Presented below are two examples, one for each case.

We often read stories about elderly couples, who have been together for many decades, dying within a few months, if not days, of each other. June Carter Cash was a five-time Grammy award-winning country music singer and was the wife of another great singer, Johnny Cash. He was one of the best-selling musical artists of all time. Remember his *Ring of Fire* (which was written by June Carter)? He received the rare honor of being inducted into all three music Halls of Fame: Country Music, Rock and Roll, and Gospel Music. At any rate, June Carter died in 2003, at the age of 73. By then, they had been married for 35 years. Johnny Cash then died four months later of a "broken heart." This is what he had to say in his last public performance in July, 2003:

The spirit of June Carter overshadows me tonight with the love she had for me and the love I have for her. We connect somewhere between here and Heaven. She came down for a short visit, I guess, from Heaven to visit with me tonight to give me courage and inspiration like she always has. She's never been one for me except courage and inspiration. I thank God for June Carter. I love her with all my heart. (Cash, Johnny. 5 July 2003, Hiltons VA)

However you may want to read "Elderly couple dies hours apart," it's always a heart-warming story, as it suggests that love does indeed seem to last beyond death. There is a physiological explanation of the death by "broken heart syndrome." However, such a scientific approach to the romantic ending of the elders does not deserve a place in my book. Indeed *hap-jang* (합장) has been quite common in Korea, where a couple is buried under one tomb. Usually, the husband is placed on the left of the wife when viewed from the front, but *feng-shui* plays an important role in specific cases. The bottom line is that the space of a needle's eye can be too big for a couple who have been in a tight embrace of love throughout their lives and beyond.

When a couple of people cannot stand each other, this world can be too small a place to avoid the dreadful encounters. A murder offers a perfect solution: having one party no longer living in this world. Once again, a married couple presents an example.

Just the other day, on June 10, the two missing children of Lori Vallow were discovered buried on a property in Rexburg, Idaho. Vallow's most recent husband, Chad Daybell, owns the land. Vallow had married four times prior. For Daybell, it was his second marriage. His first wife died under a suspicious circumstance and her body was exhumed for an autopsy. Its result has not been released yet. Vallow's third husband died from what was ruled a heart attack and his body was cremated. Her fourth husband was shot and killed by Vallow's brother, who also died soon after from "a natural cause." Before he was killed, the husband had complained in his divorce filing that his wife "infatuated at times obsessive about near-death experiences and spiritual visions." Likewise, Daybell had followed a doomsday cult that focused on the second coming of Jesus. With so many deaths around them, Vallow and Daybell must have lived freely in a wide world, until the world became so small that the law caught up with them. (06/12/2020)

258. Only a tiger can silence a hunting dog.
포수집 개는 호랑이가 물어가야 말이없다.

What type of dog a man brings to a hunting trip depends on what quarries he is after. Hound dogs are good for hunting mammals such as rabbits, coyotes, deer, and raccoons. They are very good at sight and scent. For duck hunting, the most popular ones are retrievers, spaniels, pointers, etc. They are good at locating, flushing, and retrieving game birds like ducks. This proverb is not about the skillset and capabilities of each type of hunting dog out there.

To many Koreans of the bygone era, including myself, the perception of a dog is usually associated with barking, biting, protecting, and possibly fighting. Cuddling a well-groomed lapdog was not a typical reason why we kept a dog when I grew up. Constant barking, especially during a quiet night, for no obvious reason but just out of habit, is an awful nuisance, not only to the owner but also to others within earshot.

That being said, how can one stop a dog from barking? The proverb implies that you cannot. The dog would bark until a tiger comes along to devour the dog. This is a rhetorical question and answer, on how we can stop a person from talking, yakking to be precise, endlessly without any breaks. Yes, I have come across a few such people in my lifetime. One particular man, with a PhD degree, worked for the same research and development department of a pharmaceutical firm, as I did. Many years later, he became my immediate boss as I was leaving the company. He was the type who knew everything. He knew that the sun was going to rise from the east tomorrow morning. He also knew, or pretended to know, what he didn't know or understand. One thing he did not know was that he was very talkative. Don't get me wrong: he was a nice guy and really harmless. He always meant well.

Our staff meetings would be comprised of two components; business and technical. When our manager talked about the business aspects of our department, scientists were usually quiet. We knew we were sitting at the receiving end of his directives. Once in a while, however, some smart scientist might ask some smart questions, like how high we ought to jump, why we need a five-year research plan, or why we couldn't have a reserved parking space.

The only guy who would speak, except the manager, was this motor-mouth (Let's call him Dr. V.). A unique feature of his speech was repeating what our manager had just said, and then agreeing with him all the time. Our manager, another decent man, who could even remember the name of my then-girlfriend, did not seem to mind the echo of his own words, bounced off from Dr. V. In fact, he appreciated Dr. V's endorsement of his proposals as if Dr. V's opinion was our consensus. In short, the business part of our staff meeting was a two-man show, like a tennis match. Our heads were just moving back and forth, between those two men.

As I said earlier, just a few months before I left the company, Dr. V had become my immediate boss. His yes-man-ship must have caught the attention of upper management. As far as I was concerned it was a smart move for everyone involved. His scientific contribution to our department was so-so at best. We could move forward smoothly without him at the lab bench. He was also perfect for the job, with his incessant speech, and detailed directives. Our staff meeting became a bit longer than before, but it was still tolerable. We were, at least I was, also happy knowing that his salary was still lower than some of us, his underlings.

My salary was higher than Dr. V's, my legitimate supervisor. This was possible because the company we worked for had adhered to the so-called Hay Point System. The system distinguished the scientific career pathway from the managerial pathway. Each scientist was assigned to one of the five classes, beginning with Scientist I, a new employee, to V, a distinguished scientist. When I joined the company, the company bragged about the system in which Scientist V's salary would be equivalent to that of a Director, or even Vice President. I came to doubt this claim many years later, but still, the idea comforted me greatly. The last thing I wanted from my education was to become a middle manager.

As I look back now, with the Hay Point System in place, the scientists did not need to jump to the managerial career just to be ahead of others. It also turned out to be an effective way to stop scientific and technical communities from barking at each other all the time. (06/14/2020)

259. Sprouts and babies determine their future.
푸성귀는 떡잎부터 알고 사람은 어렸을 때부터 안다.

Many people, especially horticulturists, would know exactly what plant or vegetable a sprout becomes later. As an analogy, this proverb also says that one can tell what kind of a person a baby becomes, by just looking at the baby. It appears to emphasize the importance of a beginning, as in: "First impressions are the most lasting," or "The first blow is half the battle." Another somewhat related proverb is Entry #57, "There is always a first step in a long trekking." A standard interpretation of the proverb usually begins with this premise, but there is some more to it.

When someone writes a biography of a person, a description of *their* (see the footnote of #207) youth is an essential part of the book. They can always dig out some episodes that can be built into the main development of this great person. Such an anecdotal story is presented as if it was a telltale sign of the child's future. Indeed, anyone's young life, even my youth, can offer such revealing stories. When this sort of retrospective association becomes routine, one may tend to conclude that a baby can tell what he or she would become later. This is a flawed argument or a retrofit at its best.

In my dream last night, I saw a friend whom I haven't seen for a while. It so happened that I come across him today, totally by chance. Now I remember the dream vividly, and may even tell him that I saw him in my dream. Then, I will recall this particular episode of what amounts to a chance encounter, possibly for the rest of my life, as if it were a miracle. Heck, I may even declare to everybody willing to listen how accurately a dream can predict a future event. However, let us not forget how many times we have unfulfilled dreams. Most of the time, we don't even remember what we dreamt of the other night, not to mention last night. I saw a pig in a dream, now I will find a pot of gold. A tiger or dragon, in a pregnant woman's dream, brings a boy infant, etc. So much for dream analysis.

This is to say that the second half of the above proverb, the part of extrapolating a baby's behavior to his future, is an utter fabrication. If it is so easy to predict the future of a baby, then why are there so many fortune tellers out there? In short, it is a lot easier to talk about what happened in the past, than what is coming in the future. After all, isn't that what a Monday-morning quarterback is all about? All those wise political analysts failed to predict that Harry Truman and Donald Trump would win the presidential elections in 1948 and 2016, respectively. Why then was the above proverb brought into being? It's because we want to build what we want to hear. Here is a case in point:

The cherry tree myth is the most well-known and longest enduring legend about George Washington. In the original story, when Washington was six years old he received a hatchet as a gift and damaged his father's cherry tree. When his father discovered what he had done, he became angry and confronted him. Young George bravely said, "I cannot tell a lie...I did cut it with my hatchet." Washington's father embraced him and rejoiced that his son's honesty was worth more than a thousand trees. Ironically, this iconic story about the value of honesty was invented by one of Washington's first biographers, an itinerant minister and bookseller named Mason Locke Weems. After Washington's death in 1799 people were anxious to learn about him, and Weems was ready to supply the demand. ("Cherry Tree Myth", The Fred W. Smith, National Library for the Study of George Washington, at Mount Vernon)

Teaching children the merit of honesty is highly desirable in any society. As far as I can tell, there is no harm in telling children the above story about George Washington, albeit it was concocted by a biographer. What has bothered me though was why Korean children, including myself, would learn a lesson from an American story. It wasn't like we, Koreans, did not have any inspiring legends. Just to name a few, Military General Kim Yoo-sin (595 - 673) of the *Shilla* Nation, and Admiral Lee Soon-sin (1545 - 1598) of the *Joseon* Dynasty during *imjin-oeran,* left plenty of anecdotes we can learn lessons from: see Entry #45 and #162. Indeed, why does an American story appear to be worthier than our own? Earlier, I attributed such a trend to the directional cultural flow: see Entry #27, "Another's bread looks bigger, but my child looks better." (06/15/2020)

260. Keep someone's feet warm with your jacket.
제 옷 벗어 남의 발에 감발 쳐 준다.

Once in a while, we do something good for others, purely out of kindness, compassion, and empathy. But we shouldn't overdo it, like sacrificing the expensive and warm jacket you are wearing now, just to wrap the feet of another person. There is no point to break your bone to fix another's bone, or donate kidneys to a dying person. You may die before you see the result of your kindness. So implies the above proverb. You can throw your coat over a puddle of water so that a lady can walk across without getting her shoes wet. That much we could consider your prerogative.

I do not know if it is still in fashion, but I understand that using soft bread is one of the best ways to erase a charcoal sketch on high-quality pastel paper with a rough texture. So, this artist visits a local bakery quite regularly, to buy a loaf of bread. A new owner of the shop, a lady with much compassion to spare, takes pity on him and quickly assumes that he can only afford plain bread because he is too poor to get a stick of butter. One day, she spreads melted butter rather profusely inside the bread he was buying. Now he comes home, and what happens next in his studio is your guess. Another story, this time from old Korea, is presented below, to reflect the same sentiment.

Korean men used to keep their hair long until they got married. However, once married, or passed the coming-of-age ceremony, his hair was tightly rounded up at the center of the head, as a bundle about two inches high and an inch wide. This collection of hair was known as *sang-too* (상투). Call it a topknot of hair. Although this "hairstyle" was officially banned by the then government, *Joseon* Dynasty, around 1900, the custom survived and lingered around for a while. To some, it was a traditional heritage to keep, while to others it was just another old and unworthy remnant custom.

One day, a man was casually strolling around his neighborhood and heard a low, but persistent, moaning noise coming from one of his neighbors. Out of curiosity, he wanted to investigate the source of the moan and was about to enter the house where the noise came from. To his surprise, it was definitely from a woman, and thus stopped further entry into the house. He hurriedly went home to alert his mother of what he noticed at one of their neighbors. Soon, his mother was at the door of the house and asked the woman why she was in agony and pain.

The lady of the house told the old woman that she was having a child, but stated in no uncertain terms, "I have this habit of having birth while holding the *sang-too* of my husband for support. But unfortunately, he is away now and I don't know when he'll be back." Upon hearing this urgent plea, the old woman quickly returned home and explained the situation to her son. Being the kind man he was, and not having anything else to tend to at that moment, the son volunteered to offer his *sang-too* to this woman who was about to have a baby. He went to her house in hurry.

Sure enough, the moaning had become louder, and more urgent. After hurriedly making a hole in the door with his wet fingers, big enough for his *sang-too*, he proceeded to put his topknot of hair through the hole (sliding doors at that time in Korea were covered with just rice paper over a wooden lattice in the door frame. So poking a hole with fingers wet from saliva was not a big deal. Even in my time, young kids used to do this to spy on what was happening in a room). It was not known whether or not at this point in the story, he peeked inside the room, but let us assume he did not. After all, he was a reputable gentleman from a *yang-ban* family.

"Please grab my *sang-too* tightly, so that you can discharge the baby right away," said the man to the lady inside the room, while he was kneeling and staring at the floor. She proceeded as instructed, but unfortunately, the birth was anything but quick. The woman was pulling the *sang-too* with the almighty strength required for pushing a new life into this world. And now, her moaning became a scream. At the climax, both of them heard the strong and healthy cry of a newborn. Alas, she pulled the *sang-too* too hard, and the whole hair assembly came out of his cranium, along with his skin. (A story from Naver.com was modified.)

The young man with *sang-too* could have avoided the painful accident, had he read and understood the above proverb. (06/15/2020)

261. Far-away friends are the same as the nearby foe.
지척의 원수가 천 리의 벗이라.

As in the United States and the Western World, the units for volume, length, and weight used in old Korea were never systematically defined and established, say, in a decimal system. They had been in use, rather non-scientifically, until the so-called CGS (centimeter, gram, and second) units were formally adopted. It was a relatively recent event, certainly after Korea achieved its independence in 1945, from the Imperial Japanese occupation. Even with the official implementation, old units of measurement have survived for a while, especially in rural areas and among those old school folks.

The unit of distance used in the above proverb, *ri* (리), is as confusing as the yard or mile for a foreigner. One *ri* is about 400 m; however, at some point in Korean history, it was as much as 10 times longer. It was not like the definition of one meter, the distance light travels in a vacuum during one $299,792,458^{th}$ of a second. The distance quoted in the proverb is 1,000 *ri* (천리), which we will just say is 400 km or 250 miles. The number 1,000 here really means a large number. Another unit was 척, or *cheok*. It is a Korean foot, signifying a very small distance relative to 1,000 *ri*. It says, "An enemy very close by is like a friend 250 miles away." What does the old saying imply?

Friends, relatives, and even siblings who are far away would be of little use when we face an enemy right here and now. That much everyone would agree. But do we equate them with an enemy? How are they as bad as an enemy? It puzzled me for a while, but I just cannot offer any better explanation than them being useless, simply because they are too far away. The history of recent wars may shed some light on the opposite cases. That is the confusing part, at least to me.

The 28th President, Woodrow Wilson, had been pursuing a foreign policy of non-intervention in global conflicts when the First World War broke out in 1914. He would state that America was "too proud to fight" in what appeared to be a still regional war in Europe. He was narrowly re-elected in 1916, after campaigning with the slogan "he kept us out of war."

This was despite the attack on May 7, 1915, by a German U-boat, which sank the British liner RMS Lusitania and killed almost 1,200 innocent travelers, including 128 Americans. See also Entry # 81, "Big trees face more wind." In response to a strong protest from Wilson, Germany stopped attacking merchant ships for a while. Then, in January 1917, Germany resumed submarine warfare around the British Isles. It was a calculated gamble since they had known that the U.S. would enter the War with their submarine warfare.

Along with the above development, the German Foreign Minister sent a telegram, later referred to as the Zimmermann Telegram, inviting Mexico to join the war as Germany's ally. In return, the Germans promised to help Mexico recover the territories of Texas, New Mexico, and Arizona from the United States. The United Kingdom intercepted the message and presented it to the U.S. embassy in the UK. It eventually made its way to President Wilson, who released the Zimmermann Telegram to the public. It was the beginning of U.S. involvement in the First World War. President Wilson announced the break in official relations with Germany on February 3, 1917. After seven US merchant ships were attacked by German submarines and with the Zimmermann telegram, Wilson officially declared war against Germany on April 2, 1917.

As it turned out, it was the end of any wars being regional or local. From then on, all wars on this planet - big or small, ugly or justified - have become more or less global concerns, involving many nations, each participant with varying political and economic interests. The Second World War involved the whole world. The Korean War was won with help from the U.S. and U.N. troops. Every conflict and war involving Arab-Israeli, Vietnam, Croatia, Iraq, Afghanistan, Yemen, etc., have entailed some sort of aid from far-away allies, or interference by opposing nations. This is undoubtedly owing to facilitated communication, faster transportation means, and perhaps most importantly, the understanding of global morale in maintaining peace. In this context, the above proverb appears to have now completely become obsolete. (06/17/2020)

262. The girder vibrates when a pillar is banged.
기둥을 치면 대들보가 울린다.

In traditional Korean buildings, including residential homes for ordinary citizens, the most important and "sacred" part is the girder, known as *dae-deul-bo* (대들보). It is a massive, one-piece, solid wood beam, weighs "tons," and spans the whole length of the house. It is usually pine, or Korean red pine, if you can afford it. Columns stand on the base stone and crossbeams hold them in place, all around the structure. The weight of the roof comes down upon *dae-deul-bo* (대들보), via numerous smaller rafters. During the construction, the day of raising the heavy *dae-deul-bo* is celebrated with plenty of drinks and food, besides some serious business like Buddhist prayers. It is a solemn as well as a noisy occasion of celebration. It is the day of barn-raising, so-to-speak.

The *dae-deul-bo* is an open beam above a big chamber, called *dae-chung* (대청), with a hardwood floor. It is usually the biggest room in a house, flanked by two rooms, say, a living room and a study. From the *dae-chung* (대청), through sliding doors, one steps down to a square courtyard, a few stone stairs below. If *dae-chung* is the crown of a house, the *dae-deul-bo* is its center-piece jewel. One day, when we were kids, my brother and I tied a rope around the girder to make a swing in the *dae-chung*. We enjoyed the new device of our invention, all afternoon. Come dinner time along with our father, we were thoroughly reprimanded, like dogs stealing a piece of cooked steak.

The relationship between the *dae-deul-bo* and supporting columns likens to that of lips and teeth. Without lips, teeth would feel cold. Without teeth, lips may deform. The pillars of the house will hold in place the *dae-deul-bo* and all of the weight of the roof and rafters. Without those weights bearing down, the columns may collapse at the first sign of disturbance, like a ground tremor or even a strong wind. Given this relationship, the above proverb says, "If you bang a column, *dae-deul-bo* will make noise or vibrate." They are like two sides of a coin. They need each other.

144

A standard interpretation of the proverb is that you do not have to say exactly what you really want to say outright, especially when you chastise someone. You do not need to hit the *dae-deul-bo* with a big hammer to make a point. You can just gently tap the columns that are holding the *dae-deul-bo*. Unless the listener is an idiot, he or she will get the message you are trying to convey. Metaphoric expression of one's emotion and thought, employing some inscrutable anecdotal episode, has been highly regarded in old China and in Korea, as well. Yes, it can create some misunderstanding later, but it can also spare some awkward, and possibly painful, moments between the accuser and the listener. Or, as the following story attests, gently tapping the pillar could work nicely for both parties involved.

In English, June is the sixth month of a year or a woman's name, as in my wife's. Both are spelled and pronounced the same way. Likewise, a given Korean noun can have a few different meanings. One of them is a simple monosyllable word *bae* (배). It can mean the belly, or collectively a ship, a boat, or even a yacht. Although the word is pronounced exactly the same, no one gets confused, as their meanings are completely different. Even a child can distinguish between them, based on the context of a conversation.

On a lazy, dog days afternoon, a traveler came upon a river and took a small ferryboat. As it so happened, he was the only passenger and the ferry was tended by a young and rather attractive local woman. As they were crossing the river, neither of them had anything really to talk about, and an awkward silence descended upon them, less the peaceful sound of water hitting the side of the ferry. While gazing on her, the man casually uttered words, "Now that I am on your belly (or *bae*), I reckon myself your husband." Upon hearing this nonsensical claim, she tried to find an appropriate rebuke, but couldn't find any. Instead, her face blushed to the earlobe, while the traveler kept eying her with some mysterious grin.

Just like anything adverse in her young life, time was on her side, and eventually, they arrived at the other side of the river. As the traveler stepped out of the boat, she blurted out, "Sir, now that you are coming out of my belly, I reckon you are indeed my son." (06/20/2020)

263. Excuse for letting a cow run amok.
밭에 소 풀어 놓고도 할 말은 있다.

Intentionally or inadvertently, this young man lets a cow loose, and now the cow is having a great time gobbling up the vegetables in the field that he most likely helped his master till, earlier in the season. This is a grave mistake insofar as Korean farmers used to say that a family would go down if their cow disappeared. And yet, this proverb says that the young man must have something to say, either an excuse or a justification. Most of the serious incidents, such as the above, are usually associated with power, passion, money, or a combination of these elements. If not, they are not serious, right?

We will start with the power being associated with a disaster. The idiocy of President Trump to hold a political rally today in Tulsa, OK, right at the peak of the coronavirus pandemic, is the result of his incessant desire for power, nothing else. Some 20,000 supporters, equally idiotic as the man himself, are expected to jam into the 19,000-seat BOK Center to yell their lungs out in demonstrating their adulation for the President. Speaking of shedding viruses and sharing infection, this would be a textbook case.

The gathering thus resembles a mass suicide, appropriately decorated with all the bells and whistles. It was originally slated for yesterday, the Juneteenth Holiday, the end of slavery in 1865. The organizer of the event must have completely forgotten its historic significance, despite the constant demonstrations from Black Lives Matter following the killing of George Floyd, in Minneapolis last month. Very smart people, they are; smart enough to preempt any possible legal liability in case someone gets infected with the virus at the rally. That was about all we heard from the organizers.

As to crimes of passion, or hatred to be exact, I present here two recent stories from Korea, one after another, in May and June. In both cases, stepparents were arrested for cruel treatment of a half-adopted child. In the first case, the tragedy happened in the city of Cheon-An. A 10-year old boy died after two confinements in succession, for a total of about seven hours, in a small suitcase. The first one was about 50cm x 77cm (20" x 30") in size and the second one was 44cm x 60cm (17" x 24"). The break in between was for allowing the boy to urinate. Here, the culprit was his step-mother. Two children of her own, 11 and 15-year old sons, were apparently at home when their step-brother was dying inside the confined space. Later, police discovered, on the body of the boy, numerous signs of physical abuse, including cigarette burn marks and bruises.

The second story was as bad as the above. A woman, who was driving in Chang-nyung city, Southern Gyung-sang Province, noticed by chance, a haggardly-looking girl walking a deserted street in bare feet. As later revealed, this 10-year-old girl had just escaped through a fourth-floor balcony after a series of maltreatments by her 35-year-old stepfather and 27-year-old biological mother.

The woman, who happened to have children of similar age, bought a meal for the starving girl and was able to learn more about what the child had gone through. She then brought the girl to a police station to submit a formal complaint. It became a national scandal. Apparently, the girl had been chained to a bedpost with a shackle and had to endure a constant beating. Her fingertips were "melted" on a hotplate until little trace of fingerprints remained and her body was bruised extensively.

What did these cruel parents have to say at the police station? The parents of the dead boy stated that they had just wanted to discipline the boy so that he wouldn't lie again. The stepfather of the girl who successfully escaped from hell insisted that it was just part of parental discipline, overblown out of proportion and that there had never been any non-stop punishment. Had these people been the one who lost the cow, they could have claimed an alien creature, out of the blue sky, just lifted the cow, and disappeared into the thin air.

Examples of money being a cause of discontent are so numerous that one could perhaps write a series of tomes on the topic. The infamous Ponzi scheme, run by Bernard Madoff, swindled over $60 billion from wealthy investors. In December 2008, Madoff confessed to his sons that it was all "one big lie." That was the whole extent of his say after the fraud was exposed to the public: see also Entry #4, "You steal a needle now, then soon a cow." (06/20/2020)

264. Driving a stake into a young zucchini.
자라나는 애호박에 말 뚝 박는다.

If someone drives a thick wooden stake with a sledgehammer into a young, green zucchini, what would happen to the plant? Why would someone do such a cruel act? Zucchini cannot scream in pain, but we can imagine the suffering to its certain demise. Would this cruel man also burn the tail of a cat and laugh at the flustered animal running around? I have always believed that Koreans are one of the rare, law-abiding, and most peaceful people on this planet Earth, but there have been a few glimpses of occasions that defy such a notion. This proverb is one. The following story is another one.

During the 35-year occupation of the Korean Peninsula by militant Japan till the end of World War II, Korean resistance groups, collectively called the Liberation Army, were active along the Chinese-Korean border. One of the guerrilla leaders was the communist Kim Il-sung (1912 – 1994), who later became the founder of North Korea. He was the one who triggered the Korean War in 1950. His first wife, who died at the young age of 32 during the delivery of a stillborn girl, gave birth to two sons. Kim Jong-il was his oldest son. The younger son died in a swimming accident. His second marriage produced three children; one of them was Kim Kyung-hee, his eldest daughter. It is rumored that Kim Il-sung also had other children with mistresses, but no official record is available.

Kim Jong-il (1941 - 2011) succeeded his father as the Supreme Leader of North Korea. Once again, there is no official information available on his marital history, but he married twice and had at least three mistresses. His first wife was the daughter of a martyr, who died during the Korean War. She was handpicked by his father and married him in 1966. Soon after, they had one daughter, but the marriage ended in divorce in 1969. His second wife was the daughter of a high-ranking military official. His father, Kim Il-Sung, once again handpicked her to marry his son. The two were estranged for some years but left one daughter behind.

Interesting stories of Kim's family begin with the mistresses that Jong-il kept. The mistress number one was an actress. She had already been married to another man and had a child when they met, but Jong-il forced her husband to divorce her. This relationship started in 1970 and produced one son, Kim Jong-nam (1971 – 2017), his oldest son.

His second mistress was a Japanese-born, ethnic Korean dancer. She had taken over the role of First Lady until she died in 2004. They had two sons, Kim Jong-chul and Kim Jong-un. They also had a daughter, Kim Yo-jong, who was born around 1989. After years of estrangement, the number two was rumored to have died in Moscow, in 2002. Jong-il then lived with his one-time secretary, who acted as the first lady, for the rest of his life.

To summarize, Kim Jong-il had three sons, from two different women. Kim Jong-un is the youngest son and is the current Supreme Leader of North Korea. His younger sister, Kim Yo-jong, is currently his closest confidante and has recently made a lot of publicity by destroying the Inter-Korea Liaison building. She has abruptly changed her posture toward South Korea, from a dove to a hawk. The whereabouts of Jong-il's older brother, Jong-chul, has remained a mystery, but apparently he lacks any political ambition.

Jong-il's younger sister, Kim Kyong-hui, married Jang Sung-taek, who was once considered the number two man, second only to Jong-un. Then, in December 2013, Jong-un had him "pulverized" with a salvo of Russian 14.5-mm anti-aircraft machine guns, for some nebulous reasons like corruption and conspiracy. Who would know the true reason? It could well be something to do with the women involved. But still, Jang was once his right-hand man. It was believed that his annihilated body was burned to ashes with a flamethrower so that there was no remnant of him to speak of.

In February 2017, Kim Jong-nam, the exiled half-brother of Kim Jong-un, was assassinated with a nerve agent while walking through Malaysia's Kuala Lumpur International Airport. Jong-un must have ordered the assassination. Both instances made a sensational news worldwide. The way these murders were carried out reminded me of the above proverb. (06/24/2020)

265. If you want to dance, suggest it to your brother-in-law first.
제가 춤추고 싶어서 동서를 권한다.

I do not know if it is a matter of humility or shyness, but we tend to first ask others to do what we want to do, like sing, dance, drink, eat, etc. In this proverb, it is I who really wants to dance, but I am asking somebody else to start dancing first. That somebody, in this proverb, happens to be my brother-in-law. Once he starts, of course, I will jump onto the stage, most likely before anybody else. It is like breaking the ice. Why an in-law? I cannot tell exactly why, but a brother-in-law, especially if he is younger than me, can be easier to approach. He is close enough for the suggestion, and yet he doesn't know me well enough to understand my true plan. The case also applies to a woman: If I were a woman, I would approach my sister-in-law. For the subtle and delicate relationship with an in-law in general, see Entry #254. "In-laws sing my song."

Traditional Korean folk dance, referred to as *chum* (춤) here, is quite different from what one may expect from a typical social dance of the Western World. We seldom hold a partner during dancing. It is individual and yet moves along collectively, like barn dancing in this country, but without much physical contact.

The music is usually simpler, as Korean folk "opera" or soliloquy such as *pansori* uses a pentatonic scale of E, G, A, C, and D, without any semitones. In *pansori*, a singer tells a long story in a company with a single drummer. Musical instruments are also simple: besides the barrel drum, called a *buk* (북), they could have a small windpipe, a gong, a clapper, a cymbal, etc. *Chum* also varies from a spontaneous movement of emotion and feeling to more elaborate dancing with a fan or a face mask. Needless to say, the music, instrument, and dance all depend on the nature of the gathering.

An important component of a party entailing *chum* is of course the drink, usually *mag-geol-li* (막걸리), the traditional Korean milky rice wine. It is slightly viscous and tastes somewhat tangy, bitter, and astringent. Left standing for a while, it shows white sediment, and one would stir it before drinking in one gulp. Unlike beer, *mag-geol-li* is consumed from a bowl, never in a glass. Because of its low alcohol content, no one passes out with *mag-geol-li*. It is a happy, communal beverage. Alcohol always makes people bolder than their usual selves, and as soon as someone starts dancing, everyone with a little bit of alcohol in their brain will get wild and participate in the communal dancing.

Besides the need for impetus from others to boost one's courage, let's see why we would ask others to initiate what we would like to do. Back when I was single and living in Michigan, I used to seriously date an American girl for a few years. Just before we broke up, she used to mention a lot about the soccer coach she played for, in a local summer league. In particular, I remember her mumbling about how pretty his girlfriend was. Typically, "I can't hold a candle beside her," or "Like any Briton, this guy enjoys drinking."

I learned through the grapevine that my ex-girlfriend married him. I still think she meant to send me a certain message, which I must have completely missed. It makes sense because I used to get labeled as a rather insensitive guy. It may well be unconsciously uttered words, but if a wife talks about a man rather often, the husband ought to listen more closely.

When a kid punishes himself, is it because he wishes to preempt what is surely coming, like a reprimand from his father, for some silly misdeed he committed earlier? Or is it a rehearsal for what is coming, like watching others dance before you do? No matter what, it may not be a bad practice to envisage your reflection upon others, as a third person.

In a similar vein, we can also ask why criminals often return to the scene of their crimes? I understand that arsonists usually go back to the crime scene to watch their work unfold. They may take great pride in their work and want to witness the house burning down, to see the level of destruction they've brought, or just to see how well the fire marshal can solve the case. Another post-crime behavior would be frequently engaging in a conversation about your own crime, as a third party, like O.J. Simpson's book, *If I Did It*. This regurgitation appears to be similar to the frequent talk that my ex-girlfriend made of her new friend back when I was young and didn't know much about human interactions. (06/26/2020)

266. A big house, albeit tilted, won't collapse in three years.
큰집이 기울어져도 삼 년 간다.

Even when it begins to tilt, a big house will not fall over quickly but remain standing for three years. So says the above proverb, similar to Entry #5, "Would a pagoda of labor crumble soon?" Here, "three years" is a figurative expression for a long time. A literal example may be the Leaning Tower of Pisa, which has survived more than eight centuries.

The Tower of Pisa, in central Italy, is well known for its nearly four-degree lean: one side measuring 55.9 meters (183.3 feet) in height, and the other side 56.7 meters (185.6 feet). Its total weight is estimated to be 14,500 tons. The tower is comprised of seven floors: each accommodating a bell that represents a musical note of the octave (see more below). The tower began to sink immediately after the second floor was completed in 1178. This was due to a rather shallow three-meter foundation, set in unstable ground. Because of frequent battles in Pisa with neighboring states, the construction was often halted, sometimes for more than a century. This was good news on one hand, as it let the subsoil settle and get stabilized.

On the other hand, it was bad news, as it allowed the construction, although leaning already, to continue until completion as we see now. Had the construction continued without interruptions due to wars, the tower would have toppled a long time ago. Incidentally, the famous experiment by Galileo Galilei (1564- 1642), which established two cannonballs of different weights descending at the same speed, was carried out at the Tower of Pisa. Needless to say, this experiment could not have happened, had the tower been straight.

By the time the tower was completed in 1372, it was already "curved." Many attempts to compensate for the tilt are as old as the tower itself. Most of these efforts failed, while some worsening the tilt. Fortuitously, these efforts have been lukewarm at best, because the very tilt was essential for the lucrative tourism. In 1990, the Italian government rather reluctantly decided to close the tower to the public. The seven bells were also removed to reduce the head weight. Residential homes, in the path of a potential fall of the tower, were vacated for safety. Removing soil from underneath the raised side, corrected the tilt to its 1838 position.

By 1990, when the tower was closed to the public, the tilt had reached 5.5 degrees. The remedial work between 1993 and 2001 reduced the tilt to 3.97 degrees. After a decade of corrective reconstruction and stabilization efforts, the tower reopened to the public late in 2001 and was declared stable for at least another 300 years.

Other humongous architectural or monumental structures; such as the Stonehenge in England (five millennia old), those Egyptian pyramids (four), the Great Wall of China (two), and the Parthenon of Athens (two); will last till the end of human civilization.

The British passenger liner *Titanic* offers a similar case. She was the largest ocean liner in service, at 270-meter (880-foot) long, when she sank in 1912. It took almost three hours for the ship to sink after hitting an iceberg. After the collision, the captain requested the two bands on the ship, one a trio and the other a quintet, to play together at various sites. This was the first (and last) time they played together. Survived passengers later recalled that they played lively tunes. During the last three hours of the *Titanic,* there was also a priest hearing confessions and giving absolutions on the leaning deck.

The metaphor of the proverb must be like the longevity of old money from wealthy families such as Rockefeller, Rothschild, Vanderbilt, Carnegie, et al. Their wealth, or at least their names, seem to last for centuries. For example, the Jewish Rothschild family of Frankfurt has been in the banking business since the 1760s. They have passed on the wealth of original Mayer Amschel Rothschild (1744 – 1812) through his sons, who have successfully established international banking businesses in various cities in Europe.

During the 19th century, they were said to possess the largest private fortune in the world. The family's wealth somewhat declined during the 20th century and was divided among descendants. And yet, we do not see any indication of an abrupt demise, in agreement with the above proverb. As a comment in tangent to the above, Korean jaebeols are said to last only a few generations, approximately 70 years. It makes me wonder why. (06/28/2020)

267. What's the point of bragging about the past glory on the empty lot of yonder side?
저 건너 빈터에서 잘살던 자랑하면 무슨 소용 있나?

I am the last child of a 10-member family, born to a 40-year old mother. Nowadays it is not unusual for old women, say, as old as 50 or even 60, to have a baby, but back in the 1940s, 40 was an old age to give birth. At any rate, by the time I was brought into this world, the prosperous period of our family must have already gone by.

Soon after World War II was over, the communist regime controlled the northern provinces of the Korean Peninsula, where we were born. Just like any war, the Korean War misplaced many families, mainly those fleeing the North. As I look back now, the hardship our family had to endure was not something only we had to live through. Wherever we look, I hear the dialect we spoke, a sort of comforting noise among the strange dialects heard in the strange town of Seoul.

Among those war refugees from North Korea, the sentimental reminiscence of the past was a commonplace occurrence: it was part of the introduction. Invariably, everybody sounded like a descendent of a Royal family or a well-to-do descendant. Previously they had slept in silk bedclothes, eaten dinner with silver utensils, worn jade rings, employed several housemaids and errand boys, used furniture inlaid with mother-of-pearl, and so forth. Even in our family, elder siblings missed the good old comfortable and luxurious life I never had the privilege to live in.

I knew that my father struck a gold mine during the Japanese occupation of our country and hence was well known to be super rich throughout the South Providence of Hamgyung. Although I was still a boy, I knew and understood the crux of the above proverb. What's the point of longing for past glory? I resented it all.

A generic question we ought to address must be, "What do memories serve?" Memory is a mental record of experience, be it emotional, or physical, good, bad, ugly, or pretty. It is essential to have a memory, as it serves, if nothing else, the purpose of dictating the future. Besides, if we do not have any memories, it would mean, in effect, that we do not have the past. It is then impossible to establish a personal identity. That is amnesia.

For an old person like myself, what we have plenty now is in the past tense and what we will have increasingly less of is the future. Any religious postulates put aside, memory is all we will have at the point of our departure from this world. It is up to me which explicit memory I will bring up for regurgitation out of the vast memory bank in a particular situation. The choice must depend on the emotion and sensation involved. Now, with the lock-down from the COVID-19 pandemic, time is plenty for recalling an explicit memory. But, suppressing such temptation, I go out to get some flowers for the balcony upstairs. This is a deliberate attempt to think more about the future, albeit limited.

Korea as a nation has also maintained a huge data set of collective memories, mostly sad ones. In my mind, contemporary Koreans dwell upon the past too much, as if the future is numbered. Maybe it is indeed: just look at the political turmoil and unsettled citizens.

During the Sino-Japanese war around 1937, and until the end of the Second World War in 1945, the Japanese military practiced an officially sanctioned, sexual slavery system, whose sole purpose was to provide sex to their soldiers. They lured young Korean women under false promises to what appeared to be concentration camps. Tens of thousands of women were forced to offer "comfort" to soldiers.

As to reparations for the Japanese atrocity, a serious conversation between the two nations began in 1990, some 50 years after the incident. It consisted of two components: an admission followed by a sincere apology and monetary compensation for the handful of survivors. Being cunning Japanese and stubborn Koreans, the negotiation did not proceed smoothly. By 2017 the Japanese government eventually offered a rather reluctant apology and financial compensation in the range of US$ 40 million. As is often the case involving money, early this year, some fraudulent transactions were discovered between money managers and the victim's families. My recommendation is that we should let this memory rest in peace and move on to the future. (06/30/2020)

268. Standing on his hands with a hat on.
저모립 쓰고 물구나무 서도 제 멋이다.

During the Joseon Dynasty (1392 - 1910), any man who was somebody would wear a traditional hat called a *gaat*, or 갓. Fashion must have changed the shape of the *gaat* to some extent, but the basic design has remained the same. It resembles Lincoln's top hat, but not as tall. The fabric was also completely different. *Gaat* is usually made of horsehair, which is woven into a rather rigid network of fine mesh, just like cheesecloth. Wide and flat, the circular brim is also made of the same material.

The whole assembly is usually black and accompanied by a string on both sides for fastening when needed. The rigid form of a *gaat* is maintained with fine strips of bamboo. As one can imagine, *gaat* tells the social status of the owner. One of the most expensive, and hence only high-ranking officials could afford, was a *gaat* made with swine bristle, *jeo-mo-rip* or 저모립. Let's just call it a swine-hair *gaat*.

This proverb says that someone wearing a swine-hair *gaat* is trying to stand upside-down, on his hands. The hat would surely fall off to the ground. We all would ask, "What in the world is he doing?" Considering his social status, this behavior would be most bizarre and induce onlookers to inquire as to the motive, as well as the mental wellbeing, behind this incredulous behavior. According to this proverb, that is precisely what we should not do. "Just let him be" is what it suggests, because that is his "style" and prerogative. Don't interfere with what he is up to. Who are we to say anything to anybody anyway?

As pointed out in Entry #177, "Get the land, then build the house," Koreans are conformists in the truest sense: they follow a certain *hyung-sik* in almost all matters rather blindly, and any deviations from such tradition and convention are frowned upon. The above proverb is now saying that strange acts can not only happen but also should be left alone, without any meddling from others. This is a very Western, self-centered ideal that a collective society like Korea would have a hard time accepting. We want to poke our nose into anything unusual and make sure it is corrected to the *hyung-sik* most appropriate to the given situation.

156

Just a few days ago, the Chinese government passed the national security law for Hong Kong residents, restricting much of the freedom they inherited from British rule in 1997. On paper, the new law seems very innocuous and reasonable: It is a criminal act to undermine and to attempt to break away from the Beijing government, collude with foreign or external forces, use violence or intimidation against ordinary citizens, etc. These are all standard clauses one can find in any national security law. In response to the fierce street demonstrations of Hong Kong residents against the proposed law, the U.K. and the U.S.A. earlier spearheaded an international protest urging China to reconsider the law and expressed concerns about basic human rights in Hong Kong.

The Chinese government passed the law without backing down. They argued that their business is an internal matter of a sovereign country, which no other nation can or should interfere with. Appearance-wise, this claim is once again in agreement with the above proverb: stop nagging them. It is, after all, their prerogative. What is missing here is, of course, the will and desire of Hong Kong residents. The man, who tried to stand upside down with his expensive *gaat* on, was doing as he wished.

One day many years ago, a friend of my wife visited our home with her five-year-old daughter, Anna. As they were leaving, my wife grabbed a handful of candies from a bowl and put them in Anna's skirt pocket. That is the type of generous gesture one may expect from a Korean wife. Instead of saying thank-you, Anna was quite displeased and upset. My wife was understandably taken aback by this turn of events and looked at her friend for an explanation. As it turned out, Anna wanted to pick and choose those candies she liked by herself, not by my wife, or anyone else. I heard this episode later after I came home from work. We were amazed at how early this couple taught the attitude of assertiveness.

Throughout her life, once Anna defines what she wants, she will protect it with a great deal of determination, aside from other's interference. And Anna's parents, as well as everyone around her, should respect her wishes. This is what the Beijing government should have understood. That is why the man with a *gaat* on his head was doing what he wanted to do. (07/02/2020)

269. Roads and *maal* not to take.
길이 아니거든 가지를 말고 말이 아니거든 듣지를 말라.

If there doesn't seem to be a road or trail, do not enter the woods. It could just be an illusion and you may eventually get lost in the wilderness. If the words, or *maal* (말), you hear don't make any sense, stop listening. It could just disturb the peace in your mind. So says the proverb. Easy to say, but how in the devil do we know anything about a road that we have not entered yet, or about a speech we have not completely listened to yet? It isn't logical, but that's the Korean way. Don't be too technical about it.

Which way shall I go? You ask yourself at a fork in the road. Spit on your palm and bang on it with two fingers together: index and middle fingers. See which way the saliva flies. That is the direction you ought to take. I am good at such practices. I used to roll a pencil, not a round one, but the one with six sides, to select correct answers to multiple-choice questions on exams. I've survived OK, have I not? As to the *maal* you are about to hear, you may as well ask the person in advance not to utter any words if it would hurt or offend you. How can I guess what a person is about to say?

Nowadays, we seldom get lost on the road, thanks to Google Maps on a smartphone. For this fool-proof convenience, we might have lost the ability to read maps once and for all. Most kids, and even young adults, cannot tell you which direction is north or give you the direction to your destination. They don't seem to appreciate the pleasure of poring over a Rand McNally Road Atlas to map out a long road trip with your family or friends. Thus, one part of the above proverb is no longer relevant. But, wait.

"When you find my body, please call my husband George and my daughter Kerry. It will be the greatest kindness for them to know that I am dead and where you found me — no matter how many years from now." These sentences were the last entry in the chronicle a 66-year-old retired nurse kept, while hiking the Appalachian Trail by herself. It was the summer of 2013. Her body was discovered almost two years later in the woods of Maine, by a logging company surveyor. She wandered into a wild terrain and got lost, only about two miles off the Trail. She tried to send text messages in vain, to her husband, but she was beyond the reach of the phone signal. Although her trail name was Inchworm, she had logged in nearly 1,000 miles (1,620 km) from where she and a friend had started. Her friend had, unfortunately, had to leave the trail because of some emergency at home. So much for Google Maps, uh?

As to the second part of the proverb, I have already devoted a significant number of essays to the topic on *maal*: in the first volume alone, we have Entries #1, #15 ("The tongue can break bones"), #23, and #82. The importance of spoken words and of how they are delivered is shared by many different cultures at various points in history: see, Proverbs 25:15, for instance: "By patience is a ruler persuaded, and a soft tongue will break a bone."

When do I know for sure that what I am hearing is nonsense and stop it? Am I allowed to predict what is coming, based on what I've heard thus far? The speaker may say, "Please hear me out." If I stop *them* (see the footnote of #207) too early, wouldn't I miss something important that is delivered later, or could I misunderstand the situation? We have been taught to be good listeners. Why not now?

Julius Robert Oppenheimer (1904 – 1967), a theoretical physicist who successfully led the Manhattan Project for developing the atomic bomb, strongly believed in the international control of nuclear proliferation and the nuclear arms race. It did not sit well with many politicians. He suffered the revocation of his security clearance in a much-publicized hearing in 1954. A decade later, President John F. Kennedy awarded him with the Enrico Fermi Award for political restoration. Had the short-sighted politicians and military brass listened to him, this world might have become much more peaceful.

My Mister, a 2018 Korean TV drama, is one of my favorites. The plot begins with a conspiracy to trap and get rid of a managing director, Ahn Dong-hoon, by his rivals in a construction company. A large sum of bribery money, in the form of gift certificates, is delivered to the wrong person, Ahn Dong-woon, a department head. This mistake, from a simple misunderstanding by a special delivery boy, triggers one of the most entertaining dramas involving three brothers and one young woman. (07/04/2020)

270. A black crow, a black mind?
까마귀 검기로 마음도 검겠나?

The American crow is black. Their body is covered with rather shimmering black feathers. Does it mean that their mind is also "black?" By black, it must mean inscrutable, cunning, enigmatic, etc., in a somewhat negative connotation. Whenever a Korean proverb is in a form of a question, the answer is usually no. Then why do they ask? It helps to emphasize the answer, but more importantly, to have us examine the question more carefully. Here, the underlying message is: "Don't judge a book by its cover," "Appearance is deceiving," or even to say that "Beauty is in the eye of the beholder," and "Beauty is only skin deep (but ugly goes clean to the bone)."

In this country, civil unrest stemming from police brutality towards African Americans has been simmering for many years and appeared once again on May 26, when George Floyd was killed by a Minneapolis police officer. The protest has now reached above and beyond its boiling point, and the whole nation has been seriously discussing the inequality that Blacks have endured in every aspect of their lives. Having black skin does not mean anything about their "minds," as the above proverb attests to. If skin tone has anything to do with the minds of people, Anglo-Saxons must have "white" or "blank" minds. That would be equally bad, right?

Has the opportunity for prosperity not been offered to Blacks? Or have Blacks not actively sought after the opportunity? Any rigid answer can divide the nation, resulting in a chasm between people. It is such a fundamental question that we have to consider relevant social, economic, educational, and political issues involved. There is no way one can resolve, in a one-page essay, this age-old dilemma, as old as this nation. I wish we lived in a society based on trust and comity. If a cop asked me to stop, I would stop instead of running away. As long as I am an innocent, law-abiding citizen, I can ask why I was stopped and go from there. We have now completely lost mutual trust. The only way to establish a healthy society is by rebuilding mutual trust and respect.

Once again, what we see may not be what we believe we see. In the 1987 American film, *Fatal Attraction*, Glenn Close has a weekend affair with a married man, Michael Douglass, while his wife and their daughter are out of town. What appears to be a one-time fling becomes a nightmare as the woman refused to end the affair and becomes quite obsessed with him. This modern professional woman of high fashion, Glenn Close, was not an angel. She was a terribly deranged woman. At the end of the movie, we see Anne Archer, Douglas' wife, taking a bath when Glen Close barges into the room with a knife. Douglass hears the scream from his wife and rushes in, fending off Glenn Close. A most maddening scene was when Close, presumed to be drowned in the bathtub, suddenly emerges from the water, swinging the knife. Shocking is an understatement of the scene, which anyone who saw the movie will never forget.

Cases opposite to the above are also equally plausible. Here, what appears to be mundane, ordinary, trivial, humble, and ugly, turns out to be exactly the opposite of what we might have expected: silent genius, haggard-looking millionaire, ugly but tasteful melon, quiet warrior, honest politician, and most of all, *amhaeng-uhsa* (암행어사). Besides the Cinderella story, the following paragraph from Entry #77, "Hot tea doesn't show steam," illustrates the case in point.

During the Joseon Dynasty in Korea (1392 - 1897), there were roving secret agents, called amhaeng-uhsa (암행어사), an ombudsman appointed by none other than the King himself and reporting only to the King. At a given time, only a few were dispatched to the rural countryside, to monitor any wrongdoings of local governors and their cronies. Disguised in plain, often tattered clothes, and pretending to be ordinary citizens, they were quietly listening to people's concerns and caught criminals red-handed, on the spot. They were often misunderstood and mistreated, but they endured all till their power of authority was called for, which was probably that of the FBI, CIA, NSA, ATF, and all other scary institutions of this country combined. Then, they would reveal themselves with a wooden tag of identity. Their stealthy move likens to that of hot tea without steam. (07/05/2020)

271. A mute with honey, a centipede with acupuncture.
꿀 먹은 벙어리요, 침 맞은 지네.

I do not know how our speech-impaired or blind ancestors communicated with each other, as they had neither sign language nor Braille. I spent some hours investigating this question in vain on NAVER, a Korean version of Google and Wikipedia. I came across the following fictitious story of a married couple, consisting of a blind man and a mute wife. If they were able to communicate, anyone could. It was posted by the poet Cho Jee-hoon (1920 – 1968). Apparently, he also heard this story secondhand.

One day, the mute wife discovered that their next-door neighbor's house was on fire. She hurriedly entered the room to report the news to her blind husband. Upon hearing the commotion, the husband asked, "What's the matter, dear? Why the hurry?" The wife immediately grabbed both hands of her husband and placed them on her throbbing breasts. She wrote with her finger, the Chinese character meaning a person, 인 (人), right between the two breasts. Now, the character changed to another word meaning fire, 불 (火). Those two dots on the character, of course, represented her nipples. Being the well-educated man he was, he immediately shouted, "Fire?" followed by "Where?"

The wife then proceeded to kiss his mouth, perhaps a bit longer than warranted. The man was now really surprised and cried out, "Oh, next door, Mr. Yeo's house?!" Here, two attached mouths formed a character pronounced Yeo, or 여 (몸). "How much damage did the fire cause to their house?" was his natural inquiry. As if she had waited for this question, the wife quickly stroked his phallus. He completely understood the situation and said, "Oh, only one pillar is now left standing, uh?"

Besides the excitement from the fire next-door, there was an undeniable physical elation in the room from the pulsating chest, bare breasts, wet kisses, and erect penis. They were almost beyond the half-way point to bliss on a lazy afternoon. I do not know if there really was a fire, or this was just a ploy on her part to indulge in carnal pleasure. All said or unsaid, they understood each other quite well.

How would a mute express his enjoyment of delicious honey? How does a centipede describe the pain incurred by a piercing acupuncture needle? These two questions form the above proverb. Except for the couple presented above, the answer is, of course, with great difficulty. Taken together, it portrays a person who seems unable to express *their* (see the footnote in #207) opinion well. In this fast and furious modern living, such impairments would be serious handicaps in daily life. This is despite a civil rights law known as the Americans with Disabilities Act, or 장애인복지법 in Korea, which protects them from discrimination by schools, employers, and anyone who provides services to the public.

On the other hand, many ordinary people are not handicapped, but just poor in expressing their feelings and thoughts rationally or logically. I am not simply speaking of stuttering. I do not know to what extent one can teach, for instance, to debate well, and how much it is a talent one is born with. *The Topeka School*, a novel by Ben Lerner, a finalist for the Pulitzer Prize in 2019, introduces a high school senior. His mother is a famous feminist writer, while his father is a psychiatrist, both working at the famous Menninger Foundation, then in Topeka, Kansas. A large portion of the story deals with the son's brilliant debating skills, displayed at a national competition. My impression from the book was that it was a gift one was given at birth: There was only so much one could acquire through training. I was interested in the subject matter, for I have been a poor debater throughout my life. With this conclusion, I do not regret that I did not participate in a debating club when I was a high school kid.

As a footnote, I modified the original proverb, "침**먹**은 (swallow) 지네" to "침**맞**은 (receive) 지네." My justification begins with the fact that the word *chim* (침) can mean both saliva or an acupuncture needle: the change was from "a centipede that swallowed human saliva" to "a centipede that received a needle." Some people believe that human saliva can weaken and eventually kill a centipede. There was no scientific explanation for this claim. It seems to me that there was a simple typo from the very beginning and scholars have tried to retroactively make some sense of the error. Together, the proverb covers both the pleasure of having honey and the pain of getting poked with a needle. (07/06/2020)

272. A bludgeoned deer leaves an odor on the club for three years.
노루 때린 뭉둥이가 삼 년 우린다.

I have never learned the difference between an alligator and a crocodile. Likewise, I do not know the difference in characteristics between 사슴 (sa-seum) and 노루 (no-roo). As far as I can tell, these two Korean words simply represent a deer. If I would live another 20 years or so, I may try to learn the difference, but at this stage in my life, such an effort doesn't seem to be warranted.

Deer have several major external scent glands distributed throughout their bodies. Their primary function is communicating with other deer as well as other animals. Besides, they sometimes squat while urinating so that urine would run down the insides of their legs, onto glands in the ankles. The odor from certain chemical compounds in the urine depends on the season, gender, reproductive status, and social rank of the animals, indicating urine probably plays a role in olfactory communication in deer. The upshot of this explanation is that deer are well equipped with mechanisms, thereby sending varying odors for communication to others.

Our Korean ancestors were keenly aware of a deer's often-strong smell, to come up with the above proverb: The club used in bludgeoning a deer will smell with an odor that will last for three years. Once again, the "three years" here was just to represent a long time. We have come across such an expression before: see, for instance, Entry #266, "A big house, albeit tilted, won't collapse in three years." The proverb reminds me of a scene from the 1987 film, *Untouchables*, in which the Chicago gangster Al Capone (1899 – 1947) beat some of his men, who had betrayed him, with a baseball bat. The wood grain of the bat must have been filled with brain tissue, not to mention blood, which might have lasted a very long time. Indeed the bat may say, "Crimes may be secret, yet not secure."

On August 6 and 9, 1945, the first (and the last) two atomic bombs were dropped over Hiroshima and Nagasaki, respectively, killing a total of over 200,000 people. Approximately 85 percent of Americans approved of the action. They would not forget, and will never forgive, the sneak attack on

Pearl Harbor by Japan, in December 1941. Those two atomic bombs certainly accelerated the surrender of Japan and the closure of World War II. And yet, scientists, military generals, and politicians who were intimately involved in the development and in deciding to use the bomb, were mentally tortured by what had just happened to human history.

Just five months prior to his death in 1954, Einstein regretted: "I made one great mistake in my life when I signed the letter to President Roosevelt recommending that atom bombs be made." President Harry Truman, who ultimately decided to use the bombs, and Robert Oppenheimer, who had played the key role in developing the bomb, met for the first time in October 1945. Truman wanted Oppenheimer's support for legislation that would give the government control over atomic energy, but he refused: "Mr. President, I feel I have blood on my hands." Truman always defended his decision. In a 1948 letter to his sister, he wrote, "It was a terrible decision. But I made it to save 250,000 boys from the United States, and I'd make it again under similar circumstances."

Oppenheimer, on the other hand, developed some serious depression worrying that politicians and generals would reach for nuclear bombs too readily. Just two months after the War was over, he resigned as the Los Alamos scientific director to promote the safe use of atomic energy. He had no part of the Atomic Energy Commission, as he was considered a security risk. General Leslie Groves, the military counterpart of Oppenheimer, wrote, "We had solved the immediate problem of ending the war, but in so doing we had raised up many unknowns." The crew of the *Enola Gay*, the B-29 bomber that carried the bomb to Hiroshima, were all welcomed as war heroes, but later faced questions about the morality of the bomb. (from *Countdown 1945* by Chris Wallace, 2020)

Al Capone died at the young age of 48 of cardiac arrest, after suffering a stroke, and thus did not have much time to regurgitate and repent for his crimes. The detonation of the two atomic bombs over Japan has been a subject of discussion, even nowadays, 75 years later, and will continue as long as humanity exists. It is indeed a "three-year" memory. (07/08/2020)

273. Avoid autumn drizzles under an in-law's whiskers.
가을비는 장인의 나룻 밑에서도 피한다.

In the Korean Peninsula, the autumn rains seldom pour down hard like summer showers. They seem to come and go on their own will and usually last for a short period. Those drizzles barely wet the whiskers of a father-in-law, so his son-in-law could stand underneath him to avoid the sprinkles. A strange proverb, this is. For one particular interpretation I came across, I offer two tracks of thought. The first one is that there are many trivial matters that we worry about, like a short-lived sprinkle of autumn rain. Here, it is best not to dwell on such matters and to keep moving forward with our lives. After all, even after a big torrential shower or a hurricane, time heals the damage. We ought to maintain a broad perspective of life whenever an adverse event takes place.

The second thought is more interesting. When and if a young couple faces a challenging time, say, financially, the last person the husband would seek for help would be his father-in-law. It is a matter of pride. His wife may say that her father is "loaded" or that she could talk to her father about the situation they are in now, but her pleas themselves could hurt his self-esteem. Likewise, the wife may have this urge to talk to her father-in-law. Since she knows that her husband would be upset by the suggestion, she may wish to talk to her in-law directly without telling her husband. If she does and her husband discovers it later, his disappointment and anger will be immediate and deep.

The above proverb says that these considerations are all nonsense. What pride or self-esteem exists in the dire situation you are in now! Getting help from others including in-laws, when you are in bad shape, and helping others when they are in trouble, is the very hallmark of humanity. If you could lean on your father-in-law to avoid getting wet, you could ask him for really anything. If the in-law is a wise man, with the gift of foresight, he might have already noticed your living condition. Perhaps he offered you help even before you ask and without telling his daughter. He may wink at you and say with a knowing grin, "You can pay me back later, whenever you can. Just take good care of my daughter."

166

The ideal scenario presented above can happen when the parties involved are relatively poor, as they have had chances to develop a deep sense of empathy. Among wealthy families, such an episode seems unlikely to happen. Instead of empathy for the poor, these folks appear to live in perpetual greed. As pointed out in Entry #112, "Brag about spending, not making money," relatively speaking, poor people donate more to various charities than the rich. For these egocentric people, when a need arises, there are no friends or advisors to lean on. Most of the people around them are not true friends whom they can rely on. Most likely, they could be with a special interest in taking advantage of the given situation. In many instances, siblings are their own foes. See Entries # 7, "Seas can be filled, but not your greed," and #158, "Are siblings treasure or foe?"

On December 5, 2014, Korean Airline 86, destined for Korea, returned to JFK International Airport just 20 minutes after takeoff, to discharge the cabin crew chief Park Chang-jin. The oldest daughter of the CEO of KAL, Cho Hyun-ah, was in the first-class cabin and served macadamia nuts in a closed bag, rather than on a plate. This irked Cho to the point she had a heated confrontation with Park. It was reported that Park kneeled before Cho to beg for forgiveness. And yet she repeatedly assaulted Park and summarily dismissed him right on the spot.

After the incident became public, Cho and her father had to apologize profusely to the furious public. In the end, it was Cho who was dismissed from KAL and had to stay five months in a prison for having obstructed aviation safety. The flight attendant and cabin crew chief returned to their positions by April 2016.

Cho's father passed away about a year ago and her older brother took over the CEO position. Early this year, "the lady of the *nutgate*" was conspiring with outsiders to take over the company from her brother. But then, COVID-19 hit upon the airline industry. Their business dwindled to only 10% of normal activity, and her attempt became a moot point. This was really an unsettling time for the siblings to lean on each other, but there was no such indication (disclaimer: this woman is not related to the author of this essay, although they share the same last name). (07/10/2020)

274. An injured field marshal barking orders inside a fortress.
다리 부러진 장수 성 안에서 호령한다.

If you are a war-time army general, would you prefer a desk job in Pentagon or to be engaged in the battlefield? We can ask a similar question virtually in any profession. Would you rather be in a clinic dealing with patients or become an administrator of a medical center? If you have a PhD in science, would you prefer working in a research lab or managing a big research program? If you are a professor, say, in a sizable university, would you prefer teaching over an administration position like a deanship?

For both sides of a given profession, maintaining outstanding performance, day in and day out, would be a challenging task. In terms of compensation and perks, the managerial position is better than the practitioner. In terms of job satisfaction, however, the practitioners seem happier, as they can really keep their hands wet all the time in what they were trained to do.

From what I had observed during my professional career, I would say that the transition from a technical position to a managerial position appears to be less problematic than the other way around. It was like someone with a PhD in basic science moving to a field in applied science, say, from physics to biology. This person would have a much smoother time than a biologist trying to become a physicist. See more in Entry #169, "A tree with deep roots survives drought."

If a general, who has been commanding thousands of troops on the battlefields, somehow lost a leg and subsequently got assigned to a desk job in a war department headquarter, there would be only a few at attention when he barks out an order. In essence, this is the sorry scene that the above proverb is describing.

Once you retire, you become nobody, seemingly all of a sudden. Every retiree becomes very quiet in the public domain: trend-setting philosophers, famous sports figures, highly respected political commentators, religious leaders, controversial politicians, prominent businessmen, well-known entertainers, and other idols of our time. We miss them for a while, but gradually forget their existence, till they publish an autobiography or depart this world. Then, we may say, "Is he still alive?" Paul Simon's relic of *Mrs. Robinson* ends as follows:

Where have you gone, Joe DiMaggio?
Our nation turns its lonely eyes to you
Woo, woo, woo
What's that you say, Mrs. Robinson?
Jolting Joe has left and gone away
Hey, hey, hey - Hey, hey, hey

On April 19, 1951, General Douglas MacArthur ended his farewell address to the U.S. Congress, quoting "Old soldiers never die," an old folklore song of the British army:

... but I still remember the refrain of one of the most popular barrack ballads of that day which proclaimed most proudly that "old soldiers never die; they just fade away." And like the old soldier of that ballad, I now close my military career and just fade away, an old soldier who tried to do his duty as God gave him the light to see that duty.

There is some cynical tone in the proverb as if asking, "Who cares about your marching orders now? Nobody knows or appreciates that you were once quite a commander. You are now just a crippled foot-soldier." Most of my contemporaries in Korea were all once very successful "somebodies" in their professions and are still very vocal in political opinion.

We have a chatroom in Kakao Talk, with more than 160 high school classmates, where we can belt out our complaints, protests, and dissatisfaction towards President Moon and his party in the national assembly. Although I wish our conversations stayed away from politics (and religion), having a common adversary surely unites us in good harmony. (07/11/2020)

275. For gossip, even a guy on a double-crutch comes forth.
남의 말이라면 쌍지팡이 짚고 나선다.

Gossiping is so much fun that a man, who can barely walk even with a pair of crutches, still steps forward and holds court. The above proverb uses 남의말, or speaking of or about others. For the time being, I just consider it gossiping. From an evolutionary perspective, gossiping helps the teller and listener bond, as they share information of mutual interest and spend time together. As such, gossiping is an essential form of social interaction by the means of talking about rather unflattering and negative things on a third party. It may provide them with a feeling of superiority. It is essentially the source of the wellbeing of the participants and thus the driving force of gossiping.

Interestingly, we tend to look down upon those who gossip regularly, especially those who engage in negative gossip. We consider them less reliable or trustworthy, for we fear that they may start a rumor about us from a negative angle also. At some unconscious level, we know for sure, "A gossip speaks ill of all and all of her" and "Gossiping and lying go together." Another interpretation of 남의말, speaking of or about others, and an alternate to gossiping, is poking one's nose into other people's business.

Compared with Westerners, Koreans are notorious in this regard. It certainly includes me. It wouldn't surprise me if a woman knows how many pairs of chopsticks her friend's household has, although she may not remember how many her own kitchen has. Everybody seems to have an opinion on every topic one can bring up, especially politics, children's education, social justice, ethics, etc.

For some reason, we become better chess players when we watch other people's games. In my case, my intrusion into a friend's private space seems to be somehow justified by this vague notion that it is "required" for a good friend to get involved, certainly deeper than normally warranted. Besides, I am truly interested in their human drama, nothing more. Often, this is how I become their confidante and I feel good about the privilege of such occasion where I can offer any form of support when they are in an adverse situation. Call it my mode of empathy.

Human rights in China, or lack thereof to be exact, has been a target of frequent criticisms by the U.S. Department of State, Canadian Ministry of Foreign Affairs, international non-governmental organizations, such as Human Rights in China, and Amnesty International, as well as many private human right activists. After Xi Jinping became General Secretary of their Communist Party in 2012, the situation has become worse.

With these criticisms, are we not interfering in their internal affairs, like me telling my neighbors what to do with their backyard? Just last month, the U.N. raised a wide range of concerns over the repression of "fundamental freedoms" by the Chinese government. Here, I will present only one issue involving the Uigur population. It was recently reported that more than a million Chinese Muslims are being detained in re-education camps in the Xinjiang region, in the northwest of China. Here, Muslims are to disavow their religious faith while welcoming the Communist Party. Chinese government officials claim that the detainment is to fight separatism and Islamic extremism.

According to the Chinese Constitution, the "Four Cardinal Principles" supersede the rights of a citizen. The Principles, first established by Deng Xiaoping in 1979 and on which no debate is allowed, entail upholding: (1) the socialist path; (2) the people's democratic dictatorship; (3) the leadership of the Communist Party; and (4) Mao Zedong's thought and Marxism–Leninism. Once they define human rights within this framework, they justify what they are doing with their citizens. The government claims that anyone who complies with these principles would enjoy and exercise all human rights, including economic opportunity.

At the same time, they never fail to highlight the rapid deterioration of Western societies. They always cite, among many social issues, the racial segregation we are facing nowadays in this country, which is considered a clean-cut violation of human rights. They have been implying that too much freedom is dangerous and that freedom is currently not their primary concern, as they have just begun to enjoy some level of prosperity after centuries of poverty and political instability.

It seems to me that both sides love to talk about the other, as the above proverb says. Or see Entry #115, "The pot calls the kettle black." (07/13/2020)

276. A bent stick with a bent shadow.
굽은지팡이 그림자도 굽어 비친다.

In the 1956 film, *The Ten Commandments*, Charlton Heston, playing Moses, carries a long and straight staff. He used it for the miraculous transformation of various objects as well as for dignified walking and leading. Other notables, who used a walking stick, include Winston Churchill, Woodrow Wilson, Sherlock Holmes, Charlie Chaplin, Franklin D. Roosevelt (by necessity), Fred Astaire, George Washington, Frederick Douglass, Maurice Chevalier, King Henry VII of England, Louis XIV of France, Benjamin Franklin et al. The list goes on, to which I may also add my father.

Not a long time ago, perhaps as late as in the 1950s, a walking stick was a fashion item among Korean gentlemen. Almost everyone in the older generation seemed to own one and used them differently to their liking. For some, it was like a weapon, helping define personal space on the street. Here, the bottom tip proceeds first, dropped from some height, while the handle is still more or less beside the body. As a man moves along, the tip and the hand holding the cane is way at the back.

The whole motion, in perfect rhythm, is synchronized with his steps, usually one touch-down every three steps. The total distance that the tip of the stick travels in one motion can be several feet. It is a big space on a busy street, and you don't want to be in the vicinity, lest your feet get tangled.

Other men carry a walking stick as if it were a precious treasure. It does not seem to offer any function. They are not a threat, even on a crowded street, as the stick seems to carry the man. This was a typical picture of some of our older and docile teachers when we were middle school kids. You may compare a walking stick used in this fashion, with an umbrella that a British gent of old used to carry, regardless of the weather.

Note, however, that an umbrella has not always been such an innocuous fashion item. Here is a scene, which would make any plot from any spy movie look amateurish. On September 7, 1978, a Bulgarian dissident received a stab from a passerby with the tip of an umbrella, on Waterloo Bridge in London. Four days later, he died. The tip of the umbrella had a hidden pneumatic device that injected a deadly toxin from the castor bean, ricin. The passerby turned out to be a Bulgarian Secret Service agent.

If a stick is bent, so be its shadow. Even if it is really straight, its shadow may not be if the ground is uneven. But it is absolutely correct to say that the shadow would be bent, if the stick was originally bent. There are no two ways about it. The proverb implies that if the initial intention is bad, it will be eventually revealed. In the dark, we may not see the bent shadow, but the truth will appear with light. It is similar to Entry #41, "Clean upstream begets clean water downstream," where I said that if the origin is bad, there is very little that one can help improve.

There are at least two potential attributes to the late discovery of true intention. The first case may belong to a bona fide fraud or cheating in a disguised appearance. Most of the con jobs belong to this category. The large-scale Ponzi scheme run by Bernard Madoff may serve as a good example of this category: See Entry #4, "You steal a needle, then soon a cow."

In the second case, the original intention might have been good and sincere. However, the ensuing circumstance might have made it impossible to fulfill the promise made at the beginning. In the heat of the election campaign, George H.W. Bush declared in 1988, "Read my lips, no new taxes!" But he did just that after he was elected as the 41st President. Some people have never forgiven his change of heart, but I fully understood why and how he had to. See Entry #35, "You can see a fathom of water but not an inch of mind." The rosy economic growth that Bush had predicted did not materialize, the unemployment rate hovered around eight percent, and the federal deficit rose by 45% from the Reagan era. Since he did not want to cut any defense spending and since the Federal Reserve refused to lower interest rates, Bush did not have any other choice except raise taxes.

As to the poor performance of President Trump in almost all aspects of the presidency, I am in a quandary: Was it a fraud from the beginning, or was he just incompetent for the job people assigned him to? My inclination is toward the latter. (07/16/2020)

277. A fly on a horsetail travels a thousand miles.
말 꼬리에 파리가 천 리 간다.

One lazy summer afternoon, a fly challenges a horse to an endurance contest, saying, "I bet, I can fly a longer distance and faster than you!" The stallion, full of testosterone and at the peak of his youth, is aghast at the outlandish behavior of a mere horsefly, and replied in indignation, "Anytime, anywhere!" So, they start a race. Sure enough, the stallion does not see the fly while he was running at full speed.

Soon he is running out of breath and stops to see where his challenger could be. As expected, he doesn't see the fly in the far distance but hears a buzzing noise just in front of him. To his surprise, the fly is there mocking him, "Hey, big man, let's continue." This may well have been a scene from *Tom and Jerry,* but is the crux of the above proverb. The fly in this proverb personifies people who take advantage of a person in power or fame, whom they happen to be acquainted with.

The so-called *choi-soon-sil gate* may offer a good example of the above proverb. Choi Soon-sil (1956 -) was a good friend and confidante of the ex-Korean President, Park Geun-hye (1952 -). Choi was accused of having taken advantage of her close relationship with the President, in soliciting financial support from several Korean chaebols, marginally for official use or mainly for personal gain. The scandal undoubtedly accelerated the downfall of President Park in 2017. More details are presented below, since the scandal bears some significance in modern Korean political history.

Ms. Park, the 11th President of Korea, lost both of her parents by assassination: her mother in 1974, during a Korean Independence Day ceremony, and her father, Park Chung-hee, who was the 3rd President, in 1979 during a dinner at the Korean Central Intelligence Agency safe-house. Soon after she had lost her mother, at the tender age of 22 and living a lonely life, Choi's father, 40 years senior to Park, approached her offering spiritual guidance and comfort. He was then a minister of a barely legitimate church.

We could say that the man was a Korean version of Rasputin. The latter was a Russian self-proclaimed holy man who befriended the family of

Emperor Nicholas II, the last monarch of Russia, and gained considerable influence in late Imperial Russia. Choi's father died in 1994; however, this encounter of "soul mates" led to Park's nearly 20-year close relationship with Choi's daughter, Soon-sil.

Fast forward to late 2016, and the news media began to report the unwarranted influence of Choi over President Park. Since Choi was not an official government employee, her involvement in President Park's official businesses reflected President Park's poor judgment. It included the President's schedule, speeches, and decision-making on matters ranging from her choice of handbags to state affairs, including some classified information. Besides, Choi and President Park's senior staff members were perceived to "extort" ₩77.4 billion (U$60 million) from Korean chaebols to set up two culture and sports-related foundations, Mir and K-sports.

Finally, using her tie to the President, Choi was able to have her daughter admitted to Ewha Womans University, although the daughter failed to meet the admission criteria. This episode probably angered Korean citizens more than any other of the "crimes." In June 2017, Choi was sentenced to three years of imprisonment for the conspiracy with university officials and professors. In February 2018, the Court also found Choi guilty of abuse of power, bribery, and interfering in government affairs. She was sentenced to 20 years in prison and fined ₩18 billion (U$17 million).

In the meantime, the scandal caused a series of mass demonstrations calling for the resignation of President Park. In March 2017, the Constitutional Court unanimously confirmed the impeachment proposal from the National Assembly. Subsequently, the former President Park was sentenced to a 25-year prison term and ordered to pay a fine of ₩20 billion (U$18 million).

It certainly divided the nation. On the one hand, the older conservative population believed that the current prosperity and freedom Koreans enjoy is largely due to her father's heroic efforts and showed sympathetic support for his daughter. On the other hand, the more liberal, younger generation did not care much about that particular part of history. All being said, had Choi and Park understood the true meaning of the above proverb, the tragic events could have been avoided. (07/19/2020)

278. A shortcut is a long way. 질러 가는 길이 돌아 가는 길이다.

At first glance, this proverb is inscrutable to the point of becoming an oxymoron. Following the Pythagorean Theorem, you could cut across an open field, instead of walking two bent trails in tandem. But, the field is with tall grasses and wet spots here and there. You may come across a snake or two, not to mention the blazing sun on your back.

Right in the middle of the field, you may regret your decision and wish you had taken the yonder narrow trails, lined with cypress trees. By that time, it may be too late. You must continue your ill-conceived plan. At the destination, you find all your friends who have taken the long, but cool tree-lined roads, waiting for you, each with a bottle of beer. In this context, the proverb sounds like, "Haste makes waste." The crux is, try not to cut corners.

The following is an excerpt from an article by David Kirkpatrick and Jane Bradley that appeared in the April 16, 2020 issue of *The New York Times*. If you recall, at the early stage of the COVID-19 outbreak, every nation was struggling to obtain a sufficient amount of personal protective equipment, like facial masks, ventilators for patients, and virus test kits for the general public. To make matters worse, President Trump literally walked away from all this hassle and passed the hot potato to each state governor.

Every governor was thus scrambling to get the necessary stuff in the open global markets, at a competitive bidding price. China, having gone through the pandemic a bit earlier than other nations, was the primary source of supply. Their attitude was, for the lack of a better expression, "take it or leave it." For a while, they seemed to be holding a gun aimed at our heads. It did not sit very well with many people: after all, they gave us the problem, and then we had to pay a hefty price for their remedies.

LONDON — The two Chinese companies were offering a risky proposition: two million home test kits said to detect antibodies for the coronavirus for at least $20 million, take it or leave it. The asking price was high, the technology was unproven and the money had to be paid upfront. And the buyer would be required to pick up the crate loads of test kits from a facility in China.

Yet British officials took the deal, then confidently promised tests would be available at pharmacies in as little as two weeks. "As simple as a pregnancy test," gushed Prime Minister Boris Johnson. "It has the potential to be a total game changer."

There was one problem, however. The tests did not work.

Found to be insufficiently accurate by a laboratory at Oxford University, half a million of the tests are now gathering dust in storage. Another 1.5 million bought at a similar price from other sources have also gone unused. The fiasco has left embarrassed British officials scrambling to get back at least some of the money. "They might perhaps have slightly jumped the gun," said a member of the government's New and Emerging Respiratory Virus Threats Advisory Group. "There is a huge pressure on politicians to come out and say things that are positive."

A few salient features of the story are highlighted here. First, let us examine the attitude of the Chinese companies. Understanding the desperate situation the U.K. was facing, they demanded an upfront payment and the goods be picked up in China by the buyer. I cannot make any comment on the price, but it must have been high. Also, note that the U.K. government had to purchase as many as two million assay kits since the Chinese fixed the smallest size of an order at the bargaining table.

Secondly, being the modest people Brits are, the professor was very polite when he said that the Johnson administration "might perhaps have slightly jumped the gun." Koreans would have used words like "stupid" and "idiotic" in describing the government's action. I would say they were duped, no doubt.

Only time will tell how the above misstep would have affected the overall fight against the pandemic in the U.K. However, one thing has become clear: The scandal fully supports the implication of the above proverb. (07/19/2020)

279. Even a dog recognizes its owner.
개도 제 주인은 알아본다.

Of course, a dog would recognize *their* (see the footnote of #207) master. After all, the dog spends more time with the owner than anybody else. More important, it is the owner who feeds the dog. If a dog appreciates the affection from its owner and tries *their* best to express unlimited loyalty, why can't we humans be the same to those who love us dearly: like our parents, friends, siblings, and even strangers from whom we have benefited?

One thing I want to clarify right away is that the perception of a dog, when the proverb was first in use, was not what we have nowadays. In this old saying, a dog means a lowly animal that may not deserve much care from humans. See, for instance, Entry #132, "Even a dog is allowed peaceful meals." Once again, we of course let the dog enjoy a meal without any disruptions, but the nuance is that even such a humble creature is entitled to a peaceful meal. The above proverb particularly refers to those people who are ungrateful for a favor they have received from others.

The word, *joo-in* (주인), stands for a master, owner, head, employer, landlord, etc. Its metaphor in the present context may include familial, as well as educational, pedigree. With this broader understanding of the proverb, can we now say that if we do not recognize or actively ignore where we are originally from, we are worse than a dog? I have already addressed such unsettling questions, as applied to an immigrant like me, in Entry #58, "Frogs don't remember they were once tadpoles." The following is reproduced from that essay:

If you do not keep your past alive, especially the heritage of the motherland, you will become some sort of a betrayer, if not an outright traitor. Once poor, be frugal for the rest of your life to "honor" the suffering you've gone through! This condemnation, albeit too severe, is something many long-time expatriates here in this country are keenly aware of, and struggle with, whenever they visit the country they left many years ago.

So, to what extent have I "abandoned" the Korean heritage as an immigrant to his country? I have lived in the United States since 1967, for more than two-thirds of my life, having become a naturalized citizen in 1982. This question had not surfaced till I had more time to regurgitate it. If the question was raised in the past, I must have been too busy to think about it more carefully. Retirement, and closing in on the final days of life, compels me to address the topic.

In the past few months, this country has been facing quite a bit of turmoil on two major fronts. One is the killing of George Floyd by Minneapolis police on May 25. A white police officer knelt on Floyd's neck for nearly eight minutes. After his death, protests against police violence toward African Americans renewed the Black Lives Matter (BLM) movement throughout the nation.

The second one is the arrival of the COVID-19 pandemic, in early January. This brought about an abrupt halt to the economy, resulting in unprecedented chaos in the daily lives of every citizen. The common thread on these two developments was ultimately the disparity in economic opportunity, resulting in a gap in wealth between the White and African Americans.

To my surprise, the compassion I have for African Americans, as well as the Hispanic population, was not as high as I had once assumed. I have recently struggled with the question of why. Two tracks of possible answers come to mind. First, I lack empathy, in terms of racial discrimination. My job was so technical in nature and domestic life has been so simple, that I have not experienced any serious discrimination for being a foreigner. It has been a blessing on one hand, but my life has been of low amplitude, albeit a long one.

With little experience, I may not be able to feel the pain that minorities in this country must endure. The second thought is that the eagerness with which I tried to identify myself as an American, might have unconsciously forced me to adopt the attitude of typical Whites, with apathy towards nearly everybody but themselves. Either way, it is a shame. How can I develop genuine compassion towards African Americans, Hispanic Americans, and importantly native Indians? It is not a simple judgmental question. It is a moral question. (07/22/2020)

280. Scratching other people's legs.
남의 다리 긁는다.

If you scratch somebody else's itchy leg, what do you gain? More to the point, why would you do that? Did the person beg you to? Why can't they do the scratching themselves? It isn't like the leg is not accessible. Don't you have anything better thing to do? The crux of this proverb is that what you have done with all your efforts is just for somebody else. Don't forget about your own itchy leg. Helping others comes after you help yourself. A corollary is that you should not do to others, what you would not do to yourself unless they asked you specifically to do so.

The head of a household happens to be an old carpenter, and yet they do not have a decent cutting board in the kitchen. A minister, who preaches fidelity, is having an affair with his secretary, right in his church. An old car, belonging to an auto mechanic, is about to quit of old age. Why do children of a school teacher tend to be rowdy? A chef's meal at home isn't like what we see on his TV show. An advice columnist, Ann Landers, got divorced herself. Dishonest judges, fraudulent businessmen, cops taking advantage of female drivers, and other hypocrites, are not doing what they are supposed to do. Instead, they try to scratch other people's legs.

Just yesterday, President Trump declared that wearing a mask during this COVID-19 pandemic is "patriotic," and yet he doesn't wear one. On July 9, the city mayor of Seoul, Park Won-soon, committed suicide after he had been accused of sexually harassing his secretary. This man was one of the most vocal attorneys in Korea advocating for women's rights. As I see it, Trump is not smart enough to recognize how absurd his patriotism is, while Park was intelligent enough to recognize his own double standards. That may be the reason why Trump is still alive, while Park is dead.

Most of the modern wars, in which the United States has been involved, started with a notion of helping other nations with noble ideals such as democracy and free enterprise. Such honorable intentions are, however, regardless of whether they fit well with the existing traditions of religion, culture, and social systems of the host country. In reality, such justifications may well be just a banner under which political and economic interests of the U.S. are lurking.

In the meantime, many non-governmental organizations from the private sector, especially Christian-based ones, go to a foreign country to help them be free from political oppression, poor economy, and terrible social injustice. With so much investment and effort, my question is whether we are scratching the legs of others when we have our own legs, desperately waiting for a good dose of scratching? No wonder the "Make America Great Again" movement has been so appealing to the me-first generation.

We were sent to DIE FOR EMPEROR AND IMPERIAL NATION, and everyone acted like we believed in it. But when the soldiers were dying, the young ones CALLED OUT TO THEIR MOTHERS and older ones called out their CHILDREN'S NAMES. I never heard anyone calling the emperor and nation." Nobuo Nishzaki, a Japanese veteran of the Second World War said these words in an interview with a reporter from National Geographic. The magazine article continues: *"Leaving home for the navy in 1942, Nishzaki, then 15, was given an order by his mother: 'You must survive and come back,' she said. He clung tightly to her words, even as the winds of war swept him across the Pacific, from one battle to the next, and finally to a suicide mission at Okinawa. Despite long odds, he lived – and honored his mother's demand.* ("The Last Voices of World War II," National Geographic, May 6, 2020)

No war can be justified. War for peace is an oxymoron at its best. Citizens of one nation may say that they have to fight to protect their peace. Isn't that also what the other nation says? Peace-loving people would not know the national boundary, and yet, humanity has been full of wars. Any religion on this planet promotes compassion, forgiveness, kindness, and love towards other human beings. How can we then explain the century-old conflict between Christianity and the Islamic faith? An individual who cannot have a peaceful mind, a family who lives with constant squabbles among its members, a community that cannot live in harmony, or a nation that cannot handle their domestic issues, all tend to look for something to do for others. It is like scratching other people's legs. (07/23/2020)

281. The penniless man goes after a bigger cake.
돈 없는 놈이 큰 떡 먼저 든다.

A penniless person, who cannot afford anything, grabs the biggest piece of a cake on the table. This proverb seems to say that an ill-qualified man steps forward, boasting about his ability and qualification, for a given task. This person may not recognize the limitation of his ability, or he does, but insists he is competent. We saw a similar proverb in Entry #6, "Sparrow tears legs racing against a stork." There, I said that we must live within our means and adjust our ambitions according to our ability.

Subsequent to the 2008 global financial meltdown, many U.S. corporations were forced to restructure or downsize, just to survive. The 2010 American film, *The Company Men,* shows how three families try to cope with the sudden unemployment they face. The movie features Ben Affleck, Kevin Costner, Chris Cooper, and Tommy Lee Jones. A publicly held shipbuilding corporation begins to fire employees, starting with low-ranking positions. In the movie, Affleck plays a typical ambitious, white-color employee with a six-figure salary, a wife, and a teenage son and younger daughter. They live in a well-manicured house with two cars, one being a Porsche. Their social life has been that of typical young and upwardly mobile couples. As he is fired, the company helps him transition to a new job through a consulting firm, but to no avail. He has to sell their house and his Porsche and move in with his parents. Eventually, working for his brother-in-law, he takes a manual labor job installing drywall, played by Kevin Costner. It is a big letdown, but he accepts the situation with resignation.

With an additional round of lay-offs, a senior manager, played by Chris Cooper, is let go. This man has risen from the shipyard floor to the corporate offices, after 30 years of dedicated contribution to the corporation. His immediate boss and long-time colleague, Chief Financial Officer (CFO), Tommy Lee Jones, protests the move with Human Resources and the corporate Chief Executive Officer. Instead, they also fire Jones.

The ex-senior manager's life immediately falls apart, as many potential employers tell him he is too old to start a new career or to do jobs even young people find difficult. Upon his wife's request, Cooper disappears from home every morning, as usual with his briefcase, all just to keep his dire situation secret from the neighbors. But, he cannot do anything about mounting bills, or his daughter's impending college tuition. Frustrated and depressed, he commits suicide in his garage by carbon monoxide poisoning. This, of the three families, is the most saddening case. In an ironic twist Jones, the former CFO, actually becomes wealthier as the company's stock price goes up, due to the company's downsizing. But he feels guilty about his company ruining so many lives, and thus starts his own business. Affleck is the first person he hires.

It is no longer fashionable to tell everyone within earshot that President Trump is a pathological liar. We have become so desensitized to his lies, we have acquired deaf ears. But we still have to witness his performance in governing this nation. It has been, at least for me, a very painful and unpleasant time. Lately, we have witnessed how he reacts to each of the two major crises: the COVID-19 pandemic and racial tension. My bottom-line assessment is that he is simply not qualified for the job: just like the guy who is grabbing the biggest portion of cake, without any means to pay for it.

As of today, over 150,000 Americans have died from COVID-19. Tens of millions have also encountered a possibly irreversible financial ruin. And yet, Trump walked away from his responsibility as the leader of this nation, once he realized he could not come up with any intelligent solution to the pandemic. Now, he has to come out of the closet because he is behind Joe Biden in the election polls.

In addition, racial tension is at its peak. As to the Black Lives Matter movement, he has painted all, in one sweeping brush, as unlawful violence. He sent Federal Homeland Security personnel to those cities where demonstrations were taking place. Not so much because he truly believed that the protests were damaging federal buildings, but because he chose to use "law and order" as a political mantra in a violence-filled fantasy of a dystopian society. All of us have to avoid this, at any cost.

And yet, to many Americans, Trump is an underappreciated martyr of true American value. To them, I say "amen," but strongly suggest they read this proverb. (07/26/2020)

282. A minster's cow is not afraid of a butcher.
대신 댁 송아지 백정 무서운 줄 모른다.

If you are a "somebody," with an impeccable familial pedigree from a *yang-ban* ancestry, you are entitled to a certain amount of perks in old Korea. So does their cow, is what the above proverb says. The cow has been treated so well that she is not afraid of anything, including a butcher. Their dog would probably be the "alpha male" among the neighborhood pack and their housemaid would be the matriarch of their own community. They all enjoy such status because they are related to a *dae-sin,* or 대신. This word is loosely translated as a government minister, like a department secretary in the U.S. government. Suffice to say, his household has some "power" to display, which they must have (ab)used rather liberally. In this proverb, ordinary citizens speak of their displeasure about it, tongue in cheek.

Cho Gook had been the chief secretary to Korean President Moon Jae-in, between 2017 and 2019. When he was nominated as the minister of the Justice Department, mass media and the opposition party at the national assembly, were able to dig out much dirt about his family. His wife, a professor in English, was accused of tax evasion, falsifying awards and documents, and liberal use of university property for personal purposes. These incidents had never been exposed until Cho Gook was undergoing the vetting process.

Their daughter, a student at a medical school, received unwarranted help and favors from her college. Suspicion ranged from admission to a medical school, her participation in research and internship, her resume, scholarship, etc. It was also said that their son received special attention and favors from teachers and school administrators. While he was serving as a member of a youth committee sponsored by the city of Seoul, he seldom attended the meeting, but received all the benefits offered to the committee members. Besides, there was hearsay that he entered the committee on a special provision.

Just like his sister, the son was said to be a recipient of a chancellor's award, but he was not able to produce the evidence. His internship at Seoul National University was based on special treatment, by a close friend of his father. Falsifying documents, his questionable stay at George Washington University, via a student-exchange program, and an unusual position as a teaching assistant at the Yon-se University graduate school, were all added to the dark cloud over his head. But, most of all, he had been avoiding mandatory military service. This was the last straw in triggering the furor among Korean citizens.

None of the above accusations emerged as a major criminal act. Indeed, it was difficult to establish any of those episodes as such. Two aspects were in their favor: first, Cho Gook himself was a legal scholar and should have known what constituted an illegal practice. Secondly, he had been part of the well-established ruling class of Korea. Wherever he turned, there were people who owed him a favor. In the end, it was not the facts exposed to the public, but the perception of ordinary citizens that caused the downfall of Cho from the ministry position, after just 45 days. The scandal reminds me of the so-called *Choe-Soon-sil-gate*: see Entry # 277, "A fly on a horsetail travels a thousand miles."

Let us compare the above episode with some incidents involving children of U.S. presidents. The anger and frustration that the 33rd President, Harry Truman, expressed when their only daughter received a bad review after her solo recital were those of a father, not of a president. In all accounts, Truman's daughter was not a great soprano: see Entry #41, "Clean upstream begets clean water downstream." One of the few times Chelsea Clinton made a headline in a newspaper was when she was about to get married. Apparently, she told her father, in no uncertain terms, that he would not be invited to her wedding unless he shed off some bodyweight, which he had to oblige.

Al Gore, two-term Vice President to Bill Clinton, had a son who received a speed ticket. He was driving a Toyota Prius, then a novel, hybrid, fuel-efficient car. He was driving at a speed of more than 120 MPH. What shocked and impressed people was not who the driver was, but the fact that a Prius could move that fast, a free advertisement for Toyota. One son of the 38th President, Gerald Ford, became a professional rodeo cowboy and toured the country. Daughters of Michelle and Barrack Obama have always been under the radar, without any "noise." (07/28/2020)

283. Getting hurt from a fall on even ground.
평지에서 낙상한다.

A fender bender in a parking lot is a common accident and certainly happens more often than on a freeway with a speed limit of 75 MPH. My wife has had a few. It's just a nuisance and hassle. Most of the time, the damage is trivial and the repair costs less than the insurance coverage deductible. Thus, we just pay for it out of our pockets. When you least expect it, something unforeseen happens, usually when your mind is somewhere else. Complacency often does it. When you hike precarious terrain on a mountain, you don't fall, but on even ground, it could happen. This is the crux of the proverb.

A sneak attack on a nation, without formally declaring a war, provides a tremendous advantage for the invading army. Its initial impact can last for a long time. Sometimes the country attacked off guard may not fully recover to have a decent chance of fighting off the invaders. It is like kicking the testicles of a man in a street fight. The victim would fall to the ground, with both hands on the groin, while the attacker keeps on kicking the downed man with his feet. It is an ugly win, but subsequent revenge can be uglier and more deadly.

The United States formally entered the Second World War one day after a surprise military strike by the Imperial Japanese Navy Air Service and midget submarines against the naval base at Pearl Harbor. The attack took place just before 8:00 AM, on December 7, 1941. That it was a Sunday shouldn't surprise anyone. Very likely, most of the American soldiers on the island must have been in deep sleep, possibly with a hangover. That is what young men usually do on a Sunday morning. Without any significant air defense over Hawaii, major ships sunk in deep water and made salvage impossible.

At the dawn of June 25, 1950, the North Korean army crossed the 38th Parallel behind heavy artillery fire. It was again a Sunday morning. The initial battle was so swift and much in favor of the North that within two days the Republic of Korea (ROK) had to flee from Seoul. On Day 3, in the wee hours around 2 AM, the ROK blew up the major bridge over the Han

River in an attempt to slow down the advancement of the North. It inevitably trapped many fleeing citizens and soldiers in Seoul. For instance, many South Korean National Assemblymen, voluntarily or involuntarily, remained in Seoul, 49 of which subsequently pledged allegiance to the North. Such a rapid deterioration of the ROK was happening only because of the surprise attack by the North, at the dawn of a Sunday.

Unexpected incidents happen seemingly all the time, out of nowhere, to unanticipated and thus, unprepared people. Just a few days ago, a 63-year-old woman died from an attack by a great white shark, while swimming off the coast of Maine. This was the first-ever fatal shark attack in Maine. We simply shake our heads in disbelief when we hear about someone getting hit by a car traveling in the wrong direction on a one-way street, or a golfer stricken by lightning on a sunny day. Steve Irwin, a world-renowned Australian wildlife expert, was killed in 2006 after his heart was pierced by a short-tail stingray's tip while filming in shallow water. Note that stingrays were not considered particularly more dangerous than other animals he had handled in his career, for which he had gained his fame.

According to the so-called *Improbability Principle*, "it's an unusual day if nothing unusual happens." What would be the probability for me to come across one of my students, on the beach of Cancun, during a X-mas vacation? A dear friend of mine was born at the same hour, of the same day, and year as myself. It seems that highly improbable events are commonplace. Sir David Hand, emeritus professor in statistics at Imperial College London, explains such perception with five secondary laws: the *Laws of Inevitability*, *Truly Large Numbers*, *Selection*, the *Probability Lever*, and *Near Enough*.

The first law, for instance, states that somebody must have a winning lottery ticket, although the odds are against you. Using the second one, he says that, with just 23 people, the chances of a common birthday are better than even. The last three laws deal with distorted impressions, as affected by the occurrence of the same event, slight changes in assumption, and treating similar events as if they are identical. If we follow his logic, tumbling to a fall, on even ground, is not really as rare as one would expect. (07/30/2020)

284. Being whipped together lessens the pain.
매도 같이 맞으면 낫다.

"Misery loves company" is equivalent to this proverb. Sharing a burden, including misery and punishment, is desirable in many situations, especially among friends. When one person cannot lift a heavyweight, but two or more could. Why am I the only one who gets punished, when all of us were involved equally in an offensive act? Conversely, can I somehow lessen the punishment my friends are facing, even if I was not directly involved in the "crime" they committed? I am not speaking of illegally making a false statement on their behalf. Rather, I could appeal for leniency through a letter-writing campaign, or organize a peaceful demonstration requesting mercy with other friends.

Weight or pressure, exerted on a tight spot, is certainly more intense than when it is spread over a wider area. Imagine a rod. When it is suspended horizontally, its weight is distributed along the length, with the center of gravity at the middle. As we lift one side, the center moves closer to the lower end. When the rod stands perfectly straight, the center of gravity is at the lower end, and the top end does not seem to bear any weight.

Most of the dams for hydroelectric power are designed not in a straight line, but with an inwardly curved line. See the aerial view of Hoover Dam in Nevada. Bridges are also designed in such a way that their weight is distributed as widely as possible. Having arches, instead of just a straight line, would serve such a purpose. Such basic principles in physics and engineering do indeed appear to support the above proverb, saying that sharing is always desirable.

Besides misery and weight, what we could and should share is wealth. One of the most unsettling trends I have noticed in this country, over the past 50 years or so, is the disparity in wealth. In Los Angeles, for instance, a tent-city of homeless people, in downtown Skid Row, is now on full display only a few miles away from a community of multi-million-dollar mansions. The rich become richer, while the poor become poorer. One of the most remarkable economic findings reported last year was that the top one percent of wealthy people hold more than 40% of the national wealth, while the bottom 90% of the population possess less than 25% of all wealth. I am sure that such a trend also prevails in Korea.

The so-called Gini Index measures economic inequality. It ranges from 0 to 1, representing hypothetically perfect equality to complete inequality. The absolute value may not mean much to laymen, but the Index is a useful quantity for comparing between nations or time. In 1967, the Index of the United States was 0.38. It increased rather linearly to 0.49 in 2018. Among the nations, I was able to dig out the following set of data for the year 2018: Denmark (0.25), Germany (0.29), Korea (0.35), China (0.47), U.S.A. (0.49), South Africa (0.58) and Sierra Leon (0.63).

I was pleasantly surprised to notice that Korea enjoys a very good score, much better than China and the United States. Indeed, the inequality in Korea is relatively on the lower end of the scale. I do, however, predict that the number will increase steadily in the coming years.

Economic inequality originates from many causes, each with varying degrees of contribution: job market, education, labor regulation (including union status), tax system, globalization, age and gender, wealth concentration, information technology, etc. We have understood these factors for many decades, and yet the chasm of wealth continues to grow. Some of the remedial solutions, such as education, may take a long-term, concerted effort of all citizens. Without the political will of a government to mitigate the wealth gap, there is very little that average citizens can do individually. In the meantime, the simplest deed we can commit ourselves to would be sharing our wealth, or at least align our interests to those legislations that favors such principles.

Sharing is the best form of generosity. It consists of two parties in give-and-take. We can share almost everything without losing anything. It ranges from last night's dream to dreams one had many years ago, from unconditional love to bottomless forgiveness, from monetary and physical aid to mental support, from the agony of failure to the jubilance of victory, and from happiness to pain as the above proverb says. (08/03/2020)

189

285. Even if you know, ask for the directions.
아는 길도 물어 가라.

This proverb says that we cannot be overly careful when we make a decision. Indeed, there is no reason not to confirm that everything is in good order, prior to embarking on a project. It is similar to "Measure twice and cut once," as applied to a tailor or a carpenter. Once cut short, there is no remedial recourse, except to keep cursing yourself. Also, see Entry #60, "Is this stone bridge strong enough to cross?"

When I was a professor in a pharmacy program at a state university, we had two additional satellite campuses. Each of these had about two dozen Pharm D students listening to our lectures from the main campus, in real-time, via quite a sophisticated video system. Nonetheless, our Dean constantly nagged the instructors to visit those campuses for in-class lectures, lest those students feel like secondary citizens. Since I was the course coordinator, I had to oblige with the Dean's wishes. One problem was that a round-trip, for a 50-minute lecture, took all day, as both campuses were about a three-hour drive away. This was the main reason for the reluctance from course coordinators.

Our Dean offered us a two-seater airplane to and from the remote sites. In that way, I was able to come back to my office around noon and do some "harassing" to my graduate students in the lab all afternoon. This is what I remember happening when I flew for the first time. As soon as I sat beside this old pilot, he was pulling down a tattered instruction manual from a front headspace, and going through each toggle switch one at a time. He seemed to be experienced, but still I was nervous about the possibility that this man was flying the plane for the first time.

It was a chilly and rainy November morning when I first flew with him. The trip was bumpy, and as we were descending for landing in a thick cloud, this man stretched his neck to look outside the window for a landing strip. On the way back home, I learned a few things about him: He had been flying small planes throughout his adult life, and going over the checklist had been deeply ingrained in his DNA. As I recall, it was a pleasant trip, and the class bought pizza, so I had a few slices.

On March 19, 2003, an international coalition led by the United States invaded Iraq "to disarm Iraq of weapons of mass destruction (WMD), to end Saddam Hussein's support for terrorism, and to free the Iraqi people." The battle was over very quickly, in a month or so, as the coalition troops, outnumbered and overwhelmed, Iraq forces with technically advanced weaponry. But the invaders were not able to find any trace of WMD. Even the old pilot I talked about previously was going through his checklist before taking off the ground. The U.S. started a major war without any concrete evidence for their justification. Soon, President George W. Bush and UK Prime Minister Tony Blair declared a victory. However, those powers that be must have known there were no WMD.

In February of 2002, Joseph Charles Wilson (1949 – 2019), an American diplomat, was sent to Niger, by the CIA, to investigate if Saddam Hussein had attempted to purchase uranium for constructing WMDs. After the invasion was over, Wilson published in July 2003, an opinion column in *The New York Times*, the now-famous essay was titled, "What I Didn't Find in Africa." He wrote: "America's foreign policy depends on the sanctity of its information. For this reason, questioning the selective use of intelligence to justify the war in Iraq is neither idle sniping nor 'revisionist history,' as Mr. Bush has suggested." His doubt was not something the Bush administration would have welcomed.

Just a week after Wilson's op-ed was published, the identity of his wife, Valerie Palme, as a CIA agent was revealed in public, by a syndicated columnist. She had been operating in Athens and Brussels. Nobody seemed to know why this fame-seeking journalist broke the story, but it is an unwritten taboo to reveal such information in the public domain. My impression, based on what we all read from media coverage of the so-called *Plamegate,* was some kind of retaliation from the Bush administration. Very recently, in fact, only a few months ago, Valerie Plame ran for a Congress position on an anti-Trump platform in New Mexico but lost in a primary. For many years, the story of the Wilsons had dominated the imagination of many fans of John le Carré, certainly including me. All said, the unfortunate episode could have been avoided, had the folks involved understood the above proverb. (08/04/2020)

286. The noise from a ghost crossing a swollen stream after a downpour.
장마 도깨비 여울 건너가는 소리를 한다.

By my own definition, a ghost moves around in stealth, without making much noise, especially during the dark of the darkest night. What would you hear when you stand in the wee hours of the night, beside a rapid stream, while a ghost crosses it? Let's say we still have a torrential downpour and the stream is swollen to the brim. The answer is, of course, nothing, except the threatening noise of the violent water. When do you mumble something that nobody can hear? And what are you complaining about? Addressing these questions is the key to the understanding of this proverb.

Let us imagine a Buddhist monk, with a shiny head, who has just come across a sudden summer shower. His words of displeasure won't be nasty, like a four-letter word starting with F, or expressed loudly so that everyone nearby can hear them. Now, to make matters worse, he has also noticed that he doesn't have a handkerchief to wipe the rainwater off his head.

Another man has just noticed that there is no toilet paper, after finished his business. I suppose he could yell for help, hoping someone can hear him, but his first reaction must have been a mumbling expletive. With my favorite baseball team, the Detroit Tigers, Kirk Gibson clinched the 1984 World Series in the 8th inning of the 5th game, with a three-run homer off Goose Gossage of the San Diego Padres. Gossage refused to walk him with a base open. Up to that point, Gossage had claimed that he "owned Gibson." What could have gone through the head of the Padres manager, Dick Williams, at that moment?

At the cash register of a grocery store, you realize that you have forgotten to bring your wallet. Your car runs out of fuel just a few yards away from a gas station, you almost reel in a big fish but it gets away at the last minute, there are no coins in your pocket for a vending machine, cars come in continuously from the right lane even when they saw the merge sign way at the back, you smell cigarette smoke but can't see the source, you have to retake a course next semester because you failed to answer a few questions in the final, later in the morning at work you notice your socks don't match, you go out sailing on a catamaran then the wind suddenly quits, the AC unit breaks on a hot Friday afternoon, etc. These are all legitimate causes for a quiet curse, at least initially.

So, you are saying something that you do not want anyone to hear, most likely a complaint. You don't speak loudly, maybe because you don't have anyone to blame. We do not know for sure if the current COVID-19 pandemic is indeed man-made in origin, to be more specific, a synthetic virus strain accidentally released from the Wuhan Institute of Virology in China. Some politicians in this country seem to promote such a conspiracy theory, for whatever purpose they may have to fulfill. Currently, the China-United States relationship is at rock bottom. It was already strained with trade talks, but the pandemic has shed further light on the ugly side of the relationship.

President Trump often refers to the virus as the "Chinese virus," or even the "Kung-Fu virus". It doesn't help the public sentiment, already negative if I may add, towards Chinese-Americans in this country.

Justin Tsui, a registered nurse pursuing a PhD in nursing practice in psychiatric mental health at Columbia University, was approached by a white man on a subway platform in Manhattan. The man asked, "You're Chinese, right?" When Tsui responded that he was Chinese-American, the man said that he should go back to his county, citing the 2003 SARS outbreak as another example of "all these sicknesses" spread by "chinks." The man kept coming closer and closer to Tsui, who was forced to step toward the edge of the platform. "Leave him alone. Can't you see he's a nurse? That he's wearing scrubs?" said a Latino bystander. After the bystander threatened to record the incident and call the police, the aggressor said that he should "go back to his country too." When the train finally arrived, the aggressor sat right across from Tsui and glared at him the entire ride, mouthing, "I'm watching you." (from the 07/06/2020 issue of *Time* magazine)

The racist white man should have learned from the above proverb, and muttered to himself first, just to hear out how stupid he sounded. (08/05/2020)

287. Scooping water out of a river is still a good deed for others.
흘러가는 물도 떠 주면 공이다.

Although there is an abundant supply of water in the river, you can be kind enough to scoop it up for others. It is a simple gesture of kindness one may overlook, as it seems trivial. The point of this proverb is that there is no limit to kindness, big or small. Another way to put it is that you should not stop a kind act too soon. Make sure to see it through till the end. An interesting word here is *gong*, 공, which can be translated as merit, honor, achievement, good deed, credit, etc. In the above context, I'd prefer it to mean achievement or good deed. A small effort on your part is still a significant *gong* if it originates from kindness shown to fellow human beings.

In December 2013, I visited Korea to see a dear friend of mine, for the last time. He was in a university medical center, quite far from where I was staying, a friend's place in Yong-In City. In the morning I would go to the hospital, take him in a wheelchair to a nearby restaurant for lunch, have him enjoy a smoke outside, and then go home in the afternoon. The last leg of the trip, back to my friend's place, was via a local bus line, after two separate subway rides.

It was at one such occasion, for the first time in my life, a young man offered me his seat. He just stood up, pointing with a mobile phone in his hand, to the seat he had just vacated. I knew I was getting old, but I was still surprised by the episode. I was grateful for the young man, probably a high school kid, and uttered a few broken Korean words to commend his kind act. I felt it was only a few years ago that I did the same for the elder, but now I just saw a dying friend and came across another incident that reminded me of my old age. Still, his kindness dominated my feeling then. I was assured of the basic decency of humanity.

A gesture of kindness on the part of a giver, however simple it may appear, could have a profound impact on the recipient. According to a CBS report a few weeks ago, a sheriff's deputy of a jailhouse in Georgia collapsed at his desk. He just lost consciousness, most likely due to some medical condition, and fell onto the concrete floor, splitting his head open.

Albeit locked in their cells, three inmates, who had earlier noticed the unstable deputy during his round of security procedures in the housing unit, immediately began pounding on their doors and shouted the deputy's name in hopes of waking him. Although he was unconscious, the deputy was able to rise to his feet and press the control panel to open cell doors. Later, he said he had thought that an inmate needed help. The three inmates, now out of their cells, rushed to the deputy and radioed for help.

A kind act of biblical scale is now represented here. In late November of 1950, right at the peak of the Korean War, the Chinese army, upon invitation from North Korea, launched a massive offensive and forced 30,000 United Nations troops to retreat to the port city of Hungnam for evacuation. In what was later known as the Hungnam Evacuation, Colonel Edward H. Forney organized the withdrawal of over 100,000 servicemen, along with their equipment, supplies, and vehicles, as well as the evacuation of over 100,000 North Korean refugees (140,000 according to a Korean government's estimate). It was the largest U.S. amphibious evacuation of civilians, under combat conditions, in American history.

Colonel Forney and his Korean interpreter, Dr. Hyun Bong-Hak (현봉학), had a hard time initially persuading everyone involved, certainly his immediate superior, Lieutenant General Edward M. Almond. For his successful operation on an unprecedented scale, Forney was decorated with a Legion of Merit award. His heroic efforts in humanitarian aid made him one of the most admired Americans in Korea. A road in a port city in South Korea, Po-hang, is named after him and numerous awards and memorials are dedicated to his brave and kind deeds. It was a large-scale *Schindler's List*, a 1993 American film based on a true story involving Oskar Schindler, a German industrialist. He, together with his wife Emilie Schindler, saved more than a thousand, mostly Polish-Jewish refugees, from the Holocaust.

Incidentally, like *Schindler's List*, the Hungnam Evacuation was also featured in a film: the opening scene of a famous 2014 Korean film, 국제시장, or *International Market* (in Bu-san), aka *Ode to My Father*. The movie deals with a refugee family from Hungnam Evacuation. Kindness during a war seems to be a universal feature of humanity. (08/08/2020)

288. A three-month drought is preferred to a week of monsoon.
석달 가뭄은 참아도 열흘 장마는 못 참는다.

At this writing, on August 7, 2020, I understand that the Korean Peninsula has been suffering from unprecedented torrential rains, with 30 to 50 cm (1 to 1.5 feet) of accumulated water from continual downpours for the past eight days (and still counting). The rain is submerging cars and shops on the street, destroying roads and reservoir dams, forcing cows to higher ground, causing irreversible damage to crops, instantly producing tens of hundreds of homeless refugees, and creating other flood-related havoc. The situation is the same in Japan and some parts of China. In contrast, according to the local weather station on TV, here in Las Vegas, we have not had any rain in the past 110 days! A friend of mine in Korea has just sent me the above proverb, suggesting it be included in this book as if it would mitigate the terrible situation they are facing there.

It is tough to live for almost four months without a single drop of rain, especially nowadays with the day-time high hovering around 105° F (40° C). And yet, it would be fair to say that drought, with a single-digit relative humidity, is definitely more tolerable than the water-saturated atmosphere of a monsoon season with continual rain for a week.

Muggy weather discourages evaporation of water such that we cannot lose the heat, say, from our skin. Just remember that we perspire to provide natural cooling by the evaporation of sweat from the skin. The consequence is that sweat isn't going anywhere, except to drench our clothes. Indeed, condensing water on a cool surface of a cold coil is the major component of any air conditioning system. Thus, the above proverb states that we can easily endure a three-month drought, but not a week-long spell of rain.

What are the pros associated with living in an environment with low humidity? What my wife and I noticed, immediately after we moved to this city in a desert, was the absence of mosquitos. Because of this pest, I was not able to run any significant outdoor chores, like mowing grass, when we lived in North Carolina. Insect repellents containing as much as 40% DEET

(*N,N*-diethyl-*meta*-toluamide) helps, but when the spray is mixed with sweat, it is just awful and who knows how much of the active ingredient gets absorbed through the skin. People warned us about scorpions, but we have yet to encounter one. Besides mosquitos, we also noticed that there is no mold and other pests like spiders around the house. In short, we like the weather here in Southern Nevada better than North Carolina.

To be fair, low humidity entails its own adverse effects: dry and itchy skin, eyes, and hair. However, none of these is insurmountable. We try to maintain 30% relative humidity inside the house throughout the year, but we would be happy if we could obtain about 25% with humidifiers. There are three ways to increase humidity in a room. One is a bona fide water evaporator. It constantly boils water and emits steam. The second approach is a plain room-temperature evaporator.

To provide a large effective surface area for evaporation, it usually comes with a rotating belt wrapped in porous fabric. The third option is "atomizing" water, and spraying the resulting fine water droplets. This type of device invariably employs a water-sonicating mechanism. In all cases, it would be imperative to use distilled water. Regular tap water will leave deposits of non-volatile solids, such as various salts present in the city water, on the furniture surfaces in the second and third options listed above and calcified solids on the heating coil with the first approach.

Similar to fire, a serious flood results in permanent damage to nature as well as humans. In this country, the severe water damages caused by hurricanes on the East Coast and wildfire ravaging in California, seem to have become more intensified in recent years. Pundits blame global warming for such extreme weather, in terms of both periodicity and intensity. Various models show that with climate change, the planet would experience more changes in weather patterns such as extreme heat, intense precipitation, and drought.

Given a choice, we of course want neither a monsoon season with accompanying floods nor a long-lasting drought affecting agriculture. We tend to resign to nature believing it is beyond our control. Is it really the case with the severe weather we encounter nowadays? (08/09/2020)

289. A true friend shares half of his world with his pal.
의가 좋으면 천하도 반분한다.

Here is another Korean word that is not easy to translate: 의, pronounced *eu*. According to a Korean-to-English dictionary, it means relationship, friendship, or intimacy. Usually, the word is used in a positive context, and thus we may not need "good" in front of the word when we use it to mean a friendship. The proverb says that in a genuine relationship, the friends involved would divide everything under the sky into two, each claiming only half. Such stories of a true friendship are hard to find nowadays, except for the following story. It was reported by the Associated Press on July 24 of this year and illustrates the crux of the proverb. I am reproducing the article verbatim.

A western Wisconsin man will share his millions in lottery winnings with a longtime friend because of a promise they made to each other nearly three decades ago. Friends Tom Cook and Joseph Feeney shook hands in 1992 and promised that if either one of them ever won the Powerball jackpot, they would split the money. That promise came to fruition last month when Cook bought the winning ticket for a $22-million jackpot at Synergy Coop in Menomonie, Wis.

When Cook called to give his friend the good news, Feeney couldn't quite believe it. "He called me, and I said, 'Are you jerking my bobber?'" said Feeney, an avid fisherman. Cook retired after hitting the jackpot while Feeney was already retired. Neither has any extravagant plans for the winnings but both are looking forward to enjoying more family time. "We can pursue what we feel comfortable with. I can't think of a better way to retire," Cook said. The pair said they're looking forward to some traveling. The men chose the cash option of about $16.7 million, leaving each with nearly $5.7 million after taxes are paid. Note: In Korean currency, these amounts would be equivalent to 200 억원 and 68 억원, respectively.

BTS, also known as the Bangtan Boys, a seven-member Korean boy band that debuted in 2013, has become all the rage in the contemporary pop-music world. Since 2017, BTS has led the K-Pop wave into the United States, becoming the first Korean group to top the Billboard 200 with their albums *Love Yourself: Tear* (2018), *Love Yourself: Answer* (2018), *Map of the Soul: Persona* (2019), and *Map of the Soul: 7* (2020). They are the fastest group, since the Beatles, to earn four Number-One albums in less than two years. That their success is phenomenal is an utter understatement.

They work together to produce most of their output. It is said that the lyrics of their songs are largely from their personal experiences and reflect their opinions on social issues such as mental health, difficulties faced by teenagers, learning how to love oneself and respect individualism, etc. Likewise, their musical style has also continuously evolved, covering a wide range of genres. Throughout several world tours, they have established a substantial fan base, as their performance resonates so well, not only with young people but also older generations with their own fond memories of youth.

My wife, not exactly a spring chicken herself, is an ardent fan of BTS. If someone asks her for the reason why she likes them so much, she would say it is the remarkable *eu* (의) among the seven-member family, in addition to their music and choreography. According to my wife, these young men in their early 20s share everything in both materials and emotions. It is apparently quite common for one member to pay the bill for everyone after dinner. Shopping together often results in buying stuff for other members for no obvious reasons but to show they care. They prepare meals together and generally have a great time with each other. It's hard to believe, but they have not had any significant quarrels among themselves in the past seven years together. In summary, my wife attributes their popularity to the "chemistry" of the group, or *eu* involved.

As I listen to my wife's raving praise of BTS, I cannot stop re-examining the above proverb as applied to other relevant instances such as the successful development of small businesses, communities, sports teams, and more importantly, families. (08/10/2020)

290. Charcoal briquettes burn better together.
숯불도 한 덩이는 쉬 꺼진다.

Charcoal is made by heating wood at a high temperature, without the supply of air. The resulting product of the pyrolysis is mainly black carbon. Because it is anhydrous, it is light in weight and burns at high temperatures with little smoke and soot; thus its popularity in outdoor cooking. Charcoal briquettes burn best when stacked together, with facilitated airflow. Converse to the above proverb, a single, isolated charcoal briquette easily quits burning. This implies that a concerted effort is always better than an individual attempt in achieving a common goal.

The "parable of the arrow," from the Iroquois tribe of Indians, is equivalent to the above proverb. An elder shows children a single arrow and demonstrates how easy it is to break. He then bundles a dozen with a tie and shows how impossible it is to break any of them. And the Indian chief declares, "Divided, a single man may destroy you: United, you are a match for the whole world." Numerous similar parables are found in various countries, including Aesop's Fable, each emphasizing the importance of cooperation for synergy: see also Entry #28, "Two hands must meet to make a noise" and #69, "A knife cannot carve its own handle."

The most abundant big-game species in East Africa is the wildebeest. They migrate as a herd for the best chance of survival. When isolated alone, they become easy prey for their primary predator, the spotted hyenas. A school of fish and a flock of migrating birds seem to adopt similar strategies. In the case of wildebeest, they graze in mixed herds with zebra, which are usually better aware of common potential predators.

Like a canary in a coal mine, zebras can take off quickly, as soon as they sense the presence of, say, a lion. Such inter-species cooperation, really a symbiotic relationship, is abundant in nature and well introduced in many biology textbooks. It is certainly not dissimilar to burning charcoal briquettes together for the most efficient use of the fuel. A question is why a single entity is always vulnerable in the real world.

"Divide and conquer!" has been a popular mantra in politics, warfare, business, foreign policy, and sociology. The strategy is for gaining and maintaining power, by breaking up a concentrated power into pieces. Then, the individuals to be ruled would have less power and become an easier target to conquer. Machiavelli (1469 – 1527), the father of modern political science, suggested that one of the best ways to defeat a powerful opponent is by making a man suspicious of his own subordinates, in whom he trusts. Soon, he will be alone and become a very weak man. This approach is certainly in accordance with the above proverb.

The other side of the coin is that I could make my side stronger by unifying them as one mass, just like bundling arrows together. One way to achieve this goal is, of course, by introducing to my people hatred, anger, frustration, and apathy towards the people I wish to conquer. This is to make them our common enemy, whom we would love to crush with any means available.

To unify the Germans, Adolph Hitler made Jews a common national foe. Many populist politicians of our time still adopt the strategy. The scapegoat of many revolutions has been the wealthy ruling class against, whom the population has maintained deep-rooted grudges. Witness the French Revolution, or the downfall of the first president of the Korean Republic, Syngman Lee.

President Donald Trump has been quite successful in polarizing this nation since his inauguration in 2017. From the beginning, his MAGA (Make America Great Again) movement already carried a political nuance of exclusion for non-Americans. Under the camouflage of this catchphrase with no merit and inciting hate-mongers of everyone except Americans, his administration led by Stephen Miller, a senior advisor for policy to the President, steadily promoted a notion of them-versus-us.

This guideline has been particularly painful regarding immigration policy. During his tenure, the chasm between lawless thugs and peaceful demonstrators, right-wing conservatives and progressive liberals, and Republicans and Democrats, has become so deep, we now live in the "Divided" States of America. Some people seem to thrive in such a trend. My lament! (08/12/2020)

291. *Jeong follows mae.*
매 끝에 정이 든다.

Two keywords in this proverb are *jeong* and *mae*, or 매. As to *jeong*, see Entry #153, "Easier to see *jeong* (love) leaving than arriving," which happens to be the title of my second book in the essay collection. Love or affection would be an acceptable translation here. *Mae* is a noun meaning a physical punishment, like whipping and flogging, but it could also mean fighting, arguing, or squabbling. Let us use the latter meaning first in interpreting the proverb.

After a heated argument, a young couple could engage in passionate love-making, perhaps out of exhaustion if nothing else. It clears up the "sticky air" once and for all, and could rejuvenate their *jeong*, like Entry #168, "Earth hardens after rain." It would render an opportunity of reviewing what went wrong that led them to the argument. Subsequent days would be filled with harmony, and such an event seems almost healthy and desirable for married couples. Show me any happily married couple who have not fought. I will show you the sun rising from the west. Arguments among the married are a "necessary evil" and like "cutting water with a knife." See Entry #86.

After the Second World War, the United States extended helping hands to their one-time foe, but terribly devastated, Germany, and other European nations with the Marshall Plan. For the economic recovery of Western Europe, they transferred almost $12 billion, equivalent to close to $130 billion as of 2020.

The Plan lasted for four years, beginning in 1948. Its goal was not only to rebuild war-torn regions but also to improve European prosperity. Well implemented, the plan was instrumental in preventing the spread of Communism. The foreign policy was a successful (hi)story that established a cordial relationship between Europe and the United States, including the foundation of the North Atlantic Treaty Organization, or NATO. If this history does not reflect the above proverb, what does?

Likewise, soon after Japan surrendered to the Allied Forces, the Americans showed the world what a true friend would do to a fallen enemy: between 1945 and 1952, the U.S. occupying forces helped them to reform the military, political, economic, and social systems. Nowadays, one of the most popular sports in Japan, perhaps even more popular than in the States, is baseball. It was a new sport in Japan, introduced by Americans only after the Second World War. Those cherry trees in Washington, D.C., which bring about the National Cherry Blossom Festival every spring, were gifts from Tokyo City mayor to the city of Washington, in 1912. They survived the enmity between the two nations during the War. Hot-tempered Koreans would have chopped them down in no time at all.

Corporal punishment of school children is typical of *mae*, or 매. As a child, I did homework mainly to avoid *mae*. If you have a fistfight with a classmate, you get *mae*. If you are late a few minutes to a class, you get *mae*. If you sneak out for a quick cigarette, you receive some serious *mae*. In short, we behaved as instructed, to avoid *mae*. Hard to believe it now, but *mae* was everywhere: Being the last kid in a big family, I received a lot of *mae* from not only my parents but also from older siblings. Did I resent the *mae* that was bestowed upon me, for what appeared to be minor misbehavior? Absolutely. But, even when I was punished, deep in my mind there was some troubling or rather inconvenient thought that I might have been wrong and that they might have been right all along.

As I look back now, several decades later, most, if not all, of the *mae* I had to endure during my youth, were simply a reflection of tough love. See Entry #25, "Strong plants in strong winds," for further recollection on the topic of growing up. My conclusion is that *mae* was indeed followed by a better relationship with the person who exercised it.

Currently, 19 states in this country allow public school personnel to use corporal punishment to discipline children, from the time they start preschool until they graduate 12th grade. Even with these permits, corporal punishment is frowned upon as bad practice, as if it would mar the "free spirit" of a child. I do not know if and how much legitimacy this belief holds, but that my life firmed up nicely as a young man seems to attest to some merits of *mae*. There seems to be some element of truth in "Spare the rod and spoil the child." (08/15/2010)

292. A dragon's head with a snake's tail.
용 머리에 뱀 꼬리다.

The beginning of a huge construction project, like laying a new railroad for a modern, high-speed bullet train between Las Vegas and Los Angeles, is always an affair with a great deal of fanfare. However, once the attention of the mass media and the interest of citizens fade, it seems as if the whole ceremony, with dignitaries and all that jazz, happened years ago, not just a week ago. So, the celebration begins with the head of the most fearsome dragon but quickly ends up like a mere tail of a snake. How President Trump has handled the COVID-19 pandemic may offer an excellent way to interpret the above proverb.

On December 30, last year, a Chinese physician named Li blew a whistle to alert his colleagues on a new respiratory disease in Wuhan, forcing Wuhan city officials, on the following day, to confirm the treatment of dozens of cases of pneumonia with an unknown origin. On January 3, of this year, the U.S. Center for Disease Control (CDC), Director Robert Redfield, was informed of the mysterious viral disease by his Chinese counterpart. He immediately reported it to his boss, the U.S. Health and Human Services Secretary, Alex Azar, who in turn notified the National Security Council. In early January, the U.S. intelligence community reported the incident to the President in their daily briefing.

Thus began the President's involvement in what has become known as the COVID-19 Pandemic. His daily briefings on the topic started in March with much public anticipation. It was fascinating, as well as entertaining, to watch what he had to say. His approval ratings shot up in the first months of the pandemic. With time, however, his ignorance in science and verbal attacks on reporters had become too much a distraction. I felt that watching the briefing was wasting my time; even for a retired man with all the time in the world to spare.

All in all, he was able to maintain "the face of a dragon" for a few initial briefings, which were relayed live by every major TV station. After all, he was once an entertainer on a reality TV program called *The Apprentice.*

With little to digest from the briefings, however, some leading journalists began to question why they would air the briefings.

And then on April 23, the criticism of the president hit a new high after Trump openly urged his science team to study the possibility of injecting disinfectant into patients to fight the coronavirus. This is what he said: "And then I see the disinfectant, where it knocks it out in a minute. One minute. And is there a way we can do something like that, by injection inside or almost a cleaning? Because you see it gets in the lungs and it does a tremendous number on the lungs. So it would be interesting to check that. So, that, you're going to have to use medical doctors with. But it sounds — it sounds interesting to me." It was one of the worst days in one of the worst weeks of Trump's presidency. The daily briefings largely ended in late April, like "a tail end of a snake."

His justification for quitting was on Twitter on April 25: "What is the purpose of having White House News Conferences when the Lamestream (sic) Media asks nothing but hostile questions, & then refuses to report the truth or facts accurately. They get record ratings, & the American people get nothing but Fake News. Not worth the time & effort!"

As his approval rating steadily dropped and the general election four months away, on July 21, the White House announced it would resume the daily briefings. This was less than a week after Trump announced a campaign shakeup, in which he replaced his campaign manager. Of course, it would have been the right decision, but by now too much politics had got into it. People seemed to have lost interest in watching and hearing more about, "the tail of a snake". I cannot tell what has happened to this new effort from the White House, as I have not followed the story lately. Have I missed anything? I doubt it.

The incompetent leadership of President Trump, as illustrated when he "delegated," like a hot potato, the responsibility of confronting the COVID-19 pandemic to each state, begs for an answer as to why he tried to avoid his job. Did he truly believe it was better to control the pandemic locally? Or was he plainly incapable of his job? Or was it another occasion for him to lie about the whole episode to the nation, as he kept on saying, "We are in full control. It will disappear like a miracle." (08/16/2020)

293. Making both your sister and her husband happy.
누이 좋고 매부 좋다.

There are only a few things you can do to make both your sister and her husband happy at the same time. To begin with, the relationship with one's brother-in-law is generally of formal courtesy in nature, hardly that of bosom friends, unless they happened to be as such before marriage.

Say, one night you bail him out of a police station after his post-drinking rowdy behavior, but do not inform your sister of the incident out of a man-to-man honor. Later, your sister may not be happy when she somehow learns about what you did. Likewise, your brother-in-law would be disappointed when he learns that it was you who told your sister about a chance encounter with him, in the company of some mysterious young lady at a bar. He may consider you a rat.

But, there must be something you do, which can benefit all parties involved. Earlier, I dedicated a whole essay to make a point about how similar a matchmaker is to a catalyst in a chemical reaction: see Entry #73, "How is a match-maker compensated?" Both a matchmaker and a catalyst contribute to a successful marriage and a facile reaction of high yield.

A recent novel by David Mitchell, *Utopia Avenue,* introduces a new up-and-running British rock band with four young members. One of them, a bass player named Dean Moss, is arrested unjustly after their well-received concert in Rome, for a scuffle with a cop and possession of hashish. The latter was planted by Italian cops. After three days of confinement in a "shit hole," Dean is offered a release from the jail by a compromise drawn upon by Her Majesty's Consular Representative in Rome, in which Dean is to confess his high crimes. Righteous and young he is, Dean tears up the document already signed by an Italian captain, and challenges the British diplomat, "We got off on the wrong foot. Sorry 'bout that. I was scared. But look me in the eye. If yer (*sic*) were me - innocent - would you sign that confession?" In the end, dedicated fans and British journalists, come up with a solution that not only vindicates Dean but also saves the face of the crooked Italian captain. The stalemate is thus satisfactorily resolved.

In the Camp David Accords of 1978 and 1979, U.S. President, Jimmy Carter, was able to bring together Egyptian President Anwar Sadat and Israeli Prime Minister Menachem Begin to a negotiating table, for a successful peace treaty between the two previous adversaries. Sadat and Begin received the shared 1978 Nobel Peace Prize, while the U.S. was condemned by the United Nations because the Palestinians did not participate in the peace talks.

Its historic ramification put aside, the agreement was then considered one of the most significant events that changed the dynamics of the Arab World; not least of all, it erased Egypt's sad memory of the so-called Six-Day War of 1967. All other peace negotiations in history, mediated by a third party, may be considered relevant in the discussion of the above proverb. If we can mediate a long-lasting peace between nations, why can't we help our sisters and their husbands simultaneously achieve happiness?

Given an accommodating environment, inter-species and even inter-kingdom symbiosis, can flourish. Symbiosis is formally defined as any type of long-term, usually one generation after another, biological interaction between two different biological organisms. It could be mutually beneficial or parasitic. We will talk about the former only. Head lice on humans are hardly symbiotic in my dictionary.

The most abundant gas on this planet is nitrogen (N_2), which accounts for approximately 80% of the air we breathe. It is also quite inert, chemistry-wise. However, some bacteria can convert the molecule to ammonia gas (NH_3) through the biochemical process known as nitrogen fixation. It is essential to all forms of life because it provides the nitrogen source for all nitrogen-containing organic compounds, such as proteins and genetic material, nucleic acids.

When occurring in soil and interact with water, the ammonia gas becomes ammonium hydroxide ($NH_3 + H_2O \rightarrow NH_4OH$), which is in turn neutralized by acids to form various non-volatile salts. Some nitrogen-fixing bacteria have symbiotic relationships with plant groups, especially legumes. As part of the nitrogen cycle, we could say that those microorganisms that can fix nitrogen are in a symbiotic relationship with plants and animals, and ultimately with humans. They make more than a sister and brother-in-law happy. (08/17/2020)

294. A winner is an ally, a loser a foe.
잘 되면 충신이요, 못 되면 역적이라.

People love a winner. If you fail, you are nobody. These are harsh statements but unfortunately considered as wisdom. Such Machiavellian ideal underlies the above proverb: "The end justifies the means." It implies that success means everything. To justify such a cold reality, often added are some sound-bites, like "Morally wrong actions are often necessary to achieve morally right results," or "the morality of the outcome would justify any actions." For the record, I abhor the meaning behind all of these aphorisms, including the above Korean proverb. It would create a cut-throat society if everyone followed the advice, defining the loser and the winner and ultimately the haves, and the have-nots.

What bothers me more than the above complaint is that we can love a winner for sure, but we don't have to condemn the loser as a traitor, an insurgent, or a rebel. Why can't we just leave the losers as they are? There is no need to punish them. The Korean word 역적, *yeok-jeok*, carries such a nuance. Perhaps I am too analytical: I should have just shrugged it off, attributing the use of such harsh words to the duality of any concepts. If we say that the winner is an ally or friend, then don't we have to label the loser as a foe? See Entry #98, "Handsome people necessitate ugly ones."

Trying to win all the time is hardly a winning strategy in life, as indicated by "Lose a few battles but don't lose the war." Indeed I usually win over my wife in important issues, by losing most of the time in trivial matters. The former includes what kind of car we ought to buy, where we go for this summer's vacation, whether we ought to live the rest of our lives in Korea, and so on.

The issues on which I yield to my wife, after a vigorous objection, may include: what shall we get as a wedding present for the son of my niece, which restaurant we will go to pick up our supper today, who do the dishes tonight, which ice cream should we purchase, when will we visit my sister in Arizona, etc. Here, my motto is, "Losing is winning." Letting her feel she wins all the time is a cunning, but wise, way to maintain the tranquility in this household: nothing more, nothing less.

208

Competing with fellow citizens, in a struggle for survival, is part of anyone's life. Some people become successful, while others do not. Here, winning and succeeding are viewed by others and the well-being, or happiness of the person, has very little to do with their success. Michael Phelps (1985 -), the most decorated Olympic swimmer of all time, won a total of 28 medals, 23 of which are gold, spanning four Olympics: at Athens (2004), Beijing (2008), London (2012), and Rio de Janeiro (2012). Despite all those medals, and the accolades that came with them, Phelps has struggled with depression and anxiety. In 2014, the situation was so bad that he "thought of not wanting to be alive."

In *The Weight of Gold*, the HBO Sports documentary film, Phelps mentioned how U.S. Olympic team officials and coaches viewed athletes as valuable assets during their brief windows of Olympic glory but then left them largely on their own during the years between Games. And when their careers were interrupted or over, the system moved on to the next star. Although his depression and anxiety were rampant during the peak of his successful career, I am sure that his post-Olympic letdown must have added insult to injury.

Either way, how the team officials viewed their athletes was not surprising at all. Athletes are simply goods, each with an expiration date, beyond which date their interactions with the U.S. Olympic Committee effectively end. While winning, the Olympians are dear allies, but when their tenure is over they become nobody, if not a foe.

I was 17 years old when I failed to pass the entrance exam for a civil engineering program at Seoul National University. That it was a devastating experience was an understatement. Although I received admission to the same engineering program from my second-choice university, I opted to retake the exam the following year. Thus, there was a full one-year preparation for the exam. With another friend, who also failed the exam in the first trial, I went to a Buddhist temple deep in a mountain, away from Seoul. Of several reasons for this decision, one was that I did not want to be a "loser" or "foe" among my friends as well as siblings, not that they treated me as such. I just didn't want to be viewed as begging for their "sympathy" or "punishment" for my failure. (08/18/2020)

295. Pearls become a jewel only when strung together.
구슬이 서말이라도 꿰어야 보배.

Even if you have "tons" of precious beads, it does not mean that you now have an expensive jewel. You will have to string them together for a necklace or to make something practical to wear. The amount of precious stones you have is expressed here as *seo-maal* (서말), or about 48 liters (13 gallons), where *seo* means three and *maal* is a unit of volume, each about 18 liters. It suffices to say that you have "tons" of them, but only with the potential of becoming a priceless jewel. The proverb implies that nothing is completed till you put all the parts in order. It is similar to Entry #30, "Salt beside the pot won't change the taste of its content." It is also related to "No pain, no gain."

Speaking of potential, let's imagine a man lying under a pineapple tree on a Hawaiian beach, taking a nap with the ocean breeze serving as a lullaby. In a semi-conscious state of dozing, he suddenly remembers what he learned in a physics class many years ago: (gravitational) potential energy of an object, with a mass m and positioned at a height h, is equal to $m{\cdot}g{\cdot}h$, where g is a gravity-related constant.

This memory occurs to him now, as he remembers having seen a pineapple way up high on the tree when he laid down for a rest, a few minutes ago. He hurriedly opens his eyes and sees that, sure enough, the pineapple fruit is staring at him right above his head. This rude awakening spoils his afternoon nap. The pineapple, high above on a tree, has the potential to crack open your head. It is just a potential though, as it would injure you only when it falls by a sudden disturbance.

Money has perhaps the greatest potential in our lives, as "a golden key will open most locks." Once again, it remains a potential until we use it. Thus, how we use the money is the direct outcome of the potential. It was the subject of discussion in Entry #112, "Brag about spending, not making money." Ideally, you will have spent the last penny, when you breathe the last breath on this planet. That being practically impossible, we are left with two options: dying in debt, or leaving money behind. The former scenario is perhaps not acceptable for many people with pride and integrity. The latter is OK for folks who wish to have their children take care of the leftovers.

Just like any of my contemporaries, I am conscious of getting older. With time flying by, I have begun to observe stark differences in the style of spending money among my friends. Some are aware that money is just a means of enjoying life. One particular couple seems to spend money liberally on; traveling, concerts, theater, dining, charity, parties, etc. By any stretch of the imagination, their lifestyle is exceptionally extravagant. They appear to enjoy every minute of the remaining days of their lives. When I told my friend, at such a rate of spending, their children will inherit nothing. He shrugged off my comments, saying that it was their money, and their kids are now doing much better than when they were at that age. To them, unspent money may as well be unstrung pearls.

Then there is another Korean friend, who was also a physician, and is currently living on the West Coast. They should be much wealthier than us. And yet, they live is a decent, but small house, fix their thermostat at 81°F for the summer, and 68°F during the winter; drive two old clunkers, argue with a waitress at McDonald's over a few pennies, try to bring home leftovers from a buffet-style restaurant, etc. We are close enough that I can complain about their lifestyle as cheapskates, but I know they will not change. They have two grown-up children, but leaving their fortune for them does not seem to be the main motivation for their austerity. I don't know why they live as they do at this advanced age.

Money is to meaningful spending, as talent is to a successful professional. Here, identifying a kid's potential at an early age could be an important step to a successful career many years later. How can we find it in them? Parents encourage their children to participate in a few different extracurricular activities, like sports camp, piano or violin lessons, school plays, tending a lemonade stand, and even newspaper delivery. To become a concert pianist, for instance, the child must not only have potential but also appreciate practicing. Potential is just a first step. It is certainly true that a jewel comes into being only when pearls have to be strung together. (08/20/2020)

296. Lazy students going through a book.
게으른 선비 책장 넘기기.

Distraction is always part of our effort when focusing our attention on a given task at hand. This expression, written in an incomplete sentence, depicts a scholar of a bygone era, turning a page of a book he was to study, with a great deal of reluctance and boredom. He is not interested in reading the book, period: his mind is completely wandering somewhere else.

Some time ago, I came across a cartoon where a young man was visualizing playing a round of golf with buddies, while at his desk in an office. Then the same guy, while on a golf course, was picturing a new administrative assistant with a miniskirt, at his office. I don't know why it is so difficult to concentrate, but lack of interest in what we are doing, or dreaming of something better to do, must be the source of the problem.

In the good old days in Korea, children would go to a small school in a village called *seo-dang*, 서당, to first learn one thousand Chinese characters. A dozen or so students, sitting on a wooden floor of the classroom, read the characters aloud together as if they were monks chanting in unison. Their upper bodies rocked in harmony with the sounds they generated. This was a perfect lullaby for the kids, and some fell right into sleep. An old teacher could then wake him up with a long whip of some sort. Here, their distraction would be primarily playing outside or going back to dozing off.

During puberty, teenagers and young adults would be distracted, or obsessed to be exact, by sex. It will remain as such throughout one's life. Sex is a life-long desire. If I understand correctly, towns in Florida mainly for retirees, tend to show unexpectedly high instances of sexually-transmitted diseases. Various distractions, second only to sex, would be sports, dining, social activity, some illegitimate plans, etc.

Speaking for myself, while studying for exams, I used to urinate more frequently and become much sleepier. In a boring class, I would speculate about the sexual habit of a female lecturer at the podium or daydream of a backpacking trip. During the Sunday Mass, I often drifted into a mannerism, rather than follow homily. Then, of course, my wife asks me on way back home how much I enjoyed the sermon.

So, according to the above expression, here is a scholar who is turning a page of a book he was to study, but his wandering mind is roving somewhere else. What he appears to be doing is completely separated from his mind. Despite the distraction, he is conscious enough to know that he has to turn a page of the book once in a while.

Drifting into distraction is a passive process. But, pretending can be an active form of deceiving others. The instance of turning a page of a book is a harmless pretense. Pretending that you are a normal heterosexual, while you are gay, would be nothing but spontaneous, and could be mentally draining. On the scale of mental agony, it would be at the extreme end of pain, perhaps worse than pretending to be a millionaire when you are penniless.

In my mind, pretenders of the worst kind are secret Trump supporters who behave as if they are people of tolerance and progressive mind but vote for him when the general election comes around. They are fully aware that Trump is a man of bigotry, misogyny, pathological lying, racism, and utterly without any empathy, sympathy, decency, integrity, principles, and loyalty. And yet, Trump could resonate well with them in any one of these categories, say, hatred toward African Americans or any foreigners. Essentially, they are cheating themselves. I can respect people who are vocal in public about supporting Trump with the MAGA (Make America Great Again) hats, and for all their courage if nothing else, but not those cowardly pretenders with a dark secret.

According to an article in the July 27 issue of the *Los Angeles Times*, Joe Biden's lead in various polls could be an over-estimate because there is a large reserve army of secret Trump voters who are afraid, under the current political climate, to state their true preferences. To my relief, the article stated that no such evidence was found. If people were afraid of telling the truth to pollsters, there should have been a gap between the results from polls conducted by humans and machines. There was not.

The scholar who is pretending to be studying a book may have some level of self-pity and guilt, but that's the extent of a negative outcome. However, those secret Trump supporters do a disservice to this country, effectively for many years to come. (08/21/2020)

297. A baby is my child, only in my arms.
자식도 품안에 들 때 내 자식이다.

Like any other mothers of mammals, female California sea lions, after almost a year-long gestation, become extremely protective of their pups upon their birth. When the mother sea lion comes back to the rookery from foraging, she identifies her baby through vocal communication, in addition to smell. Pups grow continuously, learning from adult behaviors as well as through interactions within their peer group. As the breeding season ends, usually after July, juvenile and nonbreeding sea lions become rather independent of their mothers and more playful. Effectively it is the end of a meaningful mother-child relationship in the life of the California sea lion. Generally speaking, their life cycle is similar to that of humans as well as other mammals.

The intimate bonding between the mother and her new infant undoubtedly begins during the gestational period: nine months in humans and, for instance, 20 days in hamsters. This, together with the labor involved in birth, provides a foundation of some ill-defined oneness. And yet the interaction between mother and an infant born from a surrogate mother is reported as satisfactory and fulfilling as the normal mother-infant pairs. This finding appears to downplay the bonding developed during pregnancy and emphasize the importance of their interaction after birth.

The intimate relationship between a mother and an infant strengthens until the child begins *their* (see the footnote of #207) puberty period. Once the child becomes independent, like starting to live in a college dormitory or leaving home for good after marriage, they are no longer within the embrace of their parents. This is essentially what the above proverb says: children are mine only when they are in my arms.

People say that a bird flying high in the blue sky envies a bird in a cage at home or an aviary at a zoo, because the birds in captivity usually do not have to struggle for food. The pet owner not only provides the food but also takes care of their general wellbeing. On the other hand, those in a cage envy the birds in the wild, because the latter enjoys freedom.

A child's life, especially *their* interaction with parents, before *they* leave home for college must be a mixed bag: sometimes they resent the excessive directives from parents, and they may often rebel rather vigorously. This is largely the consequence of physiological changes they undergo during puberty. But, other times they appreciate the love from parents and what the parents have sacrificed for them. Their affection could be on full display, for example, on a birthday or Mother's Day.

Parents would feel the same. When a child behaves against their bits of advice, they may wish that the kid would go away to college right away. The parents have simply had enough. But, then, look at how parents behave just after dropping off their sons and daughters in a college dormitory for the first time. The mother usually sheds some tears, while the father tries to console his wife. The reality hits them hard when they come home. All of a sudden, the home is so quiet with the "empty nest" the kid left behind. Deep in their minds, they know that their kid is gone. They feel the passage of time: it was just a few years ago that they brought their baby home from the neonatal clinic.

After marriage a daughter, if not working, would visit her mother with her own child, just to chat about any idling topics over a cup of tea. Sometimes, the mother may give something to her daughter when she leaves: say, a fancy tray for serving fruits or cake, as the elder does not see any further use for it. Wasn't that exactly what happened many years ago, when she was at her daughter's age?

Such gestures would also serve as a token for encouraging the daughter to visit more often in the future. Married sons usually visit parents on a special occasion, such as a father's birthday or New Years Day. They may watch some ball games together on TV or play a game of Go. Mother now dotes on the grandchildren. They are the replacements for their long-gone children. As the parents are getting older and grandchildren are rapidly growing, the visit would occur in the opposite direction: After the father retires, the parents, with plenty of time, visit their children. Playing with their grandchildren becomes one of the most cherished pleasures they have now. (08/22/2020)

298. In a single day, you come across a horse and a cow.
하루 가다 보면 소도 보고 말도 본다.

What would be the probability for a city dweller like me to encounter a horse as well as a cow in a single day? Almost zilch. And yet, this proverb says you will see them both nonetheless. That would be an outrageous claim, but it seems to have another hidden message: Here, the single-day must mean my whole life, while the horse and the cow represent "everything" under the sun. Then, I could say, "Yes, I have seen, heard, and spoken many things throughout my life." In fact, "Man, I've lived too long. Now I've seen it all," is one of my favorite phrases that I mumble whenever I encounter some unusual event.

So, what are the unforgettable experiences that I have gone through in my life? As of this writing, I am only a few years shy of 80 years old. In this long period, one is bound to have encountered many events: some were fortunate and others bad, or even ugly. Listed below, in chronological order, are such highlights. It may serve as a reference in comparing with the life stories of others.

- Immediately after the Second World War was over, the Korean Peninsula was divided into two pieces, cut along the 38th parallel north. My parents decided to flee to the South, as they were condemned as capitalists by the communists. It must have been 1947. Our family had to cross the 38th line in the dark, and since we did not know the terrain, my parents hired a guide. As I was a toddler, this drunken guide kept me on his back whenever a situation warranted, like crossing a small stream. His alcoholic smell still lingers. We were bona fide refugees and treated as such by the officials of the South. The first meal we were offered, on a train heading south, consisted of steamed rice, raw cucumbers, and salt.
- During the Korean War (1950 - 1953), I did not witness much anarchy or devastation. I do not recall seeing any dead bodies, not to mention any real battles. I did, however, encounter several orphans of the War, at the elementary school. They invariably wore unfit

clothes, most likely donated from the United States as part of humanistic aid.

- I failed to pass the entrance exam, for the civil engineering program, at Seoul National University in 1961. Up to that point, it was certainly one of the most devastating experiences I had encountered in my short life. See more in Entry #99, "All fields are fertile to diligent farmers."

- At the age of 24, I left Korea for further post-graduate studies. The departure to an unknown territory, with poor English skills and an empty pocket, was quite an adventure. It was not so much because I was ambitious in education per se, but because there was a lack of opportunities in Korea. Once I left, I seldom looked back.

- A one-year stint as a research scientist, at a Korean pharmaceutical firm, was a wake-up call. It clearly showed me what would be ahead of me in the future. And yet, I worked quite diligently and was able to achieve the production of a soft-elastic gelatin capsule for the first time in Korea. For my contribution, the president of the company bought me an airline ticket to Vancouver, Canada. Also, I lost my front teeth during the operation of heavy equipment during product development. A dental bridge has been in place since then.

- My mother passed away while I was a student in Kansas. My sister in Phoenix and I were not informed of her passing. At her funeral, a dear friend of mine happened to visit my parent for no obvious reason, but just to say hi to my mother. He then served as a pallbearer in my place. This, rather miraculous incident, is presented in Entry #140, "Parents can take care of their ten children but not vice versa." To this day, I do not understand how it happened.

- If someone asks me what the most terrible experience was while I was a professor at a university, I'd say it was when I failed to bring in a research grant from, for example, the National Institutes of Health. Grants to a researcher are what water is to a fish. "Feeding" my PhD students, and keeping the research program continuously active, is not as easy as it may sound. The competition was high, forcing me to realize how smart other scientists were. When I retired in 2013, I felt like I could fly as if the "lead" on my shoulder disappeared. (08/26/2020)

217

299. A moment is three years when waiting.
일각이 삼 년 같다.

I tried to define time in Entry #160, "Plant an acorn to build a pavilion." The classical definition of a second is the number of oscillations of a cesium atom, 9,192,631,770. This is the absolute value that every citizen of every nation on this planet Earth follows. And yet, relatively speaking, time seems to move at different speeds, depending on the situation. When one waits for something that *they* (see the footnote of #207) have been anxiously waiting for, time moves rather slowly.

Imagine a young man who has not seen his fiancé for the past few months, and now she is arriving on the plane that has just landed at an airport. He may have felt like it was years, rather than a few months, of waiting. Thus, at that point, one minute moves like a few days. Likewise, the movie one is enjoying very much ends too early. The check one has been waiting for is also very slow in coming.

The above proverb says, "I feel as if this one minute lasts three years." *Il* and *gag*, in *Il-gag* (일각), means one, plus a non-defined measure of time, like second or minute, respectively. Let us just call it one minute. As I discussed in Entry #223, "Putting off a promised visit till three births later," the number three here implies a large number, especially when used with time. See also Entries #266 and #288. For a given or similar situation, different people would feel the passage of time differently.

I have just come back from an endodontist office. The diagnosis was that I didn't have an infection. The developed cavity had not touched the nerve yet, the tooth was devoid of excess mobility, and all looked good except that the gum tissue had recessed. I can go for the procedure of a root canal now, for preventive purposes, or I can wait till I begin to feel any discomfort. Of course, I decided to wait. Most people I know would do the same. However, imagine a case where a man is to be executed by a firing squad, in a few days. In this situation, some may ask for the execution right now, rather than putting it off: "OK, let's get it over with now, once and for all." I might also do that.

When does one think the time is moving way too fast? When a person reaches old age: that is when. This is because old folks know that their lives are coming to an end pretty soon and that they have too much business to attend to in the remaining days. This is particularly true when a person with a deadly disease receives a sure prognosis of a few years, or months, to live. Here, there are two facets of wishing to live a bit longer. One is to extend their stay in this world, and the other is to avoid the unknown after death. For most, it must be a combination of both.

The emotional attachment to this world is primarily in a form of loving and appreciating family, friends, fun, fame, wealth, success, and associated perks. Essentially, it is complacency with their current, comfortable life: "Why rock the boat?" If we can still do something about extending our lives, we try hard to stay alive a bit longer. Even at the deathbed, one tries a Hail Mary. For the 2016 - 2017 football season, the Philadelphia Eagles were at the bottom of the NFC East Division, with seven wins and nine losses. Jeffrey Clayton Riegel, a 56-year-old devoted Philadelphia Eagles fan, died in August 2017. Part of his obituary read, "He requested to have eight Philadelphia Eagles as pallbearers so the Eagles can let him down one last time."

A diagnosis of a deadly disease, such as incurable cancer, still comes with various options of treatment. A risky, drastic surgery is a real Hail Mary. A few rounds of chemotherapy are another option, but with nasty side effects. Or one can become a volunteer for the Phase III clinical study of a new therapeutic modality. The dying patient can also try some esoteric approach, not supported by modern medicine.

Finally, one most appealing option (at least to me) is doing nothing and enjoying the natural course of dying as much as one can. After all, we will all die sooner or later. Why bother for a few miserable months of extension? Effectively, one can jump right into "acceptance," the last stage of Kubler-Ross' five stages of grief, skipping the previous four stages of denial, anger, bargaining, and depression. One can convince *themselves* that what remains of *their* life is indeed too short to worry about the "silly" initial four stages. (09/04/2020)

300. Ugly trees keep a mountain pretty.
굽은 나무가 선산을 지킨다.

Up close, each tree is rather homely, with bent and stunted branches, as if they have been suffering from malnutrition. But together, they would make the mountain appear coated with rush skin and look beautiful when seen from a distance. The mountain this proverb is referring to is not an ordinary one: 선산, *seon-san,* is in fact a small mountain where one's ancestors are buried. You could thus say that it is a very sacred place. Albeit significant, the site is surrounded by seemingly ugly trees. The saying means that an odd *bric-à-brac* could make something unique and valuable when put together properly.

There are many novels, plays, and TV dramas that employ a story of two brothers, usually one very successful, while the other one is not. The highly acclaimed 1995 Korean TV drama, *Sandglass* (모래시계), introduced two such brothers: the older one received a good education and became a powerful prosecutor, while the younger one stayed at home in the countryside, helping their father till a small piece of farmland. The success of the older brother was largely thanks to the financial support from their father, although they barely made ends meet. But it is the younger one who takes care of their father, ill of old age. Viewers like me were more sympathetic to this less glorified young man, who, just like the tree with bent and stunted branches, took care of the ailing father until the end.

Rich Man, Poor Man was a 1976 American, seven-week TV drama series that I immensely enjoyed. The drama was quite successful, not only among the critics but also in ratings. It is now considered the forerunner to all subsequent TV drama series of the present time, such as those from Netflix, Hulu, YouTube TV, Sling, etc. The series stars Peter Strauss and Nick Nolte as the older and younger brothers, respectively. The older one is rich, well-educated, very ambitious, and successful in everything he does. The younger brother is a rebel who eventually turns to boxing just to survive. But to their parents, financially struggling German Americans, it is the younger one they constantly worry about, just like the Prodigal Son from the Bible (Luke 15:11 – 32) and Rembrandt's drawing.

We tend to ignore anything seemingly trivial and mundane, too abundant to be of any use, too ugly for our eyes, over what appears to be fashionable, expensive, popular among the laymen, colorful to a point of being noisy, big and powerful, unusually rare, beautiful in appearance, etc. But it is a wise man who finds something extraordinary in a plain nobody, like the three wise men who followed a star to Bethlehem to find the baby Jesus in a manger. Isn't it also how they found the Dalai Lama, one of the 16 children in a humble family of farmers, in a remote part of Tibet?

In *The Ugly Duckling,* by Hans Christian Andersen, we learn that an ugly little bird hatched among ducks, suffers much verbal and physical abuse from others, simply because he was perceived as ugly. He wanders off, all by himself, to live in the wilderness, but fails as the flocks were slaughtered by hunters. He was then adopted by an old woman, but her cat and hen tease and taunt him mercilessly, and once again he sets off alone. Finally, the ugly duckling is not only accepted but also welcomed by a flock of beautiful swans. Now he realizes that he is not a duckling but a swan. He then opens his gorgeous wings and takes an elegant flight with the rest of his new family.

In a vast area of sandy beach, people walk patiently up and down with a metal detector, once in a while finding something, like an old coin. I doubt very much that they would find anything valuable in a monetary sense, but the rarity of the encounter must be what they value highly.

"I found this piece on the Outer Banks of North Carolina, near Nags Head, in the summer of 1997," the host of a party says proudly pointing to some doohickey, a rusty brown reddish piece of metal, on an expensive glass-top coffee table. When asked by a guest what it might have been, the proud founder may say, "I really don't know, but I imagine it could have come from one of the 40 guns on the *Queen Anne's Revenge* that Blackbeard the Pirate commanded, back in the early 18th century."

Finding diamond, gold, ruby, sapphire, turquoise, opal, jade, other precious gemstones, and even pearl, requires processing a large number of their source material. Come to think of it, that is indeed the definition of a gem, something from seemingly nothing. (09/05/2020)

INDEX (in essay number)